After Success

FOR CLAIRE AND KRISHAN
in memory of the Prague connection

After Success

Fin-de-Siècle Anxiety and Identity

RAY PAHL

Polity Press

First published in 1995 by Polity Press in association with Blackwell Publishers Ltd.

2 4 6 8 10 8 5 3 1

Editorial office:
Polity Press
65 Bridge Street
Cambridge CB2 1UR, UK

Marketing and production:
Blackwell Publishers Ltd
108 Cowley Road
Oxford OX4 1JF, UK

Blackwell Publishers Inc.
238 Main Street
Cambridge, MA 02142, USA

ISBN 0-7456-1333-0
ISBN 0-7456-1334-9 (pbk)

A CIP catalogue record for this book is available from the British Library and the Library of Congress.

Typeset in Times on 10.5/12 pt
by CentraCet Limited, Cambridge
Printed in Great Britain by TJ Press Ltd, Padstow, Cornwall

This book is printed on acid-free paper.

Contents

Contents

Preface and Acknowledgements

This book is driven by three themes that puzzled me and which I wanted to try to explore with empirical research. Firstly, why do people work so hard? In particular, why do men work long hours, saying that they do it for their families, when their wives or partners frequently say that they would like to see more of them? Secondly, it seems that many overtly successful people frequently suffer from self-doubts and wonder whether, in a deeper sense, their lives have been a failure. Does that, in turn, imply a 'society view' of success which people intuitively feel is nonsense? Finally, is the idea of success based on commitment to a career or a profession a peculiarly male notion, affecting the top strata of society only? Is there a single-mindedness in success that most women have happily managed to avoid through their additional or alternative expressive commitments to the family and work outside employment? Is there now an emerging notion of success based on *balance* which allows the expression of emotion or love to be combined with the development of instrumentality in employment and other forms of work? Briefly, has it taken most of the twentieth century for people to come to terms with the insights of both Marx and Freud and to recognize the reciprocal relationship between their respective understandings of work and desire.

These are difficult and complex issues which a new *fin-de-siècle* sociology is beginning to explore. The relations between character and social structure were the focus of attention in the middle of the century, but much of the work at that time was not particularly sensitive to issues of gender and few sociologists were comfortable in dealing with the work of psychoanalysts. Thus work by the American psychologist Karen Horney on the neuroses of success made little impact on those influenced by Max Weber's *The Protestant Ethic and the Spirit of Capitalism*. Drives and motivational structures that were seen as neurotic by Horney and others were glorified with a kind of male triumphalism by sociologists seeking ways of stimulating economic growth in 'backward' parts of the world. The American Dream was the incentive for many to set out on the road to success and glory: the incentive to measure this led to studies of social mobility by sociologists on another road to success and glory.

Now, at the end of the century, there is little triumphalism. The economic fix, the technological fix, the unbounded faith in individuals to strive, be greedy, seek for status and to get rich through a combination of knowledge, skill, enterprise and effort are all open to doubt. The great thrust to the modern world has been unquestionably driven by aggressive, competitive and dominant men working in the public spheres of the economy, the polity and the professions. However, in the process they have disabled themselves; they have allowed too much of the emotional and expressive sphere to remain with women. Now, women are moving more effectively into the instrumental sphere of work and are more able to keep a balance between expressivism and instrumentalism. This is producing its strains and difficulties, as Rosalind Coward's *Our Treacherous Hearts* (1993) vividly illustrates. However, men have not been so well served in analyses of their predicament of finding ways of bringing together their need for fulfilment in both the inner and the outer aspects of their selves. One of the most exciting and illuminating studies that provided a beacon of light towards a new rapprochement between sociological and psychological approaches to men's deep dilemmas was Philip Slater's *The Glory of Hera* published in the United States in 1968, a work which influenced Dorothy Dinnerstein (1976) and later, Nancy Chodorow (1987) and Miriam Johnson (1988), and has been very influential in the United States, though it has taken time to be assimilated on the other side of the Atlantic.

As I explain in the Appendix, I interviewed fifteen 'successful' men and five women at some length on at least two occasions. However, I draw on only half of this material in this book. In particular, I have omitted any reference to the three most dynamic and successful women I interviewed. The men and women I have quoted in this book have all been disguised. I have provided pseudonyms and I have changed irrelevant details to help in preserving their anonymity. It may be of some psychological interest that the two women chose real names from the maternal side of their families. I did not give the men any choice in their names but John Maltby was given the opportunity to make minor changes to the chapter which is largely devoted to him. All respondents were given copies of their transcripts and had the opportunity to take out embarrassing material. It is important to note that all respondents were able to read the transcript of their first interview before I recorded the second.

It is a paradoxical reflection of the male-dominated view of success that for me to include the women in a gender-neutral way would have been misleading. However, to write about success from a more expressive or female perspective based on such limited material seemed equally hazardous. I shall probably be criticized for what may be perceived as fudging this issue. To such critics all I can say is, 'Give me time'. Writing *After Success* makes me see the need for its sequel *Beyond Success*, which will focus more on the theme of balance to which I refer in the final chapter. In chapter 7 I do, indeed, discuss two women and two men. Both men are married with children; both women are single, childless and ambitious. Similarly, in chapter 8 I refer to both women and men struggling together with the dilemmas of the human condition. However, in general, the main theme of this book is about men after success. Its sequel will, I hope, be different.

There are, of course, no final answers in a book of this nature: the best a sociologist can do is to make us conscious of the processes of which we form a part. The two main themes of fundamental sociological significance, with which people will surely have to grapple in the years ahead, are, firstly, the renegotiations of the divisions of labour between expressive and instrumental activity in the context of a restructuring of gender-based relationships, and, secondly, the coming to terms with the flexibilization of employment and its meshing with all forms of work. Bringing the emotions back in to a rapidly changing set of work cultures is likely to cause confusion and anxiety about self-identities and much else besides. Pity the politicians who seek fairly stable targets at which to aim. As they move through life people change their distinctive mixes of work and their distinctive mixes of relationships. As their skills, employability, emotional needs and physical desires develop through the life course, they create for themselves an ever-changing kaleidoscope of circumstances. At any one point, the pattern is clear: but it is not fixed – by the time one configuration is recognized it has already changed. The British Household Panel Survey (BHPS) at the University of Essex provides evidence on changing households from 1992 to 1994 and illustrates this well:

> The more recent and quite unequivocal growth in women's employment is in the 'multiple employment statuses per year' category, in which are included those cases where women move between employment status (eg from part- to full-time, or from self-employment to employment or between employment and unemployment) in the course of a calendar year . . . part of the growth in this category is no more than switches into and out of employment during a year of birth. But when we control for this, by looking at women whose youngest child is more than one year of age, we see just the same effect. The evidence suggests that, particularly in the most recent cohorts, women's employment growth has been concentrated in 'irregular' jobs providing 'discontinuous' employment. (Buck et al. 1994)

The full implications of this flexibilization of employment and, in particular, the implications of the gendering of it for women's and men's success, anxiety and identity will be profound. Success in the sphere of employment is a problematic notion. The proportion of men in employment who are part of the flexible work-force has risen to 3.7 m (27 per cent from 18 per cent eight years ago) whereas among women it has remained stable at around 50 per cent, a total of 5.9 m.[1]

The twin driving forces of flexibilization and the changing consciousness and aspirations of women are leading to a scissors-type switch in anxiety. As women enter men's heartless world of competitive enterprise, men are entering the world of competitive parenting: both are seeking an ever-elusive balance.

People may erroneously imagine that they can achieve balance without making serious commitments. Somehow, by being free of commitments they may believe that this leaves them more free to juggle the different elements of their lives effectively. Yet, inevitably, this exacerbates uncertainty and anxiety. Being committed provides people with a security and a base from which they may grow into their full potentialities as individuals. With increasing flexibilization of employment, commitment in the sphere of work is becoming more difficult and may even be positively discouraged as a basis for long-term security and personal identity. One alternative is commitment in the sphere of love. It may not be so bizarre as it first appears, but helping young people to understand better how to make loving commitments may be one of the most positive ways of achieving greater social cohesion in the years ahead.

During the five years in which I have been thinking about and writing this book I have received advice and encouragement from many people. Often I have picked up insights from friends and colleagues who have been examining their own lives, sometimes, but certainly not always, prompted by knowing that I was writing this book. However, I have unquestionably learnt most from the women and men whom I have interviewed, who often interrupted an exceptionally busy life to talk to me. I am sure to disappoint them: those I have not discussed may feel neglected and those I have discussed may feel a little uneasy. However, I hope that all of them will recognize that without them this book would have been imposs-ible to write. I am most grateful to them all. I have explained above the steps I have taken to preserve their anonymity.

I am glad to acknowledge financial support from the University of Kent to cover the transcribing of the interviews. One of the advantages of my university is that I have a classicist and a specialist on Chaucer with rooms on my college staircase. I am grateful to Arthur Keaveney for advice about the Greek and Roman approaches to hubris, and to Peter Brown for drawing my attention to Hoccleve. It would be sad to think that such serendipitous scholarly exchanges will become more difficult when we are all tidied up into neat packages in the name of managerial efficiency.

Finally, I would like to thank Hazel Taylor for transcribing the interviews with great skill and insight, Rebecca Edwards for trans-forming my awkward manuscript, with its inserts and amendments, into the final product, and to Tony Giddens whose prompt and incisive editorial comments provided just the right balance of carrot and stick to ensure that the book was completed on time, even though I have not been able to respond adequately to many of the challenging points he raised.

Bishop's Castle,
May 1995

1

Introduction:
Mortality, the Individual and
Society: the Dialectics of Anxiety
and Success

Temporal prosperity comes always accompanied by much anxiety.

John Donne, 1631
Quoted in OED, *Select Works* (1840: 25)

After prep. and *adv.* Behind in place; later in time (than); following in search of; in imitation of; concerning; subsequent to or subsequently; in honour of.

Success fortune (good or bad); prosperous progress, achievement, or termination; attainment of wealth and influence.

This book is about shifts in the idea of success and the associated anxieties and identities. At various times in the past century or so there may have been more personal and social confidence in the idea of success. The American way of life was underpinned by the notion that everyone had the chance to succeed. The land of opportunity was, by implication, a land in which to be happy and fulfilled, not anxious and miserable. Likewise, Britain once 'ruled the waves' from the Mother of Parliaments and had an Empire on which the sun never set. The injunction was to *Rule* Britannia and the bounds of the 'Land of Hope and Glory' were to be set wider and wider, for 'God who made thee Mighty' was instructed pretty firmly to 'Make thee Mightier yet'. Clearly, God would not be expected to argue with that. In mid-century school atlases vast areas of the world were coloured a comforting pink. Evidently the United

States, the first New Nation, and Britain, the first Industrial Nation, in their distinctive ways, provided routes to success for individuals and their families. The study of social mobility provided some measures of individual success and, while the idea of rags-to-riches was more often an ideal than a reality, it offered hope for many, and, in the case of the United States, probably did much to maintain quiescence and stability in society.

The institutionalization of individual success in the form of a 'career' was largely a middle-class phenomenon. The growing government bureaucracies, the British Colonial Service, the large industrial corporations all provided secure and smoothly moving escalators of advancement for young men of modest, if not outstanding, abilities. When parents showed pride in the achievements of their offspring there was little doubt or confusion about the nature of these achievements or of their success. Their sons had 'got on' and acquired more money and a higher position in society. Women at that time achieved success in different ways – by making a 'successful' marriage or by creating a family base from which sons could leap on to greater heights and individual success could be transformed into family or dynastic success.

Of course, there were all kinds of other routes to fame and success in the twentieth century. Exceptionally talented individuals could become opera singers, professional footballers and state governors or cabinet ministers from relatively humble backgrounds. However, the main mechanism of advancement for most of those in the civil service, large-scale industry or the professions was the career. Take away the career and much more risk and uncertainty comes to surround the idea of success. Without clearly marked-out and structured ladders, it becomes less easy to prepare for advancement or to be sure that what one individual takes to be advancement has wider social acceptability. Without such social acceptance the whole notion of success becomes undermined. If people are not sure of their social position they may feel status anxiety or they may withdraw from a race in which their progress is so ambiguously or unpredictably measured.

The collapse of career is discussed in different contexts later in the book. Suffice to say now that 'flexibilization' in all its various forms has made massive inroads into professional and managerial employment: the jargon of the late 1980s – contracting out, downsizing, delayering and all the rest – has forced self-employment or consultancy on many who in the past would have settled into stable careers. The steady movement of women into areas of the labour market where they had hitherto been excluded or poorly represented has changed gendered perceptions of employment. Flexible hours, job-sharing, contracting out and teleworking have dramatically transformed publishing and other creative industries. Changes in the organization and structure of employment have produced a new kaleidoscopic pattern, where the dominant image is not of a career ladder but rather of a dynamic mass of particles moving fast, colliding, remaining stationary, coalescing into small nuclei, moving on and then splitting up again in a dynamic mass of fission and fusion. Some particles are more active, moving and coalescing more frequently. Others remain relatively stable for long periods.

This new image has not been sharply focused. The curriculum vitae of a 'successful' person in the year 2000 is likely to be of a different order from that of someone in 1960. The portfolio of jobs that someone needs to accumulate to increase employability is hard to predict. What use is a whole range of experience in the coal-mining or ship-building industry for someone who wants to remain working in Britain? There is a parallel with those who retired from the Colonial Service and returned to Britain in the 1950s and 1960s and who found it increasingly difficult to find new employment that made good use of their experience. Larger and larger parts of people's experiences have become, as it were, useless fossils with no contemporary value or use. It may, of course, still be experience of a sort but it is more likely to be disabling experience, relating to work patterns and processes that are of historical interest only. Clearly, some life trajectories of experience or job portfolios carry greater potential employability than others. But which are these? How are they to be recognized? Senior industrialists can be deposed or dismissed for creating much loss and havoc but this does not seem to prevent them from becoming substantially richer through the terms of their golden handshake and from gaining further lucrative industrial appointments. Failed politicians likewise turn their dismissal to good financial account. Presumably one way to make sense of success based on failure is that the men and women carry with them networks of influentials: this package of social entrées to those in key positions is worth more than the slump in profitability or whatever, for which the individual was held responsible and which forced the shift. Jobs that plug into valuable networks are better than jobs that are tied to potentially outdated skills and work-related experiences.

In this fluid and fluctuating world of flexible employment structures, success still exists, to be sure, but its contours have become more blurred and it is more likely to be a retrospective than a prospective concept. Furthermore, as women challenge masculine-dominated views of success, they bring in juggling and balancing skills to compete with climbing skills. Being a mother, having two part-time jobs and also leading an active social life demands different qualities from those of being a husband/father moving inexorably up a career ladder in a large corporation.

If success is becoming a more elusive concept as a result of flexibilization, is there a corollary that failure is equally ambiguous and problematic? If most young people in a particular locality have great difficulty in finding employment; if most graduates expect to have a period of experimentation and uncertainty in their twenties, including foreign travel between boring but relatively lucrative employment; if most women expect to do various short-term part-time jobs during the period when they have children under five; if most middle managers feel they have little security of employment and may well be redundant before they are forty; then failure cannot be the same as it was when most graduates were eagerly snapped up and launched on to various career training programmes, and most middle-class women had to find fulfilment as best they could outside employment.

People are living longer. A man of fifty can expect to live another thirty years or so and is likely to be vigorous until well into his seventies. Women can expect to live even longer. As people come to terms with this and see realistically that the amount of time that is devoted to full-time employment is dwindling over the complete life course, they may come to see employment in a different light. They may want to allocate the effort they devote to employment in different ways. Some may prefer to pace themselves by working part-time for much of their lives, others may prefer a great intensive burst of activity doing contracting joinery in the Gulf States or trading on Wall Street or the City of London for ten years, before moving to a less-demanding pattern of work.

These are, perhaps, still straws in the wind and may apply only to a small and self-conscious – or lucky – minority. Up to now employers who want to be 'family friendly' think in terms of flexible working hours for mothers with school-age children, generous maternity leave and, perhaps, paternity leave. The implicit conception behind being family-friendly is that men and women with young children need to be sympathetically considered. However, the time with small children is a relatively short period in the life course. Problems arising from serial monogamy create further anxieties and difficulties, particularly when families become geographically scattered. Responsibilities to elderly relatives may affect men and women in more senior positions and at different stages in the life course. If more people want more time to carry out their responsibilities as parents, as active citizens, and as people who want to grow emotionally and spiritually, as well as to acquire more material resources, then they may find themselves in conflict with employers who interpret their obligations too narrowly.

If the 'job for life' concept is disappearing, then people cannot be expected to consider over-committing themselves to an employer who is providing a mere staging post on an individual's work-life programme. While in the past women who wished to maintain their employment learnt to juggle their options, men too are now having to learn to be more flexible and adaptable. Some may find this hard.

It is not just flexibilization of the labour market that is producing a new questioning at the end of the century. The relationships between men and women have undergone a profound change which those under twenty-five take for granted and those over fifty may not fully understand. Women as appendages to men's 'success' have become anachronistic. Hillary Clinton and Cherie Blair suffer strains, to be sure, but they are both actively involved in a man's world of power and professional success. Indeed, in some spheres men are having to come to terms with what have become women's worlds of power and professional success. Women are coming to recognize the way that their demographic advantage gives them potential political power. As men cease to be 'breadwinners' for 'their' families they will come to see the need to develop their identities in more rounded and balanced ways. However, many have a long way to go. Working out new gender identities carries with it new strains and anxieties. A new literature on masculinity is emerging which so far has raised more problems than it has attempted to solve. In one of the most interesting recent collections of ethnographies the editors introduce the book by remarking 'that interpretations of maleness, manhood or masculinity are not neutral, but rather all such attributes and labels have political entailment. In any given situation they may align men against women, some men against other men, some women against other women, or some men and women against others. In short, the processes of gendering produce difference and inequality: and nowhere more obviously than in the versions of masculinity associated with (masculinized) notions of power' (Cornwell and Lindisfarne 1994: 10).

So, because of these great changes in the worlds of work and gender relations many of people's taken-for-granted assumptions are being questioned and undermined. Whatever the precipitating factor – redundancy, separation or new caring burdens – people are questioning the idea of who they are, what they want out of life and, if success is more about creating a good self, how success can be achieved if the idea of what constitutes a good self is hard to determine.[1] This idea of success is not to be confused with fame, which is inevitably limited to a small minority. Fame provides gratification and people may move beyond fame to the satisfaction of success – doing what they want to do (whatever that might be) in relation to their peers. In order to do that, they have to see the distinction between doing what they do seriously and not taking themselves too seriously. Some few people can be both famous and successful and are able to accommodate the fleeting pleasures of gratification with more lasting satisfaction. However, most people are tugged along by the compulsions of everyday life: catching buses, collecting children, getting the car serviced, visiting in-laws, step-families, grandparents and, endlessly, shopping, choosing and heating up – if not cooking. These and a myriad of other activities prevent people from stopping to think: 'And we are here as on a darkling plain / Swept with confused alarms of struggle and flight, / Where ignorant armies clash by night.'[2]

People do not ponder the meaning of life when the children are clamouring for their supper or when they are in front of their computer workstations watching the effects of half a per cent increase in dollar interest rates on bond prices round the world. When someone dies to whom they were very close, thoughts may well up at the funeral and after, but the everyday pressures of life generally keep such thoughts at bay. Yet when some experience makes people particularly aware of their own mortality they can be greatly changed in their values and behaviour. This seems most striking among those who have experienced a 'near death experience': they may have a calmness and inward serenity that makes others embarrassed in their own harried busy-ness. Perhaps those who are not saints or mystics still get glimpses of the dark night of the soul when they lie awake in the early hours with an unidentifiable pain. The routines of everyday life are probably the most powerful agents of social control and of social cohesion and for keeping unsettling thoughts at bay. Yet these unsettling thoughts are part of the human condition.

The end of the century is a time for reflection and, alas, a time for clichés. People individually tend to take stock of their lives as they pass significant birthdays – eighteen, twenty-one, forty, fifty, sixty, and probably at five-year intervals thereafter. As the jokey birthday cards remind us, there is a looking back and a looking forward, as youthful vigour gives way to mature experience – or as youthful folly is replaced by the self-delusions of mutton-dressed-as-lamb. The cringe-making clichés on the birthday cards are perhaps a way of helping people to avoid their anxieties, reflecting an uneasy recognition that one is unsure of what personal success in life might mean and is reluctant to accept new identities that are conferred upon one, or the struggles that may be involved in finding or creating new ones.

Yet however we may try to avoid the fact, the course of life rises and falls for all of us: one way of avoiding the anxieties of the inevitability of the limitations imposed by our own mortality is to transfer our thoughts about everlasting life to society, which does live on and provides some scope for our immortality. The course of history can be interpreted optimistically: the Dark Ages came before the Enlightenment; barbarism gave way to civilizing processes; pre-modern was followed by early modern, late modern or high modern; traditional society with all its superstition, fears and dangers of war, pestilence and famine gave way to 'modern', 'scientific', 'rational' society. The idea of progress might therefore provide some collective comfort and security to compensate us for the personal troubles most people face as they move through the life course.

These different thoughts about society were often barely articulated before they, too, became clichés and were then superseded by the new clichés that followed. 'Progress', 'modernity', 'rationality' acquired their own powerful critiques. Ideas of unilinear, evolutionary development flourished briefly in the 1960s and re-emerged again in the guise of the 'end of history' when the Berlin wall came down, but anything that smacked of an over-arching explanatory metatheory was very soon destroyed by the highly sophisticated weapons developed by the intelligentsia of Paris, Frankfurt, New York and elsewhere. The chaotic relativizing that then emerged had in turn to be codified, categorized and interpreted by the professionals – who otherwise might talk and write themselves out of jobs, if they too readily acknowledged that the scientific object of social science research had disappeared into thin air in a puff of multicoloured smoke. So the confusion was labelled post-modernism, although those anxious to keep something safe for study, and their own reflections, preferred to hold on to late-modernity as a less disturbing concept. Nice distinctions emerged between a 'post-modern sociology' and a ('traditional') 'sociology of post-modernism'.

Whatever labels or phrases may be used and whatever may be the assumptions embedded in them, no one can seriously dispute that technological change and development have had massive material consequences over the past two hundred years. People in the more economically developed parts of the world live longer, appear healthier, travel faster and more frequently and have a multitude of material, cultural and symbolic products available to them. This is generally held to denote success: those societies scoring highest in per capita resources of money, energy and other statistical indicators are held to be the most successful.

But these advancing indicators of economic success are, in turn, criticized by those who point out the dangers of using up finite global resources, of the need for sustainability, of the social limits to growth and of the difficulty, if not impossibility, of converting quantitative indices into qualitative satisfactions. Who wants to struggle to live in a joyless economy? In the same way that some people may feel that they cannot face ageing, decay, illness and death, so some contemporary social commentators seek an everlasting equilibrium by advocating a society that is in a steady state, balanced, and ecologically integrated with nature. There is a yearning for a new harmony, so that while individuals pass through society, age and die, society itself carries on in a self-sustaining balance. In such a society people would require incentives to devote their lives to maintaining the balance in innovatory and creative ways. Such an approach to individual life projects and society would imply a rather different view of success from that which has developed in the modern period.

It may be useful to provide a brief reminder of the roots of the individualistic model of success based on the social mobility of individual people. In order for a society such as Britain to increase its agricultural production and to develop into a manufacturing society, it is evident that there had to be geographical mobility of people from rural areas to towns based on mining, iron and steel smelting, ship-building and various forms of manufacturing. People were partly pushed off the land as the rising productivity of agricultural labour made many redundant, and they were partly pulled to the emerging urban areas by the opportunity of employment for all members of the family. Hence, while this process was bound to be disruptive, there was a regrouping of family and kin in the new context. The second main process was that small-scale capitalism had to expand through accumulation and vigorous exploitation of resources and opportunities. Families that succeeded rose as families, holding and controlling their fortunes through patterns of inheritance and appropriate marriages. These two great processes – the birth of an urban working class and the development of family capitalism into a capitalist class – have been much studied and discussed by social and economic historians of the period from the 1780s to 1914. Sociologists were less interested in the actual historical details of this process but were more concerned with the outcome of the struggle between the interests and social organization of capital and of labour. Conflict was theoretically inevitable, and considerable time and effort was devoted to justifying this, largely through an increasingly sophisticated materialistic analysis based on the work of Karl Marx. When sudden, revolutionary change did not take place, then effort went into explaining how the conflict was being diffused or deflected through the development of cultural hegemony, the development of subordinate value systems, and a variety of other subtle ways in which dominant material interests organized the cultural and ideological superstructure to maintain the false-consciousness and subordination of the dominated class. These subtle ways did not have to be conscious: 'enlightened' and paternalistic capitalists were equally at the mercy of the materialist logic of the mode of production and so they, too, might be alienated and suffer from false-consciousness as exploiters, equally compelled and driven by the mighty engine of the logic of capitalism.

Once the system of capitalism was clearly established and a massive urban infrastructure created to sustain it, a new intermediate level of managers and professionals developed between the two elemental forces of capital and labour. The expansion of financial institutions and insurance, the organization of markets and trade, the administration of empire, the training and practice of lawyers, doctors, surveyors, engineers, architects, university staff and school-teachers led to a massive opening of opportunity to those who had missed the great tide of the early expansion of capitalism. However, this time the focus was not on geographical mobility or the development of family dynasties. First individual men and then women left their families of origin and moved into managerial and professional careers into which were built ladders of individual success. The two main periods of this process were at the end of the nineteenth century and after the Second World War. It was during this second period that sociologists allied themselves with individual trajectories of success, frequently as beneficiaries themselves and also as ideological supporters, and began to study social mobility.

The two major studies of social mobility in Britain in the twentieth century were centred around David Glass and his colleagues at the London School of Economics in the late 1940s and early 1950s (Glass et al. 1954) and John Goldthorpe and his colleagues at Nuffield College, Oxford in the 1970s and 1980s (Goldthorpe et al. 1980; 2/1987). The latter study was much more technically sophisticated than the former but the assumption underlying the whole project can be seen to be seriously flawed, in the light of a critique of a notion of success limited to material circumstances and the gratifications associated with social prestige.

First, these studies relied on sample surveys, which by their nature could not isolate a capitalist or any kind of elite. The most powerful class was ignored. Hence such studies could say very little about a key issue of modern industrial-capitalist society, namely the degree to which the masses were controlled, exploited or manipulated in the interests of the minority; who constituted that minority; and whether it was permeable. There was no attempt to address the questions of whether it was maverick international financiers like George Soros or a group of salaried pension fund managers who were the controllers of a putatively exploitative capitalist system, or whether the capitalist class had given way to the capitalist system. The students of social mobility lowered their sights to more manageable issues, principally the degree of openness or closure of social categories based on clusters of occupations. These categories of occupational clusters could be brought together to form a 'class structure' or a 'social structure' which, in turn, was shown to exhibit a degree of persistence and continuity over time. This so-called 'class structure' included elements of social prestige, so that income alone was taken to be an insufficient predictor of socio-economic position. This near tautology was one of the main elements that served to distinguish sociological from economic analyses.

The focus of the Goldthorpe study was individual men, with the assumption that 'chief earners' carried the rest of their household with them into the appropriate category of the statistically determined class structure. The fundamental normative assumption of the empirical sociologists of this school was that it was somehow 'better' for there to be equal chances for the offspring of a father in any one given 'class' to arrive at a given point in his life course in any other of the classes in the structure. That is to say, the destinations of the sons and daughters from parents in any one category in the structure should ideally be distributed randomly through all the categories in the structure; likewise all the positions in the structure could be filled by people from any category of social origin. Such would be an open society with no limits to an individual's advance other than his or her ability, however difficult that might be to measure or assess. Even in such a situation of maximum social mobility, some would travel long distances and some short from origins to destinations. Also, of course, movement could be downwards and sideways as well as upwards. Mounting an empirical inquiry into such a topic is a fiendishly difficult exercise and it is surely hard to avoid means becoming ends. It is not my purpose here to discuss or to debate the large number of pragmatic judgements that have to be made in such studies in allocating individuals into occupations, in clustering these into categories, and in taking into account how occupations change in content and status over time, with the implication that the clusters themselves also change in form and content. (A present-day bank clerk who is the granddaughter of a bank clerk in the 1920s and 1930s would be termed downwardly mobile; the systems analyst son of a computer programmer of the early 1970s would be upwardly mobile. Arguably, the son of an Oxbridge professor of the 1930s, who is a professor in one of the very newly created British 'universities', is also downwardly mobile.)

The British mobility studies are based on the assumption that upward mobility is success. Downward mobility therefore implies having less success. Furthermore, the greater the shift towards a random linking between origins and destinations, the more 'equal' and open the society is held to be. Those who adopt this sociological approach to social mobility say nothing about the distribution of motivation to succeed or whether success has a common and universal meaning. This is distinct from acknowledging that there may be reasonably universal agreement on the relative prestige of occupations in a hierarchy. (I also leave aside any consideration of 'ability' or 'intelligence' in this context.) Any discussion of the merits of a more egalitarian society – which is often a tacit normative underpinning to sociological work – must assume not just that there is 'equality of opportunity' but that people are universally willing and able to take such opportunities if they are offered to them. However, it is quite clear that many individuals and categories of the population do not subscribe to a universal conception of 'success'. Occupationally based success may involve burdens that may be seen to outweigh any putative advantages. Moving away from a familiar and much-loved part of the country, spending many hours travelling or commuting, being obliged to spend long hours in employment that clash with hobbies or other interests, the difficulty of combining certain occupations with conventional motherhood or unconventional fathering, the fear of losing close ties with family and friends are among the factors that help to distort or to modify a universal view of success. Unfortunately, sociology has appeared to defer over-much to an economistic notion of success over the past 200 years and has largely incapacitated itself from developing a critical stance in relation to the modernist project. There are, of course, honourable and noted exceptions, but those who have understood sociology as being a project largely connected with collecting and analysing social statistics relating to a putative social structure have tacitly adopted an economistic view of success.

Once people are faced with viable alternatives to single-minded occupational success, it is surely an unworthy sociology that would claim that those who choose such alternatives are merely suffering from false-consciousness. Barristers who are the sons of barristers may be able to continue in a family culture they find congenial and in an occupational culture for which they are well prepared. Yet some sons and daughters of barristers may prefer to avoid what they perceive to be the world of the speciously silver-tongued for a more gritty life as a probation officer. Likewise daughters of probation officers might feel they could be more useful making sure that innocent people are not convicted, than ministering to what they perceive to be the victims of others' mistakes. Evidently this is a complex matter on which the conventional sociologists of social mobility such as Goldthorpe and his colleagues have nothing to say (1980; 2/1987). If rates of social mobility are shown to decline – however such rates are measured – the meanings of such changes remain obscure. They may indicate much increased frustration and misery or they may indicate much more choice and happiness consequent upon the increasingly divergent and variable conceptions of what constitutes 'success'. A society more at ease with itself may be more tolerant of alternative ways of exercising talents and abilities.

The unpacking of success in this way is a hazardous enterprise and produces some surprising bedfellows. Conservative leaders such as Margaret Thatcher and John Major in Britain have a vested interest in an open society based on individualistic ambition and a ruthless determination to succeed through hard work, commitment to efficiency, wealth creation and the free flow of entrepreneurial spirits. Hence Mrs Thatcher as Prime Minister attacked all forms of social closure, whether in the unions or the professions, and Mr Major talked of the need for a classless society which, he thought, would follow from releasing the nation's talents wherever and whatever they were. Some socialists believe equally strongly in the virtues of a meritocratic society, although they would use rather different language to describe it. So, in essence, many conservatives and socialists unite in seeing the good society as the product of the more efficient harnessing of the forces of production, by making the best use of the talents of workers of hand and brain. The problem for both of them is similar when material incentives are not enough.

Likewise, there is a potential alliance between conservatives of a more traditional variety who recognize the power and loyalties of locality and family, who feel that quality of life depends on more than can be set out on a spreadsheet, but who believe that one has to be born into a particular kind of English culture to know what the essence of this quality might be. Such people are in unsuspecting alliance with a certain kind of socialist in the William Morris tradition who believes in the pride and satisfaction of good workmanship and that true satisfaction can be found only in knowing that the hedge is well laid, the pot well turned or the pupil well taught, irrespective of the praise others may care to bestow. Certainly, it is gratifying to win prizes and accolades or to be paid large sums of money, but such people recognize that the inner satisfaction of the knowledge of a job well done and of one's capacities and talents fully utilized or deployed is deeper and more lasting. The woman who ceases to be a skilled craftworker in order to manage a small business, thus ceasing to have the satisfaction of working with her hands in order to have the putative gratification of earning more money, is more to be pitied than praised. She has forsaken true satisfactions for a gratification that can perhaps never be fully assuaged. Certainly, say the traditional conservatives, people should 'do well' but not ostentatiously so. Amateur sport is being ruined by the professionals, genial general practitioners are being bullied by managers and accountants – examples are increasingly easy to find. Certainly, say the traditional socialists, people should strive to develop their own skills and capacities but not in a spirit of cut-throat competition and self-aggrandizement.

It was in the context of these ideas and arguments that I began to formulate a new programme of empirical research. I was puzzled as to why people worked so hard. Most people in the Western world live relatively comfortably – despite the recent growth of serious poverty. Those with few skills and many dependents, who are paid by the hour at a low rate, would clearly have a strong incentive to work long hours. Yet, as I observed in 1987 and 1988, it was those with high qualifications and few dependents who were working very long hours in the financial institutions of the City of London and elsewhere. Why did they spend so much time earning money? Had they nothing better to do? If taxes were increased to pay for better public services would they cease to work so enthusiastically? I doubted it. My sociological response to this puzzle was to repeat the mantra of 'culture'. Different jobs, different organizations, different occupations all have different cultures. These cultures, I argued, encourage women and men to work hard and long, because that is what barristers, surgeons, vice-chancellors or managing directors of large businesses do. But, importantly, they socialize people to work hard in significantly different ways. The television producer and the surgeon work very hard but in completely different styles. My idea was to write a book called *Styles of Work*. I began interviewing very successful people in the spring of 1989 and a detailed account of my field work appears in the Appendix to this volume.

Styles of Work turned into *After Success*. The main reason for this was that the idea of writing a book to show that rich, powerful and successful people work hard for many different reasons seemed so banal that I quickly became embarrassed that I should ever have seriously considered writing a book on the subject. If, as it was claimed, senior politicians genuinely believed that lowering taxes would release a surge of enthusiasm for working even harder, then writing a book would not be likely to encourage them to change their minds. They must know from their own experience – earning so much less than the senior Civil Servants who, I hope, still advise them – that they work as politicians for other reasons and incentives. However, they must imagine that everyone else is dominated by crude material incentives.

My initial interviews were producing such a depth and complexity of material that I began to feel daunted by the task of working them into a coherent book. So many themes and ideas emerged from highly articulate and often highly reflexive people that scrambling them all together to provide, as it were, a collective image of success would produce a greater distortion than seemed to me to be reasonable. It may perhaps appear easier and more straightforward to write about 'the voice of the unemployed' or even 'young mothers with children under five' (although evidently this is arguable) but the idea of generalizing about a disparate group of highly individual and successful people in different walks of life overwhelmed me. I seemed to be caught between a sociology which applied increasingly sophisticated methods to what, to me, seemed increasingly irrelevant topics, and contemporary fiction or quasi-fiction, which had no sociological pretensions but nevertheless explored the relationship between public issues and private troubles in an imaginative and illuminating way.

Even those sociologists such as Zygmunt Bauman and Anthony Giddens who do address sociologically important questions in an imaginative and innovative way generally make modest attempts to tie their stimulating thoughts to any detailed ethnography. Some of the best anthropologists and ethnographers who might have bridged the gap have become afflicted with, for want of a better term, post-modern creative constipation, brought on by severe bouts of reflexivity. I had a great fear that it might be catching.

When I began to extend my thinking and reading beyond success towards anxiety and identity, I then realized that they were all more closely interrelated than I had originally imagined. Anxiety, as I argue later, is part of the human condition and in some form or other has plagued people for as long as they have been literate – and probably earlier. The task for the sociologist is not simply to address the general question of what causes people to feel anxious but rather to explore the *specific* contemporary conditions that cause anxieties for *specific* categories of the population. It is not a question of using a facile dichotomy to argue that in some previous time people were securely held together by the superglue of tradition – or some other catch-all concept – and that now another all-encompassing concept such as modernism, globalization, post-modernism, or risk society has put people in some kind of disorganized, rootless, anomic, stressed, insecure, anxious state. Even a modest historical exploration makes it seem highly likely that the true novelty of the situation of the 1990s is both the lack of any historical contextualization and the seemingly misguided attempt to explain confusion in terms of confusion.

Coming to terms with anxiety is a perennial problem for individuals, who may then seek solutions in the social institutions and cultural norms and values that they themselves help to create. There seem to be five main areas where men and women have sought some kind of release or solution to endemic anxiety. I refer to these, briefly, in turn.

The first is in the sphere of friends, family, kin and lovers. People can get their sense of identity and security through emotional involvement with one person or as a key member of a kinship network or circle of friends. Much of anthropology explains how this is so. Secondly, people create some kind of religious security for themselves by rituals, practices of mortification, and commitment and belief in the intervention of non-human or quasi-human deities. This remains the most important basis for identity and success for most of the world's population. Britain is untypically less religious than most places. Perhaps this explains much of the distinctiveness of its anxieties. Thirdly, people look to their work to provide meaning, stability and security in their lives. This, in turn, coalesces into identities based on occupation or 'class'. As will appear later, it is increasingly difficult for work to provide this role in the 1990s. Fourthly, people have turned to stimulants and depressants to dull the pain and to alleviate the anxiety. Alcohol and caffeine are commonly used for such purposes in many parts of the world, but there are still many other herbs and plants lurking in any remaining English hedgerows or Amazon forests that can send one high or send one to sleep. Some people manage well enough on this, particularly if the stimulants and depressants are taken in convivial circumstances. The final, fifth, source of alleviation is harder to specify than the others. It is concerned with home, place, space, locality and community. It is the geographical milieu that provides roots, a sense of continuity and reassurance. A thousand slender threads of memory unite to provide a feeling that one is part of something enduring and stable: to be known and accepted, not simply in one's role as daughter or teacher or regular attender at the live music sessions in the pub, but as someone who is part of the place, whose family has played all kinds of different roles and has lived in or near the area for generations. Continuity is maintained as much by the fact that those with whom one went to school have gone their separate ways but are still seen and gossiped about. Gossip is the cement that binds. It is right that newcomers need ten or twenty years before they can even approach becoming accepted as part of what exists and endures. They may marry in; they may have children who can integrate more readily because they were born there; but as long as important ties are outside they view the locality as a community of limited liability and they cannot be accepted. If disaster strikes – her husband leaves her, her parents die or disown her, and her children have no one else in the world to support them – then a woman may be adopted into the place as a social orphan. It is easy to romanticize 'community' as a source of anxiety alleviation and good examples may be hard to find. This is because they are mainly dominated by those who are socially and economically marginal. Communities of work are now largely limited to remote agricultural areas or are based on certain localized industries such as mining, forestry or fishing. Some artists attempt to re-create communities of work but their economic base is generally too fragile to support an adequate infrastructure. They are more likely to be eccentric outsiders than integrated insiders.

To summarize, the main areas within which people find escape from existential anxiety are love, work, religion, drugs and place. People can live successful lives by immersing themselves in four of these – the drugs solution is perhaps the long-stop for those who, for whatever reason, have missed the others. This book is concerned mainly with work and, to a lesser extent, with love. I try to show that confusions about success in work, far from reducing anxiety, may increase it. This is perhaps because the idea of success that is current is still based on the period of massive and rapid economic expansion when the goal of unlimited and unrestricted capitalistic accumulation had not been challenged by those managing and driving the system. Likewise, the dominant paradigm of the male breadwinner, supporting and sustaining his dependent family, was not seriously challenged until the last thirty years of the twentieth century. Changing patterns of work *and* changing patterns of love together make a formidable force for change. Men may be faced with a different conception of 'after success' than women, who may cope more easily with new trade-offs, balances and juggling acts.

Ulrich Beck is surely right when he remarks that the most important changes in contemporary industrial society occur 'on cats' paws, as it were, unnoticed by sociologists, who unquestioningly continue gathering data in the old categories. The insignificance, familiarity and often desirability of the changes conceal their society-changing scope' (Beck et al. 1994: 3–4). He terms these changes 'reflexive modernization' or 'the modernization of modernization', and argues that the changes imply 'difficult-to-delimit deep insecurities of an entire society'. Such ideas open up complex debates to which we shall return later in the book. However, one thing does seem clear: the interrelationships between identity, anxiety and success are at the core of a central debate of the 1990s.

The idea of success remains ambivalent and elusive and some of the elements of this are explored in chapter 2. The idea of success there discussed is almost exclusively male. Much of this chapter is focused on success as fame seen as achievement in business and commerce. It is not about more modest levels of doing anything well in the eyes of one's peers. While most people are 'failures' the abnormally successful have to be warned and pitied. The roots of a sociological understanding of success go back to Durkheim and

Weber. Perhaps there has been too much emphasis on a rather narrow male, elitist version of success which is now coming to the end of its useful life (Glass et al. 1954; Goldthorpe et al. 1980, 2/ 1987). This idea is explored in detail in chapters 3 and 5. I am able to draw on my study of managers carried out in the 1960s – the so-called 'golden age' of the career – and to compare this with managers of the 1980s to illustrate the growth of anxiety and uncertainty among middle managers over the period. The cases discussed in chapters 4 and 5 provide more detailed understanding of the styles of success adopted by senior managers and industrialists. In chapter 5 I draw heavily on the psychoanalytic theories of Karen Horney, a post-Freudian who has been more influential in the United States than in the UK, but still has not received the attention from sociologists that she deserves. She associates a drive to success as a kind of neurotic compulsion. What Horney calls 'the search for glory' leads to people creating for themselves a false self, cutting them off from their real self and turning them into 'well-adapted' automatons. The kind of obsessive tunnel vision which is illustrated by one of the cases in that chapter seems a peculiarly masculine trait. However, there is no doubt that some women can adopt very similar characteristics as certain senior politicians have recently illustrated.

For Horney the strong element of competitiveness in American culture encourages interpersonal hostility, undermines self-esteem and encourages the development of neurosis. Culturally engendered problems, such as the encouragement of conspicuous consumption, matched with the reality of limited economic resources or the injunction to show brotherly love to each other while at the same time encouraging competition with the consequent failure of firms who are not 'successful' enough to survive, all foster neurotic conflict. Erich Fromm and others have diagnosed a collective neurosis at the heart of modern society. During the period of the Cold War the strengths of the 'free world' were contrasted with the oppressions of the communist regimes. Now that the Western capitalist system has apparently triumphed, more doubts and criticisms are surfacing again. The two cases in chapter 5 provide powerful support for the ideas of Horney and Fromm.

John Maltby, the television producer, who is the subject of chapter 6, provides a pivotal case in the exploration of anxiety, success and identity. Highly reflexive and self-aware, he helped to make the interview more a dialogue between two people discussing a case who happened also to be himself. John has been a university lecturer in psychology and was highly skilled as an interviewer and interpreter of the modern world. His analysis and interpretation of himself was acute, but I suspect that my discussion is rather too deferential: others may adopt a harsher interpretation of what is presented there. For those who, for whatever reason, do not feel able to read all the case material in detail, this particular chapter is so central to the underlying theme of the book that perhaps it should not be skipped.

The following chapter is devoted to a discussion of the idea of narratives of identity based on the account of two men – a vice-chancellor and a general – and two women – an artist and a sociologist. This illustrates, perhaps better than anywhere else in the book, how the old conceptual narratives of class and career are being replaced by more shifting and problematic narratives based on gender and more elusive qualities of style and presentation. The most important theme, however, is that distinct and competing narratives of identity coexist within the same person and that the tensions between public and private sources of identity are increasing.

Chapter 8 moves on from identity to anxiety, and argues that while some may believe that traditional society did not have the anxieties of the modern period, there is much to suggest that there was considerable and widespread anxiety in medieval and peasant societies. It is not possible to contrast tradition with modernity in any simple, dichotomous way. Anxiety, as I have already claimed, is endemic in the human condition but appears in differing forms in different contexts. The distinctive characteristic of late modernity is that people are able to articulate their anxieties with greater perception and sophistication. The edgy generation at the end of the fourteenth century in England is matched by the anxious class of America at the end of the twentieth century. However, it is important not to overstate the case. The anxieties of those between thirty-five and fifty-five may not be shared by the generations beneath them. Certainly there have been dramatic changes in demographic circumstances and in personal relationships. However, we now have a language and a culture better able to accommodate and to help us to understand the causes and implications of our anxieties. Marriages may break up, partners split, people are made redundant and stress at work may be increasing. Yet, at the same time, the mass media are full of pop-counselling, and many more young people endlessly discuss their relationships as a kind of hobby activity.

Finally, it seems that the sequel to striving for success is the search for balance. This may be partly driven by the insecurities of flexibilization, which reinforces the dangers of over-commitment to employment and partly by the greater concern with a quality of life based on relationships, parenting and all the activities connected with work outside employment. Life in late modernity is based more on a determination to forge a distinctive and individual life-style than an acceptance of the conventional class-cultural patterns which developed at an earlier stage of capitalism. The relationships between the individual and society were determined largely by the exigencies of the sphere of production in early modernity; these relationships are now, in late capitalism, structured more by the choices and constraints of consumption. And as the language of class gives way to the language of life style, so solidarity, conflict and action are replaced by self-identity, anxiety and balance for most, but certainly not all, members of society.

2

Success in Shame Cultures and Guilt Cultures

The moral flabbiness born of the exclusive worship of the bitch-goddess SUCCESS, that – with the squalid cash interpretation on the word success – is our national disease.

William James in a letter to H. G. Wells, 1906

Success for men, if it ever comes, comes not unattended with difficulty. A god can end it even today. That which is fated you cannot escape.

Pindar: Odes, Pythia 12

Pleasure lies in being, not becoming.

St Thomas Aquinas: *Summa Theologica*

The struggle to achieve success is an essential element in the post-Enlightenment trajectory towards modernity. Fuelled by ambition and measured by money, often later translated into status and power, success has, for more than 200 years, been more worshipped than analysed. Trajectories of individual success, relabelled by sociologists as social mobility, have become the subject of greater and greater sophisticated computations. The greater the incidence of upward social mobility, the implication is, the 'better' the society will be by being more open, offering more opportunities and providing the rewards of success to those most deserving of them.

Success, as part of the motor of modernity, is not a static notion – simply being rich or famous is not enough. It is the *achieving* of fame and fortune which is so important. Success acquired a new meaning with the emergence of industrial capitalism – strikingly in contrast with its ambiguous meaning in the ancient world. The emergence of this new, modern conception of success was discussed by Weber in *The Protestant Ethic and the Spirit of Capitalism* (1930). Sometime in the eighteenth century the leisurely way of operating the putting-out system was destroyed. This is how Weber thought it happened:

> some young man from one of the putting-out families went into the country, carefully chose weavers for his employ, greatly increased the rigour of his supervision of their work, and thus turned them from peasants into labourers. On the other hand, he would begin to change his marketing methods by so far as possible going directly to the final consumer, would take the details into his own hands, would personally solicit customers, visiting them every year, and above all would adapt the quality of the product directly to their needs and wishes. There was repeated what everywhere and always is the result of such a process of rationalization: those who did not follow suit had to go out of business. The idyllic state collapsed under the pressure of a bitter competitive struggle . . . (pp. 67–8)

Thus the new spirit, the bitter competitive struggle, the spirit of modern capitalism was set to work. The new business men had to free themselves from the existing common tradition: 'a sort of liberal enlightenment seems likely to be the most suitable basis for such a business man's success' (p. 70). However, there seemed no way of limiting their consequent work and their success: business became a necessary part of their lives. 'That is in fact the only possible motivation, but at the same time expresses what is, seen from the view-point of personal happiness, so irrational about this sort of life, where a man exists for the sake of his business, instead of the reverse' (p. 70)

Weber went on to argue that the conditions of capitalist success were implacable: those who could not, or would not, accept them either went under or, at best, stayed where they were. The capitalist system needed this devotion 'to the calling of making money'. Weber was concerned to show how through the effect of Calvinist Protestantism the quest for grace of the Middle Ages was transformed into the quest for wealth. 'If as Gunnar Mydral perceived "Americans worship success", it was because Americans in their history worshipped a God which they were confident wanted them to be a success' (Huber 1971:107). Weber recognized that while the Puritans may have genuinely and enthusiastically wanted to work in a calling, people are now forced to do so. Whilst the early Puritans imagined that worldly goods could be worn lightly and readily cast aside like a light cloak now, Weber remarks, 'fate decreed that the cloak should become an iron cage.' If asked, Weber suggests, the men (and much of this argument is limited to men) thus trapped might well say that they are engaged in endless, restless activity for the sake of their children and grandchildren – implying a kind of false-consciousness.

The idea that worldly success and external possessions would in turn possess the possessor is part of what Daniel Bell, following Durkheim, described as the cultural contradictions of capitalism: 'Behind the chiliasm of modern man is the megalomania of self-infinitization. In consequence, the modern hubris is the refusal to accept limits, the insistence on continually reaching out; and the modern world proposes a destiny that is always *beyond*: beyond morality, beyond tragedy, beyond culture' (Bell 1976:49–50).

According to Bell, the traditional bourgeois value system was destroyed by the very essence of the bourgeois economic system, namely the free market. This is what he claims to be the main source of the contradiction of capitalism in American life. The rise of mass consumption has ensured that what were once luxuries are constantly redefined as necessities. Banks and credit card companies urge people to go into debt by suggesting that they 'take the waiting out of wanting'; buy now and pay later:

> The Puritan temper might be described most simply by the term 'delayed gratification' and by restraint in gratification . . . But the claim of the American system was that it had introduced abundance, and the nature of abundance is to encourage prodigality rather than prudence. A higher standard of living, not to work as an end in itself, then becomes the engine of change. The glorification of plenty, rather than the bending to niggardly nature, becomes the justification of the system. (Bell 1976:75)

In Britain this idea that more and more wealth and consumption is a liberating concept reached its apogee under the leadership of Prime Minister Margaret Thatcher. Herself highly socially mobile and having the good fortune to marry someone soon to be endowed as a millionaire, she set the tone for a certain style of success that made greed respectable. Any lingering post-war nervousness about getting rich, staying rich and being proud of it, had seemingly disappeared by 1988 when I began research for this book. After the Chancellor's spring budget *The Economist*'s cover showed haughty – if not insolent – rich people cavorting around the headline:

'Bourgeois Britons grow rich again'. The leading article enthused about how the 'long demoralized and impoverished' middle classes would now acquire new wealth and a new confidence – 'a self-confidence which the British have not enjoyed since King Edward VII's days before the outbreak of the First World War'.[1] This triumphalism was short-lived and many who gloried in their material success suffered the nemesis of their hubris. The cry that echoed through the writings of the ancients, 'Remember that thou art a man',[2] carried connotations lost in a capitalism with no moral or transcendental ethic.

Now, in the final decade of the twentieth century, there are signs of a new mood emerging. Superficial certainties are replaced by new anxieties. There is widespread insecurity and confusion as everything from security of career to certainty of gender identity seems open to doubt and uncertainty. For example, the dislocation of managerial lives in the United States has been dramatic. Instead of men reaching some kind of successful prosperity more and more suffer from the down-sizing and rationalization of their organization:

> The fifty to fifty-five year old male, white college-educated former exemplar of the American Dream, still perhaps living in his lavishly equipped suburban house, with two or three cars in the driveway, one or two children in $20,000 per annum higher education (tuition, board and lodging – all extras are extra) and an ex-job 're-engineered' out of existence, who now exists on savings, second and third mortgages and scant earnings as a self-described 'consultant', has become a familiar figure in the contemporary United States. They still send out résumés by the dozen. They still 'network' (i.e. beg for jobs from whomever they know). They still put on business suits to commute to 'business' lunches with the genuine article or to visit employment agencies, but at a time when more than 10 per cent of the Harvard graduates of the class of 1958 are unemployed, lesser souls in the same position have little to hope for. (Luttwak[3] 1994:6)

The iron cage has collapsed but, so, too, has the driving motivation of the careerist middle class – as future chapters will explore in more detail. The idea of success at the end of the twentieth century is not so self-evidently clear. Before relating the confusions surrounding success with those surrounding self-identity it is instructive to consider in a little more detail earlier confrontations with the problem. The ancient Greeks in this, as in so much else, provide us with insights that still have relevance to the modern condition. In some ways the Greeks seem closer to us in the 1990s than do the ambitious careerists of but a few years ago.

Success in the Ancient World

The Greek word *koros* was used to describe the behaviour of a man who overstepped the limits of acquisitiveness. Such a man is taking more than he needs and is like a gourmand, stuffing himself when he is no longer hungry. *Koros*, in turn, breeds *hybris*. Hesiod, Solon and Theognis thought that greed and the corruption of men in power was the worst evil of their times. 'Wealth does not necessarily corrupt. It is the danger, rather than any actual offence, in exceeding the due position that these writers stress. "Listen to justice, Perses", says Hesiod, "and do not practise hybris. Hybris is bad for a weak man, nor can the good man bear it easily; he sinks beneath its weight"' (Pearson 1962:72). Likewise Herodotus tells of the Egyptian King Amasis, who fears that Polycratus is doomed to disaster because of his unbroken prosperity. The danger always existed that one would go too far and take on the gods. We may call this the Polycratus complex. 'But if one water flowering wealth / in abundance of substance / and fair fame also, let him not seek to become God.'[4] Doubtless with this thought in mind Solon prayed to the Muses:

> I desire to possess wealth, but not to possess it unjustly; just punishment always comes afterwards; the wealth that the gods give remains with a man permanently ... whereas the wealth that men pursue by *hubris* does not come in an orderly decent manner, but against its will, persuaded by unjust deeds; and swiftly disaster is mingled with it. (quoted in Adkins 1972:52)

The problem for mortals is that they cannot be sure what the outcome of their actions will be. 'He who tries to act *eu* [successfully, effectively] falls unawares into some great and dire disaster, while to him that acts *kakos* [ineffectively] the god furnishes good fortune as his deliverance from folly' (p. 63ff). Solon was writing at a time of transition in sixth-century Greek society, where new sources of wealth were permitting the emergence of prosperous landowners, some of whose wealth came from crops and herds and some from plundering raids. Solon certainly wanted to be more prosperous himself but he was deterred by the fear that injustice – even if unintended – and lack of moderation would reap later punishment.

Perhaps the most famous example of Solon's views on success appears in Herodotus' account of the exchange between Croesus and Solon, the *locus classicus* for an understanding of the Greek conception of success. Herodotus describes in his First Book how Croesus first showed Solon around his palace, pointing out the various indications of his vast wealth. He then rashly asked Solon to confirm his great success: 'This urge has come over me to ask you whether you have so far seen anybody you consider to be more fortunate than all other men.'[5]

Instead of receiving the obvious flattering reply he expected, naming himself, Croesus was referred to Tellus the Athenian. Misunderstanding the implications of Solon's reply, Croesus asked who the next most fortunate might be, imagining that his great wealth would surely secure him second place. But again he was disappointed as Solon put forward Cleobis and Biton – 'Argives who made a good living and in addition to that had great physical strength.' In justification of his choices Solon explained that Tellus had honest and handsome sons, came from a good background and had died in battle. The other two were renowned for the way they managed to get their mother to an important party in honour of Hera, held in the temple. Seeing that the oxen that were due to come from the fields to pull the cart had failed to turn up, the doughty sons hitched themselves to the wagon and together pulled it the five and a half miles to the temple. When the boys got her to the church on time, the people at the feast were much impressed, and congratulations were showered on the mother and her sons. The glowing mother then prayed to the statue of the goddess Hera that her sons would receive the very best thing it was possible for humans to have, perhaps not recognizing how true success is achieved. She then went back to the party and her shattered sons lay down to sleep. They never recovered. Significantly, they had no opportunity to exult in their fame.

Croesus was extremely peeved at Solon for, as he perceived it, sending him up. Solon bravely elaborated his point:

> You seem to me to be very rich and to be the monarch of many people, but I couldn't say anything about this question you keep asking me until I find out that you have ended your life well, because the rich man isn't any better off than the man who has enough for his everyday needs, unless his luck stays with him and he keeps on having the best

of everything until he dies happily. Many people who are super rich are unlucky, you know, while many lucky people are moderately well off ... You have to see how everything turns out, for god gives a glimpse of happiness to many people, and then tears them up by the very roots.[6]

Solon left pretty smartly after giving Croesus this bad news but then, inevitably, Croesus received his come-uppance from the gods for daring to believe, simply through possessing great wealth, that he was the happiest man in the world. His favourite son was killed in a hunting accident.

The crucial point is that a man cannot be called happy [*olbios*], until he has died *kalōs*. The message is not that one is happier with a modest competence and a clear conscience than a monarch with a guilty conscience: the early Greeks were not bothered by the notion of guilt. The problem for them was 'Simply that the gods are wont to upset one's applecart without warning, with the result that a life cannot be evaluated until it is over' (Adkins 1972:81).

This uncertainty in the face of capricious deities undoubtedly caused the Greeks considerable anxieties, albeit anxieties of a very different order from those afflicting people two and a half millennia later. Clearly, there was a substantial restraint upon the pursuit of maximum success by all the means within one's power: namely, the fear that the gods would get you in the end. This belief in divine reprisal, punishing hubris in one's lifetime, underpinned the moralists' exhortations towards moderation and the necessity to aim for co-operative excellencies.

The insistence on moderation persists through classical literature. *Arete*, suggesting something like distinction or success, was not something to be sought in all circumstances and at all costs. Theognis considered real *arete* to be the middle path. 'The just man will of course avoid *koros* and *hybris*, which are obstacles to true *arete*, though not necessarily to short-lived success, and he will preserve proper *aidos*, due respect for men and gods' (Pearson 1962:79). Good parents teach *aidos* – self-restraint and sound-mindedness. They cannot teach *arete* in the older sense of the word when it was a *telos*, an end; they can only teach the means that lead to the end.

One of the problems in exploring the culture of the ancient Greeks is how to understand the significance of the individualism that expresses itself in ambition – whether for personal success or for personal fame – and to understand the analytical distinction between the two. Greek scholars such as E. R. Dodds and Arthur

Adkins consider ancient Greece to be a *shame culture* – where the reproachful party is some person other than the reproached – in contrast to a *guilt culture* where the reproach comes essentially from the self. In the words of A. W. Gouldner, 'the "shame–guilt" distinction hinges on differences between the imputed sources of conformity, between presumably "external" and "internal" mechanisms of control' (Gouldner 1965:83).

Both guilt and shame are sources of anxiety. A person will feel guilty when she or he recognizes and accepts the fact that the locus of responsibility is within and there is an internalized evaluation of how well the individual conforms to a set of absolute or ideal standards. The individual recognizes that divergence from these standards is 'wrong', regardless of personal advantage or disadvantage. Guilt, then, is a form of anxiety that arises when a person recognizes that a thought or action is deviating from some group norm that is perceived as intrinsically desirable. The form of anxiety generated by shame occurs when the individual has failed in some way visible to others, whose approval is defined as important by the individual. Fundamentally shame is an anxiety about reputation – about the image of the self held by others:

> The man who knows no shame is flawed ... the occurrence of shame requires that failures of the self be defined as derived from or imposed by outside forces; failure is taken as an indication that the person is weaker than those outside forces. The public revelation of such a weakness is one of the roots of the Greek sense of shame ... Shame rests on a concern with one's competence, potency or power; it is expressive of a desire to avoid an appearance of failure, weakness or dependency. Guilt rests on a concern with one's goodness or rectitude; it is expressive of a desire to feel right. (Gouldner 1965:85)

As we have seen, the traditional Greek belief in the precariousness of life, and the possibility that the mighty can be humbled at any time, would make it more likely that even the most successful of men would heed very carefully the opinions of others, even those of the lowest status. Perhaps by storing up gratitude for their generosity they may be able to neutralize the envy of the defeated – avoiding thereby the dangers of *hubris* – and to recognize some conceptions of the common human condition which passing differences in fortune cannot hide.

One way to avoid *hubris* is to de-emphasize a consolidated hierarchy of esteem and prestige but to provide, in Gouldner's phrase, a division of labour in the contest system. Thus Euripides remarked: 'each has his special excellence . . . one ought to place a man where he can do the most good' (Gouldner 1965:90). This Greek value of specialization is a way of avoiding *hubris* and excess. By limiting themselves to those tasks for which they are best qualified, individuals are able to reduce publicly visible failure and consequent shame. This reduction of competitive spheres to a variety of smaller contest systems – a mosaic of conflicts – 'fosters social cohesion not so much by encouraging individuals to feel a contrite sense of dependence on the larger whole as by encouraging men to lose themselves in the bitterest of struggles in a smaller and disjoined sector' (Gouldner 1965:93).

All this may work well enough for most people, but clearly those who are the leaders of the community have a degree of explaining to do to justify their prominence. They have to recognize that their actions and behaviour are more likely to be open to scrutiny. They cannot disguise the fact that they *are* more successful. They run more risk of hubris and they are open to the envy of others who may be anxious to depose them. Those who have struggled the hardest and achieved the greatest success are at the greatest risk. They have become so habituated to the struggle for achievement that they may find it hard to stop. Furthermore, the higher they have climbed, the greater may be the risks in taking further steps. The spectre of 'after success' and its inevitable punishments for hubris forever threatens. As further rewards provide smaller increments of marginal utility, they may be tempted to push their luck. The more success, the greater the danger of hubris. The nurse in Euripedes' *Medea* remarks: 'Great people's tempers are terrible, always having their own way, seldom checked, dangerous they shift from mood to mood' (quoted in Gouldner 1965:96). Today's political commentators might find themselves saying that of recent French, Russian or British leaders of the last decades of the twentieth century.

A concern for posthumous fame may encourage some leaders to disregard the opinions of their contemporaries, if they believe that those who come after them will judge them more charitably. This is an incentive to continue striving for success, despite having passed the point of legitimate contemporary acclaim. Thus, the highly successful become insatiable. 'Insatiability may serve to defend the individual and the group against the disorientation and apathy of success. "The sovereign source of melancholy is repletion", said William James. "Need and struggle are what excite and inspire us; our hour of triumph is what brings the void"' (Gouldner 1965:97).

Success, then, was a cause of considerable confusion, if not anxiety, among the Greeks. Seemingly, success could very rarely be free from *koros* – the complacency of the man who had done too well – and that in turn generated *hybris* – an arrogance in word or deed or even thought. So what is the secret of success? How can one be happy? A common refrain among the ancients both Greek and Roman was the injunction to 'Remember that thou art a man'.[7] In Versnel's detailed analysis of the Roman triumph – the formal rituals and celebrations that Roman heroes were given on their return to their home city after winning their battles – the various customs surrounding the triumphator are explained (1970). 'A successful man is from all sides threatened by "feindliche Mächte", whether demonic or divine.' At the peak of the celebrations a slave was employed to whisper in the ear of the triumphator *respice post te, hominem te esse momento* [Look behind you and remember that you are a man] (p. 380).

Aristotle addressed the problem with his characteristically penetrating and humanistic analytical focus: Solon's injunction to 'Call no man happy before his death' he considered to be overdogmatic. For Aristotle the quality of a life was determined by its activities and there seemed no good reason to him why a run of good luck should not add to happiness and the truly good and wise man should be able to cope with considerable bad fortune. A crucial element in Aristotle's ethics is the need to avoid excess or deficiency in one's actions. The observance of the mean – *mediocria firma* – is central to his position. 'Putting the matter into general language, we may say that there is no mean in the extremes, and no extreme in the mean, to be observed by anybody' (J. A. K. Thompson 1955:67). Pleasure is an essentially desirable thing and should be sought for its own sake and not as a means to something else. Pleasure – or satisfaction – comes from virtuous activities: 'What sort of pleasure should we affirm to be distinctively human? I suggest that the answer may be found after a review of the human activities. For these are attended by their own pleasures' (p. 300).

Aristotle was one of the fundamental influences in the rebirth of intellectual life in the Middle Ages. The study of Aristotle was revived in the thirteenth century by Albertus of Cologne and, overwhelmingly, Thomas Aquinas, who elaborated further on the virtuous mean. 'Pleasure lies in being, not becoming.'[8] 'To know and appreciate your own worth is no sin.'[9] 'Evil comes from tipping the balance when there should be an equilibrium, the bad being overweight or underweight.'[10]

It seems as though, in our contemporary confusions about success, to be explored in more detail in what follows, the ancient Greeks can speak to us more directly, as we shall see when we discuss the fear of success that has emerged over the last century. However, the ideas of balance and moderation, so firmly established in the medieval mind, may also be ripe for re-evaluation. In a world where wild swings between communism and fascism or between multi-ethnic unity and bloody inter-ethnic conflict occur with appalling speed, the case for the middle way should still be heard.

The Return to Modern Success

The new view of success that provided the motor for industrial capitalism had an unpromising seed bed in medieval thought. 'There is no place in medieval theory for economic activity which is not related to a moral end', wrote R. H. Tawney in his *Religion and the Rise of Capitalism*. 'At every turn, therefore, there are limits, restrictions, warnings against allowing economic interests to inter-fere with serious affairs. It is right for a man to seek wealth as is necessary for a livelihood in his station. To seek more is not enterprise, but avarice and avarice is a deadly sin' (Tawney 1938:45).

'He who has enough to satisfy his wants', wrote a Schoolman of the fourteenth century, 'and nevertheless ceaselessly labours to acquire riches, either in order to obtain a higher social position, or that subsequently he may have enough to live without labour, or that his sons may become men of wealth and importance – all such are incited by a damnable avarice, sensuality and pride.' Two and a half centuries later, in the midst of a revolution in the economic and spiritual environment, Luther in even more unmeasured language was to say the same ... The true descendent of the doctrines of Aquinas is the labour theory of value. The last of the Schoolmen was Karl Marx. (pp. 48–9)

However, from the late sixteenth century there was a gradual spread of Calvinism, with its new scale of moral values and a new ideal of social conduct. The middle classes were transformed. 'Calvin did for the *bourgeoisie* of the sixteenth century what Marx did for the *proletariat* of the nineteenth' (p. 111). Without entering the debate about the relative importance of material conditions and religious ideology, it is clear that economic individualism spread – gradually in the seventeenth century, with increasing speed in the eighteenth century and on to a triumphal peak in the nineteenth.

The first edition of *Self Help* by Samuel Smiles was published in 1859, and provided the charter for twentieth-century students of social mobility. 'On the whole, it is not good that human nature should have the road of life made too easy . . . indeed, to start in life with a comparatively small means seems so necessary as a stimulus to work that it may almost be set down as one of the conditions essential to success in life' (Smiles 1905:315).

Success, inhibited by the shame culture of the Greeks, diverted by Aristotle and the medieval Schoolman into moderation and satisfaction in work and activity, now appeared to have triumphed in a new guise. People justified their rise in society by their hard work and pious assurance that their wealth and success was patent evidence of God's approval.

Guilt-free success seemed to flourish best in the United States, as Richard Huber has thoroughly documented (1971). America was the land of opportunity and the way to make good was to make money. The acquisitive, success-dominated ideology of the mass of American people evaluated social worth largely in terms of dollars. Success spells money was a judgement echoed by social commentators and novelists with increasing confidence from the late nineteenth century. '"What this country needs above everything else", Woodrow Wilson declared in 1913, "is a body of laws which will look after the men who are already made"' (Huber 1971:112).

The Failure of Success

Nought's had, all's spent,
Where our desire is got without content:
'Tis safer to be that which we destroy,
Than by destruction dwell in doubtful joy.
W. Shakespeare: Macbeth, Act III, Sc 2

So much the more surprising, indeed bewildering, must it all appear when as a doctor one makes the discovery that people occasionally fall ill precisely because a deeply-rooted and long cherished wish has come to fulfilment. It seems then as though they were not able to tolerate their happiness; for there can be

no question that there is a causal connection between their
success and their falling ill.
Sigmund Freud: *Complete Psychological Works*, Vol xiv: Those
Wrecked by Success, 1915

By the end of the nineteenth century sociologists and psychologists
were exploring the fear of success in a guilt culture. If success
implied achieving something that was undeserved or taken at the
expense of others, than people might feel guilty. Partly they may
fear the envy of others, and partly, some have argued, there was
guilt associated with an unresolved Oedipal complex. The successful
and assertive one was perhaps risking castration from some general,
all-powerful father. Of course this begs the question of whether
success is primarily a male concept. As Huber comments, 'when
made of money the ladder of success is a topless ladder' (p. 116) and
'a cynic once remarked that "a man is a success if he can make more
money than his wife can spend" . . . The cultural definition of success
was the same for a woman as a man in American society if the
women competed with the man in the world of work' (p. 5).
According to this view a housewife could never be a success however
good, efficient, qualified, or happy she was. This became a major
source of dissatisfaction for women in the 1950s, and did much to
fuel the discontent sparked off by Betty Friedan's book *The Feminine Mystique* in 1963.

Maybe when the Americans caricatured themselves as slaves to
the 'coy mistress' or 'bitch-goddess' success the gendering of the
personification is significant, and it is clear that, unlike the ancients,
Americans had confused and conflated 'success' with 'fame'. The
fear of success was very often the fear of fame. Maybe the American
dream of success was not actually American but rather a European
fantasy about America. The dreams of finding a new Paradise, an El
Dorado, a Golden Fleece, a new land of unlimited possibilities, came
to reality in the Great Frontier and the lure of the West. It was left
to the great American novelists such as Faulkner, Santayana,
Fitzgerald, Steinbeck, Bellow, Salinger and others to record the
great disappointment (Lynn 1955). Arthur Miller's *Death of a
Salesman* is the classic account of the failure of achieving success.

It is important that we keep two themes distinct: there is the
failure of success – the disillusion with the American Dream – and
there is the *fear* of success, which has complex social and psychological origins and which emerged in its contemporary form at the end
of the nineteenth century. Following Simmel we may recognize that

'the essence of the modern is psychologism': perhaps characterization of success as a female figure may indicate that men's fear of
success reflects a fear and uncertainty about their sexual identities at
this period. Jacques Le Rider, writing of *fin-de-siècle* Vienna, claims
that: men (or fictional male characters) were seeking a redefinition
of their sexual identity: sometimes by a 'masculine protest' against the
femininity they discovered in themselves, or against the feminization
of modern culture; sometimes by a 'cult of the feminine' linked with
criticism, and 'deconstruction' of masculine values (1993:166).

The fear of success led to a questioning of what success *is* which,
in turn, led to anomie and a confusion about how to secure a stable
sense of self-identity. All that was left, seemingly, for men was to
get a sense of self-identity by 'providing for' their families as
described by Weber above (p. 23) or documented in the 1960s in my
study of *Managers and Their Wives*.

The anxieties of success were noted in their different ways by
Marx and Durkheim. Admittedly Marx did not spend long worrying
himself about the alienation of the capitalist, or as he somewhat
mischievously called him, the 'non-worker'. 'Everything which
appears to the worker as an activity of alienation appears to the
non-worker as a state of alienation';[11] but having asserted that the
capitalists are alienated Marx produced little further serious analysis:
the manuscript breaks off, unfinished. The capitalist's role in his own
alienation is fundamentally passive:

> The requirements of competition take as great a toll of his initiative as
> that of workers. He is forced to do with his product what the market
> demands – making it more or less different, selling it here or there, for
> this price and that, and so on. Hence, he is in some respects as much
> under the control of his product (of what trying to make it and sell it
> get him to do) as it is in other respects under his control. (Ollman
> 1971:155)

Capitalists suffer from greed, cruelty and hypocrisy. The dehu-
manized capitalists, lacking human powers, can only use objects by
buying them. Hence their greed for the money which enables them
to buy more and more objects. But since the sole goal of buying
things is simply to have them, then retaining the ability to buy has
to involve amassing money. Thus, according to Marx, 'greed is the
subjective means through which capitalists appropriate nature as
well as an omniscient and unruly passion' (Ollman 1971: 157). The

problem of success did not really exist for Marx, being more concerned with social relations than social relationships.

Durkheim, on the other hand, recognized in *Suicide* that new-found success could contribute to a situation of anomie where 'appetites, not being controlled by a public opinion become disoriented, no longer recognize the limits proper to them ... With increased prosperity desires increase. At the very moment when traditional rules have lost their authority, the richer prize offered these appetites stimulates them and makes them more exigent and impatient of control ...' (Durkheim 1952:253). The lack of any restraint on people's desires when it is most needed leads to the inevitability of unfulfillable demands. 'Over-weening ambition always exceeds the results obtained ... Nothing gives satisfaction and all this agitation is uninterruptedly maintained without appeasement. Above all, since this race for an unattainable goal can give no other pleasure but that of the race itself, if it is one, once it is interrupted the participants are left empty handed' (p. 253).

Writing in 1896, Durkheim noted that for a whole century industrial relations had been consistently freed from all regulation: religious influences had declined, 'And government instead of regulating economic life, has become its tool and servant' (p. 255). Both what he called 'orthodox economists and extreme socialists' unite in the main goal of achieving industrial prosperity and success, with opposed systems equally driven by economic materialism. Instead of being a means to an end, greater prosperity becomes an end in itself – the supreme end of individuals and societies alike – 'the appetites thus excited have become freed of any limiting authority ... Their restraint seems like a sort of sacrilege' (p. 255). This limitation of desires, Durkheim claimed, has been made worse by 'the almost infinite extension of the market'. Perceiving in the 1890s the implications of globalization, Durkheim recognized that for the new captains of industry with almost the entire world to provide customers, desires could not possibly be restrained in the face of apparently limitless prospects:

> From top to bottom of the ladder, greed is aroused without knowing where to find ultimate foothold. Nothing can calm it, since its goal is far beyond all it can attain. Reality seems valueless by comparison with the dreams of fevered imaginations; reality is therefore abandoned but so too is possibility abandoned when it in turn becomes reality. A thirst arises for novelties, unfamiliar pleasures, nameless sensations, all of which lose their savor once known. Henceforth one

has no strength to endure the least reverse. The whole fever subsides and the sterility of all the tumult is apparent, and it is seen that all these new sensations in their infinite quantity cannot form a solid foundation of happiness to support one during days of trial. The wise man, knowing how to enjoy achieved results without having constantly to replace them with others, finds in them an attachment to life in the hour of difficulty. But the man who has always pinned all his hopes on the future and lived with his eyes fixed upon it, has nothing in the past as a comfort against the present's afflictions, for the past was nothing to him but a series of hastily experienced stages. What blinded him to himself was his expectation always to find further on the happiness he had so far missed. Now he is stopped in his tracks; from now on nothing remains behind or ahead of him to fix his gaze upon. Weariness alone, moreover, is enough to bring disillusionment, for he cannot in the end escape the futility of an endless pursuit. (p. 256)

This fine passage has been quoted at length since it provides a remarkable sociological account of the phenomenon of 'after success', almost exactly one hundred years ago. Clearly, the *fin-de-siècle* anxieties were well recognized in Paris, Berlin and Vienna in the 1890s. Le Rider claims the Viennese modernist writers of the period all mused in their diaries on the theme of a crisis of identity which was at the heart of their work. Little wonder that Freud, the giant *fin-de-siècle* figure in Vienna, when discussing different character types that he met in psychoanalysis, should head a section on 'Those wrecked by success' (1915). In the United States Kenneth Lynn's analysis of important novelists of the period shows how they explored the horrors of winning and the emptiness of success. In a powerful documentation of Durkheim's anomic theory of suicide, Lynn concludes 'the pace that killed had to be kept up, but the enthralment and the exhilaration attendant upon the rise were now replaced by monotony, exhaustion – and death' (1955:242). Suicide was a haunting threat.

The fear of success in the first half of the twentieth century was discussed more by psychologists than sociologists. Success neurosis or success phobia was, as mentioned above, linked to the Oedipal dilemma. Discussion developed around the issue that for both men and women the inhibition of aggressive success striving might be experienced as castrating and a substantial psychoanalytical literature emerged on the rise and fall of people who attained success and then sabotaged it or fled from it. The fear of success was seen to be a pathological state. In one such analysis by Melanie Klein in *Envy and Gratitude* she developed an explanation based on how the infant experienced the mother's breast – the infant's first object relation: 'The good breast is taken in and becomes part of the ego, and the infant who was first inside the mother now has the mother inside himself' (1988:179). Under these circumstances the infant will acquire gratitude and appreciation for the goodness in self and others. However, if, by contrast, the early experience of the breast is not good the baby's ability to experience new sources of gratification is impaired and in consequence he cannot sufficiently internalize a really good primal object. The breast can be experienced as mean, grudging and depriving. This may be the source of a later compulsion to deprive oneself of success. Klein argues that 'People who have rather precariously established their good object suffer under anxiety lest it be spoilt and lost by competitive and envious feelings and therefore have to avoid success and competition' (p. 218). Envy in Kleinian terms involves an individual experiencing anger that others are able to possess and enjoy something desirable. Individuals may not want to be like another person nor want to have what the other has, but simply envy the contentment or pleasure. Associated with this envy is a desire to spoil what one cannot have. Those suffering from these primal feelings of envy may undermine themselves by devaluing and distancing themselves from what is good in their lives. Even when such people attempt to work through their problems in therapy – discussed in some detail by Klein – they may feel compelled to denigrate or undermine the process.

In his useful overview of some of the main psychological theories to account for the fear of success David Tresemer notes, 'Further writings on the psychiatric literature have linked the phenomena of fear of success and success avoidance to masochism and self-injury, "moral masochism", debilitating manic-depressive attacks, reactive depression and passivity, guilt and shame. In nearly every case, the presenting symptom, or vehicle of the earlier difficulties has been debilitating anxiety' (1977:7–8).

It is clear that there are different sources of anxiety. Anxiety from within can arise from individual psychodynamics. It can also result from a socially generated unease that the wheel of fortune inevitably turns to bring down the mighty from their seats. The Chorus in *Antigone* by Sophocles reflects this pessimistic view of success: '. . . greatness never / shall touch the life of man without destruction' (quoted in Dodds 1951:51).

So we 'touch wood' and hope that Fortune will continue to smile on us. Yet as Carl Jung observed, the process of getting older and wiser could well lead many people to a re-evaluation of what had appeared at an earlier age to be success. If success has been single-minded and at the expense of other aspects of life, then those things that have been repressed to achieve success may well resurface later in life. Doubts about the real worth and validity of earlier triumphs may be put into question and one's auto-critique may be a source of strength and personal growth and fulfilment, or these same doubts may generate melancholic despair and a world-weariness about the meaning and significance of glories that turn to ashes and gratifications that provide no lasting satisfaction.

It is because the idea of success is so full of ambiguity that it generates its own set of anxieties. Sociologically the disenchantment of worldly success can be associated with secularization, the intellectual retreat from the triumphalism of the modernist project and the uncertainty about the idea of progress.[12] If there is no clear certainty about the broad goals of society, there can be no universally acceptable ideas of success. The goals of the successful scholar may not coincide with the goals of the successful manager in an educational institution. The more complex the society, the greater the number of alternative models of success that will coexist. Faced with conflicting messages, conflicting role models and conflicting sources of social reward, people try to work out a self-identity that will maintain credibility among more than one salient audience.

Success as an indicator of a good self implies the privatization of success, which avoids one kind of competition but generates others. A young woman who has completed higher education may seek success in a profession. One or other of her parents may see their success in terms of being able to boast about their grandchildren, and long for her to get married. The young woman's partner may resent her commitment to her career as a lawyer or investment analyst and may want her to take long holidays to exotic places. How should she be a successful woman? These and other similar questions will be examined in the following chapters. Problems associated with success were of one sort when it was almost a simple question of the generals, political leaders and top capitalists avoiding hubris. In contemporary Western society, success can generate positive or negative compulsions and neuroses which may be more associated with gender identities than with propitiating jealous or capricious deities. Single measures of success – like the old-fashioned notion of social mobility – are fading as a more turbulent trajectory of jobs replaces conventional career structures. Does a man have to get satisfaction from the way he expresses himself at work as the source of his potential success, or does he also have to consider his success as father, son and partner? How should a man or woman be sure that they have been successful? Whose judgement counts? Are wealth, high office, or sporting or creative achievement and so on still examples of the main criteria for determining those who are the most successful in our society?

People are not sure any more. In the chapters that follow we explore the ambiguities, anxieties, neuroses and frustrations of success. We also consider some fortunate people who are not over-burdened by self-doubts, who are pre-eminent in their fields, are enjoying their lives, and who do not take themselves too seriously but who undertake what they *do* seriously. They have learnt from Anarcharsis to play so that they may be serious (quoted in J. A. K. Thompson 1955:302). Finally, we consider what this *fin-de-siècle* view of success may tell us about the kind of society that will emerge beyond 2000.

3

Managing without Success: 1960–1990

This and the following two chapters are concerned with the men who manage, own or control the wealth-creating enterprises of contemporary Western society. There is little dispute about the centrality and importance of these businesses and organizations and the need for those who rise to the top to be recognized and rewarded as being successful. These are the natural heirs to those pioneers of the Industrial Revolution who built up the great wealth of the West. They are now, presumably, the new officer class in the international economic war of competitive advantage. Certainly successful lawyers, architects, musicians – and perhaps even sociologists – create wealth if only by attracting students to spend money in their respective countries. However, it has to be conceded that orchestras or universities are rarely completely self-financing. If one is looking for surplus value to be taxed to provide public infrastructure, then it is not unreasonable to focus more on industrial organizations than the liberal professions.

I have explained in the Preface why I do not specifically discuss women managers; a further reason is that I wanted to draw on the research on male managers I did nearly thirty years ago, in order to explore some of the changes that have taken place in the last part of the century. Since the first study was focused on men I could not avoid perpetuating the bias to some extent. The ethnography on successful women will be better handled in a different context.

Economic and material success in modern societies, it is often claimed, depends upon the quality of management. If public and private organizations are run inefficiently or incompetently, public sector borrowing will be unnecessarily high and the competitive advantage of one nation-state's private companies will suffer in relation to those of other nations. Many institutions of higher education in these societies have hurried to establish some kind of business school, and hopeful managers bustle along to learn about organizational behaviour, human resource management and similar people-oriented skills. Being a manager means co-ordinating and controlling the behaviour of others. As the managers returned with their degrees and certificates to the organizations that sponsored them, or perhaps moved on to better positions, they discovered the great irony of Britain in the late 1980s and 1990s: their organizations were being trimmed, slimmed and down-sized, so that they themselves formed a significant number of those being appraised and controlled. Colleagues are costs. It is little wonder that the supervision and motivation of staff has become demanding and problematic. 'As jobs are "redesigned", "collapsed" and "renegotiated", managers are often required to perform duties for which they have neither ability nor inclination' (Scase and Goffee 1989:25).

Increasingly, it seems, managers have a succession of jobs rather than the 'career' which may have existed in some previous golden age – for a few years perhaps in the 1950s. Some may claim that at that time managers 'could be reasonably optimistic about their career prospects' (Scase and Goffee 1989:3), but it is generally the case that those who argue thus base their position more on American than on British material. W. H. Whyte's book *The Organization Man* (1957) became a benchmark from which some felt change could be measured. F. H. Goldner's article on 'Demotion in Industrial Management' (1965:714–24), despite its seemingly greater relevance to the British situation than Whyte's book, has largely been ignored. The assumption that American mid-twentieth-century cultural traits applied equally significantly to European countries is highly questionable. The interchangeability of ethnography of that period between America and Britain was a product of the intellectual convergence which came with the fashionable notion of convergence of industrial societies (Kerr et al. 1960). British sociology in the mid–1960s was at a pretty modest level of development and there was a tendency to follow American lines of thought more uncritically, perhaps, than would be acceptable thirty years later. We now have our own stars to give us light.

Clearly, we must be careful not to create a fallacy of relatively privileged managers enjoying what Scase and Goffee call their 'customary benefits' in the 1960s, to serve as a contrast to what became the insecure, 'Reluctant Managers' of the late 1980s. Nevertheless, there have been changes – not least in the introduction of new technology and in corporate restructuring – but there are also many more managers proportionately and absolutely now than there were in the 1960s and an increasing, although still small, proportion of these are women.

The changes for the British managers in the second half of the twentieth century in Britain have, indeed, been substantial. There were some hints in the 1960s of what was to come. In 1969 the British Institute of Management published a Report entitled *The Experienced Manager* as part of a programme designed to explore the training and development needs of older managers. Reflecting the thinking of that period, the author described the 'career progress of the average manager'. 'On entering the company, especially if he [*sic*] joins as a trainee, he will normally be put through a form of processing. In addition to indoctrination in the ways of the company he will be encouraged to see his career as one of uninterrupted and loyal advancement' (Mant 1969:16). If one substituted the phrase 'communist party' for 'company' in that quotation most people reading it in the 1990s might well consider that it made better sense. Certainly it illustrates how little the so-called liberating 1960s affected management thinking. But there were worrying clouds on the horizon. The author of the report goes on to note: 'The time may well come when that in which the experienced manager is an expert is of diminishing value to the company. The cycle of usefulness of expertise is shortening as the technological and economic operations of the companies become more complex' (Mant 1969).[1]

Twenty four years later 'the cult of insecurity' could be discussed as part of the conventional wisdom of the middle class. As one commentator observed:

A new branch of management theory says that the 'casualization' of the middle classes is not just the result of cost-cutting in a recession but an efficient and rational response to the modern world. In a language that sounds like a second cousin to English, they justify the sacking of middle managers with talk of 'down-sizing' and 'right-sizing' of 'delayering' and 'flattening' of 'shedding' and 'process engineering'.[2]

The same account, written in 1993, claimed that 8 per cent of Civil Service jobs – 44,250 people – have had the management of their jobs put out to tender. This process of 'market testing', whereby officials compete against private companies bidding to manage their work, is planned to continue 'until all 555,000 civil servants have been confronted by the market'. British Telecom reduced its managers and staff by 80,000 from 1989 to 1993. The feature was headed 'Nobody is Safe'.

This shift from 'uninterrupted and loyal advancement' to a situation where 'nobody is safe' is one of the greatest changes of the last quarter of the twentieth century. It will do much to modify our views of success in the next century.

Over the past thirty years, I have had the opportunity to discuss managers' ideas about success, since my own research interest in the topic spans that period.[3] I can reflect now on the material reported in *Managers and Their Wives* (Pahl and Pahl 1971) and compare it with interviews I have carried out over the last five years in preparation for this book. The study by Scase and Goffee (1989) provides an additional valuable source, since it is based on a larger sample than I was able to gather, and was drawn from six large organizations. The oldest manager in my sample, interviewed in the 1960s, was born in 1921; Scase and Goffee's managers were mostly born after the Second World War, and my small group of high-flying City bankers and corporate lawyers was born after 1960.[4] So it is possible to present a fairly broad perspective on the ambiguities of managerial success and ambition in the second half of the twentieth century in Britain.

In the 1960s I was puzzled why managers in industry worked so hard; I questioned in an ironical way whether they were 'willing slaves to the system': they appeared to have internalized an ideology of self-coercion and were suffering the full force of the competitive society. Commenting at the time on the men I first interviewed in 1965 and 1966 I suggested that: 'they must work hard to produce more, for if they did not, somebody else would; markets would decline and even managers can become redundant. They have no security'[*sic*]. Their only reassurance seemed to come from moving forward and upward through a succession of jobs:

> For them life is a hierarchy and success means moving up in it . . . very often it is the fear of falling rather than positive aspiration to climb which pushes these men on. Those who had an experience of downward social mobility in their family history were among the most determined to have a successful career. They work, then, because they are trapped in a competitive society: above all they do not want to fall. The men were not, however, usually prepared to admit that they were driven on for selfish, materialist reasons. They would talk of 'challenge'

and 'responsibility' as well as family commitments. (Pahl and Pahl 1971: 259)

Yet, paradoxically, a firm commitment to achieve 'success' was not, in general, typical of the managers of the 1960s. Few men were advancing along a clear and structured career line. I got a sense, when reading through the list of all the jobs they had done, of their being pulled up the management hierarchy by luck or by having a patron – or mentor as they are now called – who knew their name and suggested it at a critical time. It was a reflection of my status in the 1960s that I refer to them all as 'Mr'.

Mr Ash, a forty-seven-year-old distribution manager in the 1968 sample, knew the men who pulled or pushed him on and he felt more acted upon than acting:

> I never set target dates . . . partially because I am basically superstitious . . . I am certainly or probably going to be disappointed if I plan too much ahead. As far as getting ahead in the world is concerned, to me it means nothing specific. In fact it is slightly distasteful and smacks of people with ruthless ambition. I have never taken business seriously. Others rate business success worthwhile for its own sake. I don't. Success means no more to me than my personal job satisfaction and more money. I don't admire successful businessmen . . . I plan things mentally but don't like to recognize that I am planning it . . . I think about it a lot but won't talk about it. This is probably because I am superstitious as I said before . . . I don't have much choice – in fact I choose not to have much choice. (Pahl and Pahl 1971:99–100)

Mr Bridge was a forty-seven-year-old head of department in 1968, and he revealed a nervous insecurity:

> Taking a job like this is often a way to fall flat on your face. There's a danger at my age of not reaching a plateau but of reaching a peak and then going down on the other side. This is a definite danger. I've now got to engage in rat-race politics. I apply for promotion thinking only of my masters – there is a need to be seen to be ambitious. (p. 100)

A younger man, Mr Petham, born in 1928, was a sales manager in 1968 but hoped eventually to get on the main board of his company.

> I always have doubts if I can do a job and I often wonder if the benefits are worth it in terms of the quality of life that I have to lead as a result of the job. The financial position that we are in does not improve

generally because of the increased expenses of a bigger house ... I don't think I've made any conscious choice about my career other than taking promotion when it was offered ... I don't see my career as a logical process apart from staying in the technical sales side. It's more a series of sharp jumps. I think I've come a very long way. (p. 102)

The false image of the golden age of managerial careers seems to be based on the notion that all managers were working for companies like Unilever or BP. The reality was different. Most men moving between moderately responsible jobs in small or medium sized firms experienced their working lives as going through a collection of jobs which they retrospectively termed a career. As various surveys of the 1950s demonstrated, many managers had worked their way up, having left school at fourteen but gaining skills and experience during the war. Many had studied in the evening for professional qualifications, had come a long way and were suspicious of 'success'.[5] Only 38 per cent of my 1960s sample were graduates, the rest had risen on the escalator of the post-war recovery from the 1950s. When I first took part as a tutor on a course for managers in the early 1960s, many of them – maybe up to a half or more – would describe themselves as production engineers, happy amid the oily, noisy machinery of the plant and sceptical of the smooth-talking people on the sales side or those in the unreal world of personnel. Accountants were particularly despised as people 'who did not know what industry was all about'. Mr Ickham who, as a thirty-one-year-old management consultant in 1968, was a high-flier, was still absolutely sure that he did not want a son of his to be an accountant. I remember in 1961 or 1962 having a debate with managers on an AEI staff course on whether the goal of the company should be to sell what it could make or make what it could sell. The engineers, used to producing colossal turbo-generators for India or wherever, could not conceive of an alternative of selling what you could make. Arnold Weinstock and his consumer-durable revolution was yet to come.[6]

I feel that, looking back on my main 1960s study, I was fortunate in being able to catch glimpses of the stability and security of mid-twentieth-century Britain. One of the men in my sample was a Civil Servant born in 1926; his father, also a Civil Servant, was probably born during the last years of the nineteenth century. As he remarked, 'I think life is fixed in the London suburbs. Except in terms of the technology (for example the television) the style of life is now remarkably similar to what it was thirty years ago ... I simply see the 1960s as the 1930s writ large' (Pahl and Pahl 1971:253). Mr Bourne's son was born in 1956 and we asked him what sort of person he would like his son to become:

> Much as he is now ... I was flattered when I was talking to his housemaster at school, when he remarked that my son is a very civilized boy ... He has got a sense of humour and the same funny stories amuse us both. He is considerate. I wouldn't say he is a repository of all the virtues but I think he is an engaging personality and would be a pleasant sort of young man. I think he will ultimately make a good citizen. That sounds really corny and square, doesn't it? As far as the job is concerned one would hope he would finish up in some professional capacity. I have no strong feelings one way or the other about this: it's just a case of seeing which way he is going to develop. (p. 253)

Mr Bourne thought that true happiness was more likely to come out of having good relationships with someone else and he hoped his son would discover that for himself. He doubted that happiness could be found in any other way. Mr Bourne provided a clear benchmark of traditional security and confidence, free from the anxieties and tensions that later appeared to afflict so many in the 1990s. The younger Bourne will be much the same age as his father was in the mid-1960s in the middle 1990s, but I doubt if he will be as relaxed as his father was then who remarked: 'In the Civil Service, as compared with industry, I think that it's part of the game to pretend that you're not really trying. If you are open about wanting to succeed you are regarded as an outsider and it won't get you anywhere' (p. 254).

The middle-class managers of the 1960s emphasized the import- ance of a 'rounded personality', a 'full person' and while they always said they did not mind what their sons did, the assumption they made, either explicitly or implicitly, was that 'a lawyer would be nice', or a similar professional position. It did not occur to me to ask 'And how would you feel if your son dropped out and became a New Age Traveller?', but I am pretty sure of the answer I would get. I suspect that when the age cohort of the established middle class is quite small – as it was in the 1930s – it could afford to be quite relaxed about being ambitious. A stress on stability, style and 'gentlemanly' values was possible because it was not necessary to be otherwise. For a generation brought up on the world of *Winnie-the-*

Pooh, those expressing lovable eccentricity were much to be preferred to the rather pushy, busy Rabbit (Milne 1965:71).[7] Indeed,
there is a positive encouragement to the youthful readers of *Winnie-
the-Pooh* to be unambitious and rather laid back. It was very bad to
be too pushy and far better to sit around and have a chat than to be
'busy' in an embarrassing, if not officious way. The following
dialogue picks up the style very well:

> 'Rabbit's clever', said Pooh thoughtfully.
> 'Yes', said Piglet, 'Rabbit's clever.'
> 'And he has Brain.'
> 'Yes', said Piglet, 'Rabbit has Brain.'
> 'There was a long silence.
> 'I suppose', said Pooh, 'that's why he never understands anything.'
> (pp. 127–8)

This must have been a great comfort to many not very clever
middle class children whose capacities gave out at prep school after
only modest advancement into *Kennedy's Latin Primer*. Rabbit's life
was made up of Important Things, but there was little encouragement to take Rabbit as a role model. Much more sensible and
civilized to visit Christopher Robin where they stayed 'until very
nearly tea-time, and then they had a Very Nearly Tea, which is one
you forget about afterwards, and hurried on to Pooh Corner, so as
to see Eeyore before it was too late to have Proper Tea with Owl'
(p. 128). The names will change to Henry and Caroline, the drink
will be a rather good white Burgundy and Pooh Corner will be a
wine bar or club, and life will chunter on with weekends in the
country in Old Rectories in Wiltshire or Hampshire.[8] The Winnie-
the-Pooh world seemed to have a solidity and a security that would
stay the same for ever. The Revolution of 1979 had yet to come.

John Raynor (1969) has described success as 'an almost compulsive drive' for the middle-middle class yet it was hard to find much
of that among the Madingley managers of the 1960s, but the forces
of change were waiting in the wings. The estate agents, accountants
and city traders who would make greed acceptable in the 1980s had
already left primary school by 1968. Furthermore, the first major
post-war attack on British industry was just about to begin. The age
of mergers, take-overs and asset stripping was short-lived but very
dramatic. Post-war *parvenus* were not socialized by the public
schools. Beneficiaries of the 1944 Butler Education Act did not
necessarily remember the unchanging London suburbs or Christo-

pher Robin. Nor were they socialized into submission as Richard Hoggart (1988) describes in his autobiography, internalizing what Frank Parkin (1971) called the subordinate value system. They were angry young men eager to upset the establishment, whose 'gentlemanly values' were perceived as hypocrisy. Clever sons and daughters from the skilled working class and lower-middle class went to university for the first time in the history of their families and became social workers, housing managers and academics. Sociology grew dramatically and its acolytes spent much time investigating class and the social mobility through which so many of them had benefited. Indeed, social mobility became something of an obsession for some sociologists, despite the fact that the results did so little to explain the cultural changes that were having such important social consequences.

I was particularly fortunate in that I was a participant observer in this crucial period of transition in British industry between 1969 and 1973. Together with Jack Winkler, we had received a three-year grant to look at what directors in British industry actually did, perhaps as a way of reducing their perceived stress and anxieties.[9] Many of the most senior and powerful men in British industry were extraordinarily generous in allowing us to observe board-level politics at first hand by shadowing them wherever they went and in whatever they did or by sitting unobtrusively in their offices. This was the period of what at the time Prime Minister Heath called 'the unacceptable face of capitalism'. Small businesses were bought solely for the site value of their offices or plant; family firms were taken over and family directors bought out or given sinecures; large firms were restructured, divisionalized and regrouped; a new breed of over-smart-suited young men with MBAs appeared one week as 'consultants' and a few weeks later mysteriously became finance directors on the board. Fortunes were lost and fortunes were made (Newbould and Jackson 1972). I sat in the offices of a long-since bankrupt property development company and watched a portfolio of offices and shops in south-east England being revalued over a sandwich lunch. I cannot remember now whether it was £50 million or £80 million that was added to the company's assets through this 'working lunch'.[10]

At the beginning of the 1970s we made some tentative predictions in *Managers and Their Wives* about the changes that might follow. We noted that the wives of our managers were much more reflexive than their husbands, and had more doubts about the right of 'management thinking' to impose itself on home and family life.

They wondered whether all the long hours of their husbands' effort were worth it. Furthermore, we suggested that:

> So long as wives accept a passive role or a supportive, work-oriented one, all may be well. But the spread of the ideal of a close, companionate type of marriage, coupled with the rising level of education of women, may mean that the sacrifices will become increasingly unacceptable . . . We found little evidence among the women in our sample of dislike of the nuclear family, resentment against the marriage tie, or very great frustration in their chief roles of wife, mother and housewife. But we *did* find a sense of uncertainty about identity among the women [emphasis added now]. (Pahl and Pahl 1971: 235–6)

We went on to conclude that the main force for change would not be the managers but their wives. We noted the changing conceptions about the position of women in the British society of 1970, and the emergence of different expectations about the nature of marriage and family life. We suggested that the next generation of middle managers would be unlikely to be willing slaves to the system. 'We would expect the tension to become greater as the drive for greater efficiency in British industry meets increased concern about the quality of personal relationships, and of marriage in particular' (p. 236).

My experience of the early years of the University of Kent led me to add, rather quaintly I now think:

> The 'feminization' of young men, which has been one of the unintended consequences of the expansion of co-educational higher education, may have helped to make many more young men sensitive to the feelings of the young women they know or live with. Marriage is probably entered into far more seriously and on a basis of greater equality than it has been at any time in the past. It seems less likely that young men who have been to university since the mid-1960s will ever imagine that they are marrying a docile housewife. (p. 267)

I return to the issue of the new anxieties for men and women in chapters 6 and 8. Here it is curious to notice how tentative we were a quarter of a century ago, despite claiming to be trained observers of the social scene. We expected that there could be a demand for more time for men and women to develop their relationships – maybe even at the expense of more money. However, we acknowledged that: 'It is possible that this category of people in our society will become more materialistic. Most of our couples have achieved only a modest degree of affluence: the incentives of a larger house, a second car, more lavish and longer holidays may keep middle managers in Britain hard at the grind until the end of the century' (p. 267).

The oil crisis of 1973 ended the post-war boom. Inflation in the mid-1970s became almost uncontrollable. Public expenditure had to be contained. Britain was humiliated by tough demands from the International Monetary Fund in 1976. As industrial strife increased in the late 1970s the 'incompetence' of management and the 'greed' of the workers led to the final collapse of a kind of corporatist consensus. On Christmas Day 1976 *The Economist* published a special survey on 'The Coming Entrepreneurial Revolution'. Norman Macrae, the deputy-editor, was remarkedly prescient when he began by stating, 'The world is probably drawing to the end of the era of big business corporations. These institutions were virtually created during 1875–1910. During 1975–2010 they may virtually disappear in their present form . . . Many services now provided by government will need to be "recompetitioned" and "reprivatized".' The end of organization man was at hand.[11] (In chapter 5 we consider in more detail one of the men who was largely responsible for privatizing one of the largest of the previously nationalized industries.) The economy limped on ineffectively for two or three years. Managers may have thought they were having a bad time – but far worse was to come. Margaret Thatcher was elected with a large majority in 1979 and the second attack on British industry began. De-industrialization advanced at a manic pace (Rose et al. 1984:137–57). Some who saw the writing on the wall jumped sideways into the service sector. A few, benefiting from the massive capital gains during the short-lived period of house inflation, sold up and headed for the hills. It was unclear whether successful managers were those who kept their jobs or those who got up and ran, with or without golden handshakes.

Scase and Goffee began their work on *Reluctant Managers* in the mid–1980s in order to explore the changing experiences and attitudes of middle managers and, perhaps to their surprise, they rediscovered the ambiguities and uncertainties about success that had been described in *Managers and Their Wives* a generation earlier. However, what is of particular interest is that the *reasons* for the Scase and Goffee managers' being reluctant about committing themselves to employment seemed to be substantially different from those we put forward. Perhaps it is worth emphasizing that another study, also referring to middle managers in the 1960s, also documented a degree of distancing from complete work involvement: 47 per cent of Cyril Sofer's example expressed significant reservations about the work they were doing and were resistant to total commitment. As one said: 'I don't live to work. I work to live' (1970:247). The authors of *Reluctant Managers* make it clear that compared with how they imagined the 1960s managers to be, the mid–1980s managers are not prepared to put employment first. 'Managers of all ages, then, seem concerned to improve the quality of their personal life-styles outside rather than within work ... they have consciously reduced their psychological dependence upon employment' (Scase and Goffee 1989:100). The authors discovered growing feelings of cynicism amongst junior managers; middle managers also became affected by the apathy that surrounded them and ended up adopting a similar stance. They quote a male manager in accounting and finance in his late forties in the mid-1980s: 'Staff are expected to work much harder than before ... But when they see their hard efforts being lost by the stroke of a pen, it's rather frustrating and people are beginning to wonder whether it's worthwhile slogging their guts out' (p. 32).

Managers appear to be showing signs of fatalism, alienation and anomie, which Marx and Durkheim foresaw as part of the cost of a capitalist market economy. Like instrumentally oriented manual workers they may view their work as something they do for the money but their true identity develops outside employment.[12] Many managers now may seem to be little more than highly qualified technicians. Increasingly, senior managers now monitor very precisely the ranks of middle and junior managers, creating considerable pressure for them to reach specific targets. Individual respondents in the Scase and Goffee study objected to the short-term nature of the targets. Any success is short-lived: if a target is reached or bettered the target is then raised. This approach engenders fear. Working relationships become more aggressive: people are increasingly watching their backs and struggling for personal survival. All this destroys organizational commitment.

In answer to the question put by Scase and Goffee: 'What do you think should be the major inputs in management training?', 69 per cent of the men and 82 per cent of the women mentioned personal and interpersonal skills such as assertiveness, team-building or leadership. The more technical aspects of the job were mentioned by much smaller proportions of the sample. Since most managers have been promoted into their present positions because they have demonstrated various forms of technical, functional and specialist knowledge, their perceived lack of interpersonal managerial abilities may generate insecurity and anxiety. Furthermore, since the appropriate interpersonal skills differ between companies with different organizational styles, and since men and women are likely to move between these different contexts in the course of their working life, the scope for confusion and increased anxiety is great.

Whether or not the golden age of orderly careers ever existed, the experience of most managers in the 1990s is of considerable insecurity and uncertainty about their future prospects. I suspect that in the past a disproportionate amount of social science research was focused on large organizations such as Unilever or the oil companies. Thus, while Scase and Goffee acknowledge that Sofer's study was based on a few large-scale organizations, they make the unwarranted assumption that his conclusions would apply to all managers. As I pointed out above, the Madingley managers did not feel secure about the future but at that time certainly one of the most unlikely options was redundancy or dismissal. Thus, Scase and Goffee's assertion that few managers are committed to career success may not be particularly novel. However the idea that there is now an alternative idea of *personal* success is indeed new, and non-work criteria play a large part in self-assessed ideas of success. In particular, and crucially, Scase and Goffee discuss the way that managers and their partners work out some joint survival/development strategy for themselves and their dependents. Men are becoming more like women in recognizing the futility of working out detailed career plans. Rather, they take jobs that suit their various circumstances or, indeed, make the best of a bad job. Forty-seven per cent of Scase and Goffee's male managers said they were sometimes frustrated, and a further 38 per cent said that they were sometimes or always frustrated. The percentages were much the same for both men and women.

Some people struggling with resentment and anxiety may show symptoms of sub-clinical depression and succumb to various dependencies. Relationships with partners may stretch or snap.[13] Increases in divorce and suicide rates among this category may indicate with different degrees of tragedy the personal crises which the contemporary way of organizing society seems to produce. Maybe the thrusting and aggressively written management textbooks are partly to blame, in suggesting that career failure is due to some kind of personal inadequacy: character or moral weakness produces failure, not the system. This is a neat trick which Merton discussed so well in his classic essay on social structure and anomie (1957:131–94).

Anxious managers appear to be an exceptionally gullible market for evangelical 'consultants' or gurus, who prey on their fears and insecurities and peddle the latest brand of psychobabble, which they could get free from their grandmothers if they simply translated it into jargon and put it on transparencies for the overhead projector.

In a witty and perceptive review of more than a dozen books on management written in the mid-1980s, Patrick Wright pointed out that their authors have a new-found confidence. No longer under any obligation to consider management as a properly constituted 'academic' subject, borrowing from more established disciplines to justify its recommendations and prescriptions, the new management thinkers do not even attempt to bring the movement of enterprise under a rational description which might identify professional management with stable administrative functions of planning, resource allocation and control. Far from trying to take the guesswork out of the corporate game, the tendency now is to celebrate it (Wright 1987:8). The new magic words are 'excellence' and 'change', often approached with a religious fervour. 'The excellent company knows that the pace of "change" – one of management thinkings' catch-all reifications – is escalating, and also that constant innovation is the prerequisite of success' (p. 8). The new gurus urge companies to encourage those who, under the old rational model, would be dangerous deviants or oddballs. Now they are to be feted, encouraged to make mistakes in the search for innovation and to go hard for the 'vision thing'. 'The new entrepreneur is a survivalist surrounded by "change" – an external force which comes at him with the irresistible power of the Megatrend ... where traditional management thinking tries to help corporations get better productivity out of the Organisation Man by "tacking on skills to the same old person", the peak performer is interested in complete personal transformation' (p. 9).

If excellence is to be limited to a maverick minority then most managers are likely to be nervous and insecure. How do they *know* that they are capable of becoming excellent if this is all a matter of intuition and personal idiosyncratic style, and being unafraid of risk and uncertainty? At least with the traditional model of career and organizational hierarchy, hard work and persistence might well lead eventually to success. In the study *Reluctant Managers* it is interesting that only 35 per cent of the sample positively disagreed with the statement that the personal costs of career pursuit outweigh the benefits; what then did the other 65 per cent consider to be most important as the basis for their non-work identities? While they might long for a magic balance and insist that the most important things in their lives are their family and personal relationships, there is very little evidence to suggest that there has been any radical shift in the domestic division of labour. While it may be a fine thing for a man to say to an interviewer, I doubt if most male managers really want to spend their time ferrying their children to music lessons or trying to get cat sick off the carpet. Men may be disillusioned and anxious in their jobs but they have no better alternative to turn to, apart from taking early retirement. Two-thirds of Scase and Goffee's managers want to retire in their fifties. This appears to be a much more seriously desired option at the end of the century than it was in the middle.

All these problems affect women managers too, but they have the further problem of working in predominantly male environments which can yield a distinctive source of stress. They also have the additional burden of being primarily responsible for the home. If men are yearning for a better balance between home and work, they should pay more attention to what their partners say before trying to delude themselves and those who interview them. The distinctive problems faced by women managers now receive much academic and journalistic comment,[14] but are likely to be more acute at the junior and middle levels of management discussed by Scase and Goffee. There are some indications that, as managing involves more interpersonal skills, women may come to have the edge on men who are stereotypically less in touch with their feelings and less able to cope with emotional problems. If these are now some of the central problems of management, then much depends on whether the fashion lies more in the macho, assertive, task-oriented approach to management, which men may find more congenial, or the more people-centred style which women may find more congenial. Scase and Goffee are ambivalent, if not confused, about this point, claiming, at different places in their book, that each is in the ascendant (1989:68,122).

Perhaps the nub of the argument put forward by Scase and Goffee was reflected by one of their respondents, a man in his late forties working in engineering and maintenance:

I believe that if I go any higher . . . I will be working for the Company twenty four hours a day. Then I should be married to the company. I don't want to marry the Company. I want to stay married to my wife and family. That's it, basically in a nutshell. Which is why I've got no ambition left. (p. 143)

We are not told who cooks the meals in that man's house; who decides when to change the sheets; who washes and irons them; who is caring for an elderly relative; and who carries the traumas of teenage rebellions. It may be that this appears as a potentially more satisfying alternative to being a Company man. If, however, being married means living in a mini-hotel where the main responsibilities are cutting the grass, cleaning the car and serving the drinks when friends come in, then who would not have less of a dull, frustrating job at the office and more of the life of Riley at home?

Scase and Goffee conclude: 'Very few couples are totally immersed in their work and overwhelmingly preoccupied with career success ... Accordingly, conflicts between work and domestic life are controlled' (p. 175). 'If, in the past, there was a pronounced work ethic which fostered a desire for occupational achievement and nurtured work-based values around which personal identities could be constructed, this has now diminished' (p. 180).

This conclusion applies primarily to middle-aged middle-level male managers and not to male senior managers. In the next chapter those higher up in British industry will be considered in some depth. How do those who are largely responsible for the anxieties and insecurities of their subordinate managers construct a firmer and more secure identity for themselves?

4

Styles of Success in Business

The men and women discussed in the last chapter were junior or middle managers, most of whom would not rise to become senior managers. I now turn to discuss two cases of senior managers and a company chairman to explore the idea that while success in business is unlikely to be effortless it need not be burdensome, anxiety-making toil.

Those preparing themselves for employment in the decade before the Yom Kippur war of 1973 were in a curiously transitional position, as will emerge below. The three men I discuss in this chapter are in a quite different league from the junior and middle managers discussed in the last chapter. Scase and Goffee (1989) claim that 23 per cent of their male managers were 'senior' but only 6 per cent of their male sample earned more than £25,000 only a few years before my interviews, indeed, 80 per cent earned less than £20,000. Of the two senior managers discussed below, one (aged forty) was earning £65,000 in 1990 when I interviewed him, the other, who was forty-five, earned £95,000. The company chairman that I discuss later is a very wealthy man: as a multi-millionaire with shares in his company he can pay himself what he chooses.

Not only are the senior industrialists of this chapter successful, they are primarily responsible for what happens to the middle managers whose anxieties and insecurities were introduced in the last chapter. Charles Griffin is a leading director of personnel of a British company and an authority in his field. He is now working on his second book. The first case, Richard Scott, works for a very large multi-national company with the potential, perhaps, of becoming its next chairman. In 1990 he was writing a report on management training and development for the board and, uncharacteristically for him, was reflecting on broader policy questions. Previously he had been marketing director or managing director of various parts of the parent organization throughout the world. He is one of the top forty or fifty managers in the group's global operations. By the end of the 1990s he says that he expects to be a main board director of a large company or a chief executive of a smaller or medium-sized one. He enjoys his work; he likes it to be fun and he expects to continue to enjoy it when he moves on to greater responsibility.

These two men epitomize, perhaps, the people who are setting the pace for the style of work that will be the pattern in *fin-de-siècle* British industry. Since I am giving these two men particular prominence, illustrating styles of success towards 2000, it is necessary to say something about how they were selected. I explained to a colleague at the London Business School, who had a wide experience of observing high fliers in a number of companies, that I was looking for different kinds of reflexivity among successful managers. I was then directed to a very senior consultant, who commented on my ideas before meeting me and taking me through a short-list. I chose the two who later agreed to be interviewed. Presenting cases like this is an uncharacteristic way for sociologists to proceed, although, of course, case studies form the basis of other disciplines, such as social anthropology or psychoanalysis. While it is hard to say whether the study of civilization has been advanced more by Freud's analysis of Dora or little Hans (1977) than by Raymond Firth's study of the Tikopia (1936), few scholars would dismiss such case studies as mere epiphenomenal tales.

Since I am trying to relate biography to historical contexts and social structures, I will present my accounts of these men, their successes and their ideas separately, although there are certain similarities as will appear. All three men discussed in this chapter were educated at Oxbridge.

Business is Terribly Simple

One learns a lot from the body language of the successful. Richard Scott lounged in his chair in a rather crumpled way, smoking from time to time but otherwise showing himself to be at ease and giving the presence to his claim that he was basically a lazy person. His father had also been a senior manager and director of a multi-national corporation. Richard had been a boarder in a minor public school before going up to Cambridge to read economics and history. He had felt no urgent need to find a job on graduation but went off travelling the world and writing about rock music. He recognizes he was part of a very small generation squeezed between the post-Second World War generation and the one following the Yom Kippur War. Those who went through university or into business in the decade after the Second World War were 'largely "conformist" style people' who accepted hierarchies and who also tended to have served military service which may well have reinforced their dominant style. 'My generation ... was brought up in a land of relative wealth, relative plenty, and I suppose one's formative years in terms of social values were really in one's teenage/early twenties years when all that structure was being challenged by so-called hippies and all that stuff. It was very much consciously part of my university education and there was a very narrow window. It lasted, I think, about nine years ...' When Richard returned to Cambridge to get his MA his tutor complained to him that life had become so boring: 'at least with you guys you either got a first or failed. These people are all straight 2 : 2s.'

Being part of this privileged generation may do something to explain Richard's success, yet everything about his career suggests that he is very able: 'I work very fast, I've got a very quick brain'; and he used his talents to very good effect as he moved from one post to another throughout the world. To begin with, he stumbled into jobs by being in the right place at the right time and by being very laid back and confident. When he returned to London after travelling and working in the Far East, he claimed that he got a job with a well-known company because he replied to the question on the standard application form, 'How do you know this company?' by writing: 'I used to be your chauffeur.' On leaving Cambridge he had paid off his overdraft by being a chauffeur for a company, one of whose main clients was the firm he was seeking to join. He knew most of the management but they did not know him. It was an amusing story, illustrating well his characteristic nonchalance, and which helped him to be appointed as a sales administration assistant. He quickly realized there was no great scope for any growth and development for him there as a manager, so after eighteen months he replied to an advertisement in the *Sunday Times* for a job in his present organization, an off-shore company, with subsidiaries all over the world trading under local company names. He had been recruited for the fast-track stream to top management, but he did not know that at the time. The only formal training he ever received were short in-house courses. Mostly he learned to manage by being thrown in at the deep end and doing it. Nevertheless, being posted to a variety of jobs without any apparent connection between them had certain advantages:

> You experience a whole variety of cultures and circumstances which I think allows you to separate the wheat from the chaff. You really see what is important in running a business. Secondly, you get responsibility at a relatively young age and you learn, by sinking or swimming really, how to manage things ... Had I worked inside a monolithic UK company ... I'd be much more narrow-minded than I am now.

The extraordinary aspect of Richard's career is that there was no attempt by his seniors to move him on gradually to posts of greater responsibility. Often he resented being bored. In one job he reckoned he had only three hours' work to do in a week, in another he had fifty-five to sixty. Half-way through this period he discovered, for the first time, that 'what we should be concerned about is profit and stuff everything else'. When Richard was not sufficiently stretched in his jobs he got depressed and took to drinking too much at lunchtime. It seemed to be largely a matter of chance which overseas post he would get offered next. While he calls himself an 'Organization Man', his organization did very little specific career planning for him. However, when he was given chances he took them: he turned around marketing in one country, increased profitability and market shares in another, and in another excelled himself by tripling the profitability of the local company in two years. I asked him what qualities he felt he had that, perhaps, others didn't have:

> Our training is all about management education; it's not about managing people: we're taught none of the 'soft' skills. I found I had a natural ability in management. I made a lot of mistakes, but what I think I bring to these jobs is that ... I establish a 'vision' (rather a grand word), a sense of purpose and a sense of direction. And then I identify what are the strategy elements – normally in terms of functional responsibilities – and then I delegate them. And you get people to share that same view and, hopefully, to partake in that decision. Then they will do it themselves. I can delegate very well I think ... I think it's because I'm lazy, to be honest ... I get bored by

detail. I've always felt, the bigger the job, the less detail, and that sounds great to me.

Because Richard had developed a good track record and because he had caught the eye of a member of the main board on the chairman's Policy Committee, he was brought back to London to do the management development exercise. He began by thinking that this would involve him in planning something like a university course to teach people a few tricks, but it gradually became clear to him that the essential task needed for the expatriate managers was to teach them 'people skills'. By this he meant

> the ability to manage people, to manage laterally, manage upwards, manage downwards, the ability to communicate, the ability to negotiate, all these so-called 'soft' skills. The management of managers rather than the management of businesses. We concentrate very much on hard data. If I look at the objectives that have been set me ... they were always about numbers; they were never about people.

Once Richard had convinced himself of the importance of this new discovery, he realized that his present chairman and present company were a very long way from thinking along similar lines. He described his own organizational culture as:

> autocratic, paternalistic, a lot of lip-service to decentralization but doesn't [implement it]. A lot of interference from the top on decision-making. Very particularly the more senior end very confused – a great deal of confusion between accountability and responsibility. That's partly organization structure and partly personal style. They're a very secretive organization – and dishonest. Not a great deal of honesty in communication ... There's just no trust. If you make people responsible you also ought to trust them and that just doesn't exist.

Clearly Richard was in serious danger of being the messenger thrown over the battlements for bringing the bad news – which he fully realized. His future in the company was at some risk when I interviewed him in 1990. He knew the chairman would not like what he felt obliged to say.

Richard's great strength is that he recognizes that he has to have other things in his life from which he gets satisfaction and which balances his involvement with his work life:

I found that I deliberately tried to develop interests that I can carry around with me. I've always felt very strongly that you've got to have a much wider range of interests than simply business. I think that narrow-minded focus on what you're doing makes it very difficult. If you're that kind of style – just business-driven – you can't understand how other managers work.

He does not just say that in the rather pious way middle managers are inclined to do. Richard has already written a novel which he is hoping to get published, and he is working on mechanically renovating a vintage car. He reads twentieth-century novelists such as Anthony Powell and is not at all interested in reading business theory books. 'I'm hopeless at just sitting down, doing nothing.' People like working for him, he says. 'I can encourage other people to have their own ideas. I think also because I treat people with respect. I think that's a kind of key.' For Richard, 'management is very simple and business is very simple. And when you see Mintzberg's 400 pages it really is making the whole thing far too complicated and the simplicity of the message of management is completely befuddled by that . . . Business is terribly simple.'

Richard has worked for his organization very effectively but he doesn't feel completely committed to it: 'I haven't given my life to it . . . it's given me . . . a fairly good career path and it's given me a reasonable salary and things like that but I'm not a company man . . . [though] I need to work within an organization.' What he most enjoys:

involves juggling short-term, serious, trivial, long-term, all those things . . . going on at the same time. I'm quite good at dealing with complex issues and dealing with people . . . I don't think I could ever be an entrepreneur. I like having targets, like having goals, and it's much more difficult to set them for yourself, I think . . . I've taken each job as it comes and tried to leave behind or develop it with something better than it was when it started and that is actually enough for me . . . I see myself as a professional line manager and as a very professional marketing manager.

Unless he is chairman, or at least a senior member of the board, Richard will have moved on by the time this book is published. On one of his trips to North America, as part of his job in preparing his report, he was greatly impressed by a chief executive who had grasped that 99 per cent of all management is lateral. 'It's taking . . . in a manufacturing company the raw materials, processing them, putting them together, packaging them, getting them out to your distribution channels, out to your consumers – it's all lateral. But we've always organized ourselves vertically.' Richard was very struck by the organizational simplicity and the effective way the laterally structured company worked. He was also very impressed by the way this North American chairman

> wrote a thing called 'the Business Plan', which is effectively like an extended mission statement which he reviews occasionally. And he said to his VPs, 'Look, I think you should have meetings without me being there because I don't want to be involved. I don't want to act as a bloody judge on all this stuff and, even at your level, it's lateral and so you can handle these things on your own.' He said for the first year round they argued, for the second year they began to work as a team and the third year he knew who his successor was.

Richard really admired this man for being 'incredibly lazy' but having

> the nicest life-style I've ever seen of a chief executive ... he's got lots of outside interests. He had a lovely time in there. He only worked four and a half days a week – eight till four and so-called forty-five minutes for lunch. But they have some anachronisms: they have a senior mess and they go up there for two hours at lunchtime, play cards. It's just great.

Furthermore, 'It's the most successful company we have in the group.' The Cambridge 1972 graduate who was an expert on rock music and wanted to travel has revealed himself. He likes doing a good job but he is not prepared to let work dominate his life. He has discovered that if you have a clear head and trust others, business need not be complicated. But if he became chairman of a company in the next few years he will behave very differently from those at present above him. 'I'm not a hire-and-fire person. I think you've got to respect the individual. In a well-managed environment that should not occur.' The crucial thing is that managers should learn to step back from the process they are involved in: 'I think all good managers have always got that sense of distance.' Richard, perhaps unusually, would recommend people to read twentieth-century novels rather than management textbooks to appreciate more about how people relate to each other. He quoted his North American role-model, '"Keep it simple", and I think he's absolutely right'.

It may be some time before business schools look to those who teach literature to come and play a key role in the training of managers. Disabling mystifications of so-called management science and organizational analysis appear designed to prevent junior and middle managers from 'keeping it simple'. Of course, not all managers are able or would like to write a novel, but Richard has developed in his thinking from the time when he believed profit was all. One way, perhaps, to reduce *fin-de-siècle* anxiety would be to help others to make similar discoveries for themselves.

Balance as the Secret of Success

While Richard Scott could be seen as a traditional middle-class Cambridge graduate, Charles Griffin feels much more conscious of coming from what he called a 'semi-self-made background'. His father, who became an engineer without going to university, had always felt frustrated: he was determined that his son would not suffer similar frustration. He lived his ambition through his son, who became a classic grammar school success of the post-war period. Charles was born in 1945 and learned to jump through the examination hoops in the achievement stakes. Now he feels: 'When I'm not working or achieving there's something missing'. It was assumed that he would follow a smooth trajectory through school and university with a 'good job', but neither he, nor anyone else, had much idea of what it should be. He read geography and history and then drifted into management because he felt he would be more likely to get 'to grips with people in a working environment'. He began in general management and then later specialized in industrial relations. He eventually joined a large engineering firm in the Midlands with whom he stayed for ten years, being appointed to the post of industrial relations director for the UK when he was still only twenty-nine. This particular firm was well known for the quality of its industrial relations staff, and he served a very valuable apprenticeship 'learning at the feet of the master' as he put it. He was thrown in at the deep end – much like Richard Scott had been. He, too, was given very great responsibility when still in his twenties:

> I don't think I could have had a better grounding in terms of responsibility at an early age, getting to grips with what working life was really about and being in the sort of issues I was involved with . . . the job was literally so demanding there was no time for any study. I

was on call twenty-four hours a day. In a way it was like hell on wheels because the phone would go in the middle of the night about the night shift stopping. Looking back, it wasn't the best way to run industrial relations, and I've got a much clearer view now on how people are best managed to be most productive. But at the time, in terms of managing myself and managing a unit and managing a whole organization, it was a terrific experience.

However, Charles also recognizes that there were many things wrong with the style of managing in that company. He learnt many negative lessons: 'the things not to do in terms of developing the best way to get the most out of people at work'. He was beginning to develop better practice as he rose to be in charge, but when he came to recognize the inevitability of a manufacturing recession in the late 1970s he decided to move. He was now looking specifically for 'somewhere where people wanted to work and contribute their best and I wanted to go somewhere where there was good growth, there were actually resources to manage people properly – because it does actually take money – and where there was a basic philosophy that I could build on in terms of managing people properly'. He was fortunate in seeing an opportunity in a rapidly expanding firm in the service sector. Its philosophy was to hire good quality people, pay them well, expect them to work hard and to look after them well. 'They believed in sharing success and the company had gone on from strength to strength ... There had been founder shares, there were share option schemes, there were profit-sharing schemes, so everybody was able to participate economically in the organization's success and a terrific sense of fairness and equity pervaded the organization.'

Charles went through an extremely strenuous selection process lasting about twelve hours, finally being offered the job at around midnight in the chairman's huge manor house. In terms of salary he was making a sideways move earning £13,000 in 1978. Twelve years later when I interviewed him this had increased to £95,000. He has undoubtedly been a great success. 'I've really got total trust now in the people that work for me.' He gives the air of being relaxed, completely in control of his work and confident that he can handle almost anything. Not much can keep him awake at night now, although he does find it hard when he has to tell people that they need to be 'downgraded' or that they no longer have a job when they may actually be friends who have been with the company for twenty years.

He works long hours: he is always in the office at about seven forty-five and rarely leaves before six-thirty.

> I've got high standards and I work hard, and I suppose I expect other people around me to do the same, and I want to be part of an organization that's like that ... I think that people should get a buzz out of working and they shouldn't just drag along for the money. They should actually enjoy it and take pleasure and satisfaction from it.

The problem now facing Charles is that he has been too successful too soon. His gains in the company's share options scheme have provided him with substantial capital. He is almost financially independent and certainly he could take a job at half his present salary. But what should he do? He has got as far as he can go in his present company and he does not know a better one. As Personnel Director he is unlikely to be put on the main board of the holding company. He likes to know that he is in charge of 'an industry-leading professional outfit', and he feels that Charles Griffin the manager is a different person from the family man. 'I'm two people, I think ... I seem to turn into a different person when I enter the office.' When his wife gives him a lift to work, 'she says when she sees me walk into work I actually, physically, sort of stand up straighter ... I suspect I'm actually playing the "leadership" role, whereas at home I suppose I'm the informal leader.'

But what should he do 'after success'? He's forty-five and if he is going to make a move it has to be now. He cannot imagine retirement. He does not see himself as a consultant: he feels he is insufficiently out-going or confident, and he would not like the travel that would prevent him getting home every evening. He has been doing what he has been doing for so long that he now feels a true 'organization man': 'I suppose there's an element of comfort in working in an organization. It would be a bit like leaving the womb ... my mid-life crisis has come upon me!' He came to his present company:

> to institutionalize our approach to people without losing flair and creativity, and to get a clear statement of values that would apply for all time, whatever the business cycle or size of the company. And I just want to do something of that size again in a big organization because they're more difficult to manage in and to get these things through. And I think I want to face a new situation with different problems and issues, and actually think it all through and create a solution, with others, that's lasting and is almost a sort of testament to

the profession – discipline – but I do see it as a profession ... There's something in me that says you can't really stop. You need to go on and do something else and be challenged. There's something driving me and I can't just stop and do nothing at the moment.

Unlike Richard Scott, Charles Griffin relishes not the simplicity but the complexity:

Getting an organization effective is actually quite a difficult thing to do. It looks simple when you've done it but it's difficult because you've got about twenty strands you need to pull together. So you've got to look at everything from remuneration through to the objective-setting process, through to the management hierarchy, through to the way you hire, through to what you expect of people and what they can expect from you in return. And all those things need to be thought through and woven together. So you are actually making a rope from various strands and the tricky bit is getting all the strands in place ... and coming together. So integrated personnel strategy very rarely happens, and that is why I think the discipline has such a poor reputation, because it very rarely gets it together.

Charles Griffin is the senior manager most of the middle and junior reluctant managers discussed in the last chapter do not have. The company is facing down-sizing:

In the past we hired people who were very ambitious, totally career-oriented, and we came to realize that we can't actually accommodate all those aspirations in one company and we'd have to get a better balance of recruit. And so what we now say is ... there's room for all sorts of levels of aspiration in the organization and we can't take everyone who's career-oriented ... not everyone can be promoted ... so there's a distinct move away from the vertical salary and grade promotion to the horizontal broadening and extension of learning.

What sort of people with what kind of qualities has he recruited in the past?

Our essential qualities have been ... largely interpersonal and social skills, so that you have a good mould of people who work well together. Good intelligence, adaptability, the ability to cope with a job that's likely to change quite a lot, just because of the nature of the business and the rate of growth. So people who are energetic, adaptable, lively, relate well to others, a sense of fun, sense of humour, with the result that we've recruited people who are actually quite alike.

Charles frequently used the word 'balance' as an objective both for individuals and for the organization.

When I look for senior people I'm looking for achievement and balance in life outside work as well as achievement within working life ... people do need ... distraction or they become terribly introspective within the organization. They become over-committed and they just become dull and boring. They become sort of too much company people with nothing else to offer ... they've got nothing to relax into outside work ... You've got to have balance ... we've found that people who are over-focused on work become either less productive or just plain ill ... I think we'd now encourage people to take their holidays when they look like they're getting less productive. We'd encourage them not to work all the hours God sends, to try to keep the weekend free from work ... if you don't do that then performance suffers and the contribution to the company deteriorates.

Charles is dealing with the legacy of the 1980s:

We've come from a situation where we had terrifically high growth and commitment which was giving us all sorts of problems ... Marriages were strained, people turned to the bottle – all sorts of under the surface problems ... and we matured to a situation where we realized that people needed a balanced life.

I think a lot of organizations are coming at it from the other way, where people don't actually work hard enough and they probably get their satisfaction in their outside life because they can't get it at work, so the balance is the other side.

Now in the 1990s:

the emphasis is on targets, on objectives, on paper performance – on individual paper performance ... Organizations are now not so concerned about people putting in hours or where they work as about what they're actually delivering ... As long as people actually deliver and contribute, organizations aren't particularly worried about what they do in their spare time and are happy in many ways to support them in having fuller, more satisfying lives outside. I mean, the incidence of sabbaticals, I think, is going up, the incidence of second-ments and so on for people who are actually good performers, just to recharge them, is becoming more apparent ... there's a distinct shift now: everyone's demanding more performance ...

There's another huge dilemma creeping up for the 1990s and that's what the role of a manager is ... targets are being set bottom-up by teams – more so than I can ever remember. In fact it's much more normal for people to sit down together and work out what can be achieved, and for the component parts of that team to go away and then work out how best to achieve it, than I've ever experienced before. Hierarchical management is ... actually fading in terms of its direct influence. People don't respond very well to being told. They want to be involved, they want to plan jointly. They want to have a say in how a task is going to be achieved.

It is interesting that, if Charles is right, industry is moving closer to the way universities used to be run with departments and faculties deciding what should be done and how it should be achieved. However, universities are picking up the hierarchical line management style of the 1970s and in the process destroying some of their greatest organizational strengths.

When people have to be recruited to fit into teams certain team types are sought. Ideally people who are adaptable, who can fit in with a number of different team types are most sought after. The adaptable person is the key social type for the 1990s. At last management has recognized the dangers of recruiting in its own image.

I returned to question Charles on the watershed that he recognized in his own life, and to ask how it related to the shift of emphasis he described between the hierarchical model of the 1970s and 1980s and the team-project driven model of the 1990s. He was disarmingly frank:

I've enjoyed the way I've worked over the last twenty years and I've begun to wonder how adaptable I really am. I preach about these qualities to other people but ... I think my natural inclination is to look for more of the same in terms of pattern of working ... you talked about the shift from employment to consultancy. I think I'd find that a very difficult and threatening shift. I'd come to the conclusion that I'm an 'organization man', so I'm nowhere near as flexible as I ought to be. I ought to be flipping in and out of organizations and self-employment – according to Professor Handy anyway – and I'd find that quite difficult to do. I think a lot of people are like that: they like the security of employment and self-employment to them is a threat ... I don't need to work in a hierarchy necessarily. I'm very happy working in project teams, multi-discipline, multi-level project teams.

So I like groups – working with different groups within an organization. I think I'd be quite lonely working as an individual, as a self-employed consultant. I think it's hard actually doing the cold calling and following up the leads as well as delivering the end product. I think I'm more of a social person than that ... There are very few genuinely entrepreneurial people. Interestingly, though, at the moment ... because of the down-sizing situation we're actually putting a number of our professional people out to sell our services in the wider market. It's interesting that people find that difficult. They aren't naturally attuned to going out prospecting for business and for getting interviews and actually doing deals. It's very difficult for them, very alien.

Thus Charles, like a small group of twenty or so senior managers in his organization, have a distinctive 'after success dilemma' for the 1990s. 'I'm probably no longer working to live but I can live to work and I need to go through the same sort of exploratory process I went through when I left university ... I can choose, as you say, but I haven't been educated to choose.'

As a result of recognizing this new dilemma he and his senior colleagues have been going to counsellors who work as consultants to his organization:

They hold the mirror up and you can actually see the thing in the round ... I think I'm actually becoming broader ... [I'm] looking for different roles in different organizations and not necessarily seeing career as something that only exists within this organization ...

I'm going back to sailing this year for example, getting more into music and reading ... so generally leading a better balanced life ... You've been working towards conventional economic values – size of house, car, education, net disposable income. Then suddenly all those things have been achieved and they don't, in themselves, bring intrinsic satisfaction. You've got to look deeper into values that are non-economic, non-material ...

Increasingly people will only work because they want to, rather than because they have to, and I think my problem will become a wider problem with the young of tomorrow. I think what you've got to offer them is work that they will find intrinsically satisfying and developmental, and that will become increasingly challenging because society will still want things made and we still actually make things in a pretty demoralizing way ...

Like Karl Marx and Herbert Marcuse, Charles believes that society must recognize the dehumanizing consequences of alienation and the suppression of the pleasure principal by returning again and again to the notion of the young Marx, who imagined a flexible pattern of work combining manual and non-manual activities in congenial social contexts.[1] Again like Marx, the short-term solution would be to shorten the working day or develop flexible work patterns. However, the great thrust to 'relevance', or training for 'wealth creation' may not prepare people appropriately for this better, balanced life. 'I think the worry is, a lot of people haven't been educated sufficiently well to know what those other things are, and so we might end up with destructive leisure time rather than constructive leisure time which is a worry.'

The problem of 'after success' is widely understood in Charles's organization:

> There are a number of people around who have a mid-life crisis at the moment. We, all the senior executives, tend to be around mid-forties ... People are thinking quite widely and differently what they do next. Some people are thinking that they're going to retire at fifty-plus because they happen to have strong extra-mural interests. Some people want to go on and do the last big career challenge; some people want to go out and do philanthropic things – so you're getting quite a range of approaches.

Whatever the popular perception of the aftermath of the materialistic ethos of the so-called entrepreneurial eighties, I did not find much evidence of personal selfishness and greed among most of the very successful people I interviewed. Charles Griffin is professionally concerned with the human side of enterprise and is, perhaps, more thoughtful than most:

> I think if you've got Prime Ministers talking about 'classless societies' (whatever he meant by that), there's the beginning, perhaps, of a new socialist dawn (with a small 's'), and that people are concerned that there shouldn't be too wide a gap between the rich and poor in society ... if it does get too big then destabilization will occur and then everybody loses ... we might be waking up to the fact that we do need to actually pull the bottom up as well as push the top on, and I think that has to be right.

Before bringing together my discussion of Richard Scott and Charles Griffin's ideas about 'balance' and 'after success', I turn to my third case – a captain of industry and one of Britain's richest individuals.

Playing at Success

A manservant opened the door of the large house in an exclusive part of London. With tennis courts and swimming pool, this was the home of a very wealthy man. I was shown into the library – certainly not a status symbol: it was stuffed with an intellectual's collection of books. Clearly Hugh Sherriff had plenty of time to read: there was a large collection of modern novels and many very expensive books on the arts. While I waited I thought maybe I should have been an industrialist instead of a poorly-paid academic.

Hugh Sherriff entered energetically, wearing blue jeans and an open-necked shirt. He looked as if he had just come in from some vigorous physical exercise and he appeared very fit. I asked him to introduce himself and he began: 'My name is Hugh Sherriff and my age is sixty'. His account of his life was clear and well constructed. He had evidently told it many times before. He is the sort of man who is profiled for business journals as well as life-style or chatty magazines. Quite exceptionally for an industrialist, he agreed to be interviewed because he is actually interested in sociology, with more than an intelligent layman's understanding of the subject. He came from a relatively prosperous professional family, and he gave the impression that becoming a multi-millionaire was not a very arduous undertaking. By the age of twenty-four or twenty-five he had done his National Service, read law at Oxbridge and been called to the Bar. However, the very ease of his success worried him: he was afraid of 'this life-sentence of a career'. So when an influential family friend suggested that he should join a company of which he was chairman just to see what it was like, Hugh agreed to spend the six-months' trial period in the company. In a couple of years he was managing director.

Hugh made it all sound ridiculously easy, but he claimed it was very easy to succeed in industry in the mid-1950s – particularly in a traditional and not very dynamic sector:

> I was the sort of 'one-eyed man in the country of the blind', I suppose. I mean, if I'd stayed at the Bar, I would have been competing with some extremely bright people. If I'd gone into any of the careers that people coming out of Oxbridge at that time did go into, I'd have had some [serious competition] ... I didn't really have any serious competition in industry ... I think it would have been pretty bad of me if I hadn't been a candidate to be managing director. But I never thought of it as a serious career ...

By the time Hugh had been in the same company for ten years he realized that he was probably going to stay as an industrialist for the rest of his life. That being so, he felt he might as well have the advantage of owning his company. Having made that decision, he simply 'went to the City, borrowed some money' and bought his own company. Again it all sounded so easy and, he claims, it really was. He had proved himself by running the company for eight or nine years of the ten he had been there and, in the mid–1960s, the City was highly receptive to an emerging entrepreneurial spirit. For the second time he was in the right place at the right time. 'I met somebody at a dinner party. Several people offered to back me and I chose the one that offered the best terms . . . ones that left me with control, more than 51 per cent of the shares, which I wanted, which I got.'

Hugh, as well as being charming, extremely intelligent and financially astute, had luck on his side. The industry he had fallen into was moving into a new phase through technological innovation. Because Hugh retained a rather academic or scholarly approach to life, he read all the business school-type books by reviewing them for a weekly. He knew the market governed business whereas his industry had operated for years in a situation where demand exceeded supply. Those who recognized the new economic situation had an enormous advantage over those who did not. Furthermore, Hugh exploited his undoubted social skills to make up for his lack of technical expertise:

> I never knew anything about machines, except I rang people up and said, 'You've brought these machines, are they reliable and do they produce at the speed the manufacturers say they will and do they produce the right quality?' And if they said – enough people whom I trusted said – they did, then I'd buy the machines.

So, somewhat casually, Hugh became an exceptionally successful industrialist. He had no formal training: he read *The Economist*, the *Harvard Business Review* and 'a few books'. He was committed to the idea that the company had to be ruled by the market and he built up his company almost entirely on his own. I asked him whether all this had been very hard work:

> No, I don't think I've ever worked hard in the conventional sense. I've never really believed that was the answer. I've never worked long hours or long days. I think I've worked in concentrated bursts when

I've worked but I've never been a very early starter or a late goer-home and I've never been a chap who worked at weekends . . . I used to turn up at about ten – now I turn up a bit later than that – and I generally leave about six. There were long periods in my life when I used to go out at lunchtime and not come back, wander around bookshops, go and meet friends, go shopping, because I didn't have enough to do.

It took Hugh Sherriff three years to get his company to make more than £100,000 profit and to have money in the bank. He paid back his loan after three or four years and started to take long holidays and relaxed weekends. He was able to do this, he claimed, because there was very little competition in his particular industry and 'the other people in the industry came from such a different sort of background'. After eight years, in 1972, Hugh, who by then owned 100 per cent of the company, sold off a fifth of the shares to City institutions. This made him a very rich man, able to retire comfortably at the age of forty-two.

One of the main reasons why I wanted to interview Hugh Sherriff was that he did not retire. On the contrary, having achieved 'success' his life after success became more demanding. 'Suddenly I realized that I enjoyed my work. That was quite interesting. I didn't want to stop working.' This surprised Hugh as previously he had always had something else other than work that seemed more interesting or more socially or intellectually rewarding. Now that he did not have to work he 'became slightly more ambitious because I realized I wasn't working to support myself, I was working for some other reason. So I decided, well, in that case I'm going to make this company more successful.'

Part of the banal conventional wisdom of the 1980s was that people worked largely for money and so the best way to make the successful work even harder was to reduce taxation. Hugh's motivation was the opposite of this. Only when he did not have to worry about making money did he start to clarify his own interests: 'I was simply interested in running a good, solid, profitable company which gave a reliable and honest service to its customers and dealt in a civilized way with its workforce and in a civilized way with the people who supplied it.'

Once he decided to re-enter his career as an industrialist he brought in new people, profits expanded and other companies were taken over as part of the expansion. When he floated the company in the 1980s, 'quite a few of my colleagues became millionaires and became really interested in the whole thing'. Just before I interviewed him *The Economist* did a survey of the most admired company in each sector and his was the most admired one in its sector.

Hugh was particularly self-perceptive in exploring his motivations for his working career after success. He admitted that, having been so successful, he wanted to see how far he could go, but he also wanted to have the respect of his peers and, interestingly, these included sociologists as well as industrialists. He prefers to be known to have done a good job than simply to be very rich. Also he is now recognizing the satisfaction of being more fully stretched. As we have seen, in the early years he was able to operate in his words on one-third capacity. He now finds new, interesting and challenging problems as his company acquires a global dimension. But even now, he says, he is only 'nearly' fully occupied. Finally, Hugh recognizes that he needs to have some kind of structure to his life, and that if he had retired earlier that might have posed problems for him.

Despite running a major British company with an increasingly global component, Hugh is still not collected by his driver until ten. Before that he will have had a swim and been for a walk or played tennis before reading the papers over breakfast. He will then get ready for the office, where he can lunch with business colleagues in his own dining room at one. He will leave the office between five and six, often going to the Royal Opera House or, perhaps, to a dinner engagement. However, he gets great pleasure from having a quiet supper with his wife and spending the rest of the evening reading. I am sure that he had read more contemporary novels than most of my colleagues in the Common Room.

Hugh admits that he is now dealing with much brighter people than those he met when he was lower down the ladder. He believes that if the job is going to remain stimulating it is necessary for him to aim for new peaks. 'If I woke up in the morning and didn't know what I was going to do and didn't have any obligations, I wouldn't enjoy my leisure in the same way as if I had work as well . . . I would lose my sense of self-worth if I didn't do something.' However much Hugh stressed the importance of his work, he would also stress equally the importance of his social life, his leisure and his physical activity. He would not do a job that did not give him the freedom to do these things. He reckons that on average through the year he does about four hours' work a day for three days in a week, largely because he spends most of the summer in the south of France and enjoys skiing. He believes his commitment to the idea of balance prevents him from being as successful as those who are completely and utterly obsessed with their work:

> I don't enjoy spending time with people who don't read books or haven't got any cultural interests. I find that very boring and I suppose for that reason I don't really spend any of my leisure time with people who work in my industry, or indeed hardly any with people who work in business of any sort because, on the whole, people don't have those interests.

Hugh consciously strives for a style of work that is relaxed. He approved of the use of that word when I put the suggestion to him. In all sorts of obvious ways he was very successful and he was also very skilled in coping with interviewers seeking the secrets of his success.

When I returned for the second interview it was somehow easier to explore more personal aspects of his private life. Hugh had had to face some extremely difficult and tragic circumstances at the very time when he was starting up his new company in the 1960s. By approaching his work through his private life I was able to see glimpses of quite another perspective on his business life. Unlike his first interview, when he implied that the mid–1960s was the time of an effortless canter into profit and the repayment of his debts in the City, Hugh now confessed that 'everything that could go wrong with the company was going wrong anyway. It always does at the very beginning and we very nearly went bust.' As he is basically optimistic and has great confidence in himself, he was able to pull through. He covers his scars very well.

Our more wide-ranging discussion of family, religion, getting older and the way men face the inevitability of decline, encouraged more philosophical responses. I asked Hugh what he thought was the best thing he had done in his life and he shied away from the question. I pressed him to consider whether the answer would more likely relate to his public life or his private life. He again found it difficult to answer. Finally, and with an effort, he said: 'I don't know. I think you've got to live your own life to the end, and you can't stop at any point and say I've achieved something, because you haven't achieved it, not really, until you've got to your end.'

This, of course, is exactly the same reply that Solon gave Croesus two and a half millennia ago. Hugh Sherriff is not only successful, but is also wise.

Discussion

It would be wrong to imagine that successful men in industry or business owe their positions to reading novels and having a relaxed temperament. However, it does seem that an obsessional or compulsive workaholicism is not obligatory either. These men in their different ways are exploring ideas of balance, if not the meaning of life. As Patrick Wright (1987) observed, when reviewing books written in the mid-1980s on managerial excellence: 'It is ironic, given what has been happening in British Higher Education ... that an education in the Humanities or Liberal Arts may form a more appropriate background for tomorrow's managers than the business schools with their more rigid MBAs.' That is, of course, a rather extreme statement, but it is supported by many current management gurus such as Tom Peters. Before coming to even the most preliminary conclusions, it is necessary to explore alternative styles of work. In the next chapter the case studies illustrate almost the opposite approach to work, reflecting a kind of compulsive neurosis. Both this chapter and the next one are based entirely on men. This is partly for the ease of exposition. I do not mean to imply that women's styles of success are necessarily different on gender grounds alone.

5

The Neurosis of Success

During the 1980s certain kinds of work became exceptionally demanding for those involved in it. In this chapter two men illustrate some of the strains and problems very well, and also raise the question of how far the public issues or organizational contexts created their private troubles, or how far distinctive processes in the development of their personalities produced the men who then sought out punishing environments.

Both men are very successful. They also work extraordinarily hard. They recognize that this unbalances their lives but they have propelled themselves on to a trajectory which they cannot now see a way of leaving. They are enthusiastic and well-meaning, and spoke with great frankness. They exposed their souls, sometimes with painful clarity. As with most of us, their parents still lived within them, providing them with inspiration and feelings of guilt, anger and sometimes pride.

They did not have to be encouraged to provide amateur psychological accounts of why they were as they were. They saw the importance of parents, peers and mentors. They recognized their compulsions and their anxieties. They claimed that they were in control, in charge of their lives: one now works for one of the largest British multi-national organizations, as managing director of one of its subsidiaries; the other had recently started up his own business which, in the three years since I interviewed him, has gone on from strength to strength. I fear that both may feel rather hurt that I suggest they are exhibiting certain neurotic characteristics. However, most people suffer from neuroses of one sort or another, and highly ambitious and successful people should not expect to be exempt.

As with all my case studies I had a considerable amount of material on which I could draw, and some may wonder how idiosyncratic are the accounts I present. The reader has to trust me, the research instrument, to be honest and not to create false impressions through sly editing. One way to reassure is to provide extensive quotations, but this could become repetitive and would make the book impossibly long. It did sometimes strike me that I could have written a dozen books based on the cases of some of the people who spoke to me at length. Some of my respondents may permit their transcripts to be deposited in an appropriate data archive, allowing others in the future to check my interpretations. I have had to make compromises, but I hope that by letting these two men speak for themselves as much as possible, I am allowing readers to develop alternative interpretations. Inevitably I am interpreting very strongly through the selection of their quotations. Sometimes they are simply giving information which I could well have summarized for them. However, by putting it in their words, I hope that the reader can get a better idea of the individual concerned. I am providing an interpretation mainly based on the psychoanalytic approach of Karen Horney: some may want to dispute her general approach, my interpretation of it and the appropriateness of my interpretation for the two cases I discuss. I have made judgements: there is no other way of writing about the men and women who are the subject of this book.

Finally, by way of introduction, I should emphasize that I am not able to make more than suggestions about psychological processes. In a competitive society to be neurotic is normal. The highly successful may simply reveal general neuroses in a more extreme form.

Selling off the Family Silver

David Clifford was seconded from a large multi-national company to work in Whitehall on a massive privatization programme. A major nationalized industry had to be transformed into pseudo-public companies which could then be sold. Margaret Thatcher's Conservative government had stumbled on the idea of privatization, and there was considerable political pressure that each exercise should be – and of course be seen to be – an unqualified success. David was seconded from the private sector for his managerial and 'business' qualities. In his new environment he had to understand and to fit into what was, for him, an unfamiliar Civil Service culture; he also had to create his own, new culture for something that had not been done before: he had to create a 'flotation culture'. He began by thinking that he knew about share sale tasks as he had had some experiences when working for his home company. He had been involved 'in a lot of business planning about cash flow business plans which has a lot to do with preparing companies for flotation'. However, he discovered that 'the managing of a giant flotation is incredibly more complex than I thought at the time'.

> It was ghastly for a bit actually. I was trying to do two things at once. So much to do and also a new environment, trying to understand the laws and the methods, bed into a brand-new working environment at the same time as trying to get something done – a very unpleasant experience ... Things had to be done, they were trying to get the Bill through. They wanted guidance on what to do about special shares (and that was an issue in itself) and what to do about the investment limits in the company, government control, all the commercial bits of the Bill. And also they had the public expenditure control. Just in the background the companies themselves that were ultimately sold – you had to go and visit them and start to get involved. All the day-to-day things at the same time as trying to cast your eye ahead and plan the whole operation. And it was just murder trying to balance the two and still press ahead, and at the same time bumping into more and more people, having to begin to hire advisers to get me in a position to go ahead when one hadn't actually got a clear view about how we were actually going to do it. So the first few months were pretty hairy.

David began with a staff of one. 'I thought, I shall just about be able to do it, but, Christ, it's difficult, it's much more than I thought.' First had to come the restructuring:

> I offered to go over and work on the project management of the restructuring, a job that hadn't existed before ... I worked like mad because I thought I've got my neck on the line – this bit depends on me. I produced a project plan to say how to do it ... they needed 300–400 people to do it. I said, 'It's much bigger than you think', and I did the whole management stuff, project plan, staffing profiles, the management structure. It all became suddenly very high profile and we had twenty-six weeks to do it. We did it in twenty-six weeks, it was done on time and it was an incredibly demanding thing but it *was* done

on time. At the end of the day we had 1500 people working on it, here and there, both our Civil Servants, advisors, industry people, their advisors, experts – hundreds of people. It was a fantastic achievement. It was the largest commercial restructuring ever. Then the time came when I was exhausted. I had a couple of weeks off. Then I came back and said, 'Now let's get down to the flotation.' We had nine months to float. We've almost finished it now, which has turned out again to be a vast task, more complicated than we ever thought . . . the restructuring had actually made the flotation complicated. No one's ever floated something that's just been restructured . . .

When first I talked to David he was thirty-eight and evidently proud of his success but he could not stop and enjoy it:

Now I'm thinking what the hell shall I do next . . . I'm actually roughly where I want to be and I can't see a good place to go on from here . . . In a way I'm hooked on the treadmill. It's very difficult to get out of this hard work, sweating it, producing results under pressure, long hours . . . At the moment [I work] twelve or thirteen hours a day plus about a day at weekends. It's a particularly bad time. It's got to the stage where it's almost monolithic . . . My life has become so dominated by work – which I'm very annoyed about – that I can't get off the treadmill at the moment, that I don't know what else I can do. I don't know what else I can be and so – What are you? I am my job.

David has lost touch with any real self. He has become a machine for getting jobs done. Why does he do it? How has he become like that? He lives a life of fictions trying to live up to his idealized self. Is he a victim of his own success or, in his striving for super-success, has he created for himself a kind of monster that is devouring him?

He admits he is not happy. 'I wish I could find a target that I could understand that would get me out of this in a way . . . I actually can't find a decent new target . . . I can't think of anything practical to do . . . I just can't see the alternative any more, because I don't have enough time to look . . .'

When I interviewed him on the first occasion he was just about to leave the department and he did not know where he would go next. He recognized that his only alternative is to carry on achieving. This would inevitably lead him on to the treadmill again: 'Just because of the job rather than the money. I'm not in this job for the money. I've got easily enough money – I've got no problem. You're in the job for entirely different reasons as well . . . One's in the job for the apparent reward of the job.'

David knows he has a problem but is completely incapable of doing anything about it. Even the process of doing the work provides little pleasure. He took me through a typical day:

Alarm at six-thirty. I'm usually exhausted when the alarm goes off: I'm very tired. I drag myself out of bed ten or fifteen minutes later ... I tend to be out of the house at eight-fifteen, typically, and be either here or in a meeting somewhere else by nine ... The day would run from nine to eight ... This week has been particularly bad so far. It's been past nine every night. The day from one end to the other doesn't have any particular breaks. There's no such thing as lunch, as you may have noticed ...

David's endless dash from one meeting to the next cannot give him much time for reflection. I asked him when he found time to read:

Read? Read means my in-tray. I read a newspaper over breakfast quickly. At the moment the in-tray is a real problem ... often I find myself these days storing long-term items and dealing with them on Sunday, though on issues that are quick I can flip through an in-tray ... I might get home at eight-thirty at night, have a meal with my wife and then say – sorry, let's have a meal in the study and I will just hit the in-tray. If there's something that really has to be done, I might be doing it until two. I don't do this all that often ... I need sleep ... If I go to sleep after ten at night I suffer the next day. I know what a fatigue headache feels like ... I do need eight hours, I really do. And the tension of this job at the moment. Almost permanent stiff necks. And it's very difficult actually to get a good night's sleep, and you're knackered the next day. It's hard to know how a human being can survive and live to be a reasonable age the way I'm playing it at the moment.

After the interview I was personally concerned about David, who seemed to be driving himself to a state of utter exhaustion. However, at the time, I imagined that he had been offered an opportunity to serve his country (if that's what 'selling off the family silver', in Harold Macmillan's description of privatization, allows one to do), and that he had been determined to do it well. Perhaps this was his chance in a lifetime to be a key actor on the stage of history.

Some months later, I went to the head office of a subsidiary of David's original multi-national where he was now managing director. He was very proud of that. He welcomed me warmly and was anxious to help me as much as possible. Sandwiches and apples from a working lunch were strewn around. David showed off his new office proudly. I congratulated him on becoming managing director. He quickly interjected: 'I'm chief executive too.' We spoke a lot about his new job, the challenges he faced and the ways he hoped to overcome them. Proudly he mentioned that a London Business School team had been interviewing him as part of a project on high fliers in the company. He was revelling in dealing with a whole new array of issues: 'It's like a game of football, a game of cards or something, that you begin to enjoy it because it's working, it's elegant, it's a success, it's coming out right.'

But getting it to come out right was once again taking its toll. David admitted he was up until two the previous night. Now he no longer has the pressures of White Papers, statements in the House, ministerial promises and pressures of his Whitehall job, where, I wondered, does the pressure come from? He answered unequivocally:

> It's entirely self-imposed here. I mean I could probably let this company drift on for a year and almost do nothing, and just have nice long lunches and read the newspaper and sign whatever papers were put to me for signature, and that would be that. I would have a very easy-going life. But I wouldn't like that because this company, I believe, is in trouble and I want to fix it. I just feel I want to fix it. Not because I was put in here to fix it, because I just think that's something that I'd like to do. So I start imposing my own deadlines. I start imposing my own pressures. I say, 'Well look, what's the business plan for this year? What's the operating plan? Let's see how we're doing – Jesus, this is hopeless.' So you begin to say, how shall I run this business? How shall I drive it? How shall I put pressure on the business? And the way you put pressure on the business is actually you put pressure on yourself as well.

David is a compulsive worker. 'I am married to my work and my wife and one of the problems is being married to two things. I'm sure that's true.' Clearly not everyone who is successful is driven by such compulsion and has become so much involved in his job that he is able to say, unselfconsciously that he *is* his job – and then couples this with the narcissistic notion that he is married to himself. Since David provides a very clear example of someone alienated from himself in his search for glory, we need to outline the psychoanalytic background to the notion of neurotic success, before exploring in more detail something of the psychodynamics of David's personality.

The Search for Glory

Human beings need to grow up in an atmosphere of warmth to provide them with feelings of inner security and an inner freedom that enables an individual to have his or her own thoughts and feelings, and to express them. He or she needs the goodwill and healthy friction of living with others to help him or her to grow in accordance with his or her real self. However, if the people in the growing child's environment 'are too wrapped up in their own neuroses to be able to love the child, or even to conceive of him as the particular individual he is', then 'their attitudes toward him are determined by their own neurotic needs and responses' (Horney 1991: 18). If this happens, the child may develop a profound insecurity and a vague apprehensiveness which Horney terms a basic anxiety. 'The cramping pressure of his basic anxiety prevents the child from relating himself to others with the spontaneity of his real feelings, and forces him to find ways to cope with them. He must (unconsciously) deal with them in ways which do not arouse, or increase, but rather allay his basic anxiety' (p. 18).

The child needs to find a substitute for the self-confidence that he lacks: one way to do this in a competitive society is to lift himself above the others. The individual needs something that will give him a feeling of identity. 'Gradually and unconsciously, the imagination sets to work and creates in his mind an *idealized image* of himself' (p. 22). Imperceptibly he becomes this image and the idealized image becomes an idealized self. Fictional definitions may be reinforced or further imposed by parents, teachers and other significant people. Horney refers to self-idealization as a comprehensive neurotic solution which offers a way of banishing feelings of being lost, anxious, inferior and divided. When such a solution appears the person tends to cling to it compulsively. Self-idealization turns into a comprehensive drive – what Horney calls *the search for glory*. The drive towards external success is fuelled by neurotic ambition.

It is not possible to explore here in any detail the full range of neurotic conditions discussed by Horney. However, it is important to understand something more of the neurotic consequences of the compulsive search for glory. Very often, of course, people may achieve the success of whatever it is they have been working towards. Yet:

> when they do attain more money, more distinction, more power, they also come to feel the whole impact of the futility of their chase. They

do not secure any more peace of mind, inner security or joy of living. The inner distress to remedy which they started out for the phantom of glory, is still as great as ever. Since these are not accidental results, happening to this or that individual, but are inexorably bound to occur, one may rightly say that the whole pursuit of success is intrinsically unrealistic. (p. 26)

Horney makes it clear that she recognizes that it is hard to avoid being competitive in a competitive culture. 'But the fact that compulsive drives for success will arise only in a competitive culture does not make them any less neurotic' (p. 26). These drives are compulsive because they arise out of the neurotic solution of self-idealization and do not follow from spontaneous wishes or strivings, as an expression of the real self. This is an important distinction: healthy strivings are based on spontaneity; neurotic drives for glory are based on compulsion.

One element of this compulsion is the need to control. Ruzicka explores this most perceptively in the case study which forms the basis for his discussion in *The Nightmare of Success*. He creates a composite successful man, Marc, who in a number of psychotherapeutic sessions gradually comes to understand: 'I have a tremendous aversion to being controlled ... I guess that's how I developed this need to control myself perfectly ... It's a paradox ... I must like being controlled, too, because I obviously let other peoples' expectations influence me. I achieve goals they set for me' (1973: p. 28). As we shall see, David provides much evidence of similar inclinations.

David's Route to Neurotic Success

I did not set out to probe David's psychology: I am not qualified to do so and I would not know how to set about unlocking his unconscious. However, as with my other respondents, I prompted him to think about such issues as the way his past influenced his present, and what feelings he had towards his parents when he was a child. This was not done systematically. However, since David volunteered many connections and cheerfully acknowledged that certain matters in his past were highly significant for him, a pattern emerged in my mind which seems to relate closely to what Horney and others have written. Obviously, I have no way of knowing whether my interpretations are valid in this case, except that they do not seem implausible and they illustrate very well the argument I wish to make. David began by encouraging me to 'dwell on my family circumstances which I think have – well, quite explicitly – determined my early career path and, I think implicitly or subtly determined a lot of my later career decisions'.

His mother came from 'a very rudimentary background' and worked desperately hard to get a scholarship to Oxford, although she was 'not a natural Oxford sort'. Then in 1949 she 'bailed out and married my father. I still don't know why.' David was born in 1952, but 'I have almost no memories of anything of substance in my childhood, all the way up to about fifteen. It's a tragedy to me that I really have almost no memories of how my mother behaved or what sort of person she was.' However, he agreed, in response to my question, that he was sure she would be proud of what he had achieved: 'I think she enjoyed achieving, she enjoyed getting to Oxford.'

Her marriage to David's father was not a success. She 'even had affairs'. Apparently, 'she just didn't enjoy being a mother particularly'. His father was a self-employed commercial artist and the emotional troubles of the 1950s were compounded by economic troubles in the 1960s:

> I remember in the middle sixties things started getting very bad and money started getting short. They started living hand to mouth. It was a very, very bad time. They were on tranquillizers too, I believe. At that stage in history tranquillizers were very easy to come by. A number of things sunk in at that time. I think I have a very clear idea of where drugs lie in one's life now, and also a very clear idea of the damage that a very basic lack of income can do to people . . . Towards the late sixties both my mother and father, at different times, had nervous breakdowns, and eventually my mother died through leukaemia. The family was just torn apart at that stage . . . [at] the same time I was going to university. I was damned if I was going to miss university. I really could not break it up because of this. I must continue. I had to achieve that credential.

Later on, during the second interview, I returned to his relationships with his parents to probe a little more into his feelings at the time. He was reluctant to say more:

> The most vivid characteristic perhaps of my parents was that they were – that they failed if you like. My mother died after rather a turbulent

marriage I thought. That's the message I was getting. My father had some sporadic successes and ultimately died, and at one stage had tremendous troubles. So, if you like I'm always trying to succeed . . .

I asked David if he ever felt any anger against his father:

Yes, there were times, not for what he was (but) what he did. I was pretty angry with him. There was quite a phase in the sixties where I felt that he had let us down. That's put crudely. He was failing. Why the hell couldn't he do better than he had done? I was twenty years younger than him and I'd already sorted things out, and I was actually managing to hang on to things and he was failing. What, in God's name – why can't he do this properly? I don't know if I ever mentioned this – for a while – part of my salary went to keep him afloat, for a year or two I think. I felt it was an honourable thing to do, and I was glad to do it, but I resented it – a rather curious mixture.

Yet they did not have rows. David suppressed – or repressed – his anger. He kept it to himself, as he said: 'Perhaps I was always a bit of a loner, but certainly the relationship was always rather distant and, in a way, tense.' That is perhaps why David went on to create his idealized self.

I'm always trying to succeed

David was much concerned to get the 'true' or 'right' answer to events and circumstances as a defensive mechanism to make order and sense of a chaotic world which he wanted to control. The more he proposed something 'right' or 'true', the greater his feeling of accomplishment. He even wanted to provide me with the right answer to explain why he did certain things. At the beginning of the first interview he admitted, 'So there's always the risk that, in going back now I give you the result of the analysis rather than the raw material, so I hope I'm going to do the analysis right or I'd be clouding the issues.'

Throughout the first interview I encouraged him to be very frank and, in common with all my other respondents, I sent him the first transcript before going to see him for the second time. I then asked him whether on reading it he had had any feelings about what he had said:

I was quite surprised. I thought there would be all sorts of things I said there that I would have regretted saying, but I just read straight through it, and it was just like me talking back at me. I didn't find it at all surprising. I found it rather mundane, I'm afraid. I'm sorry if I'm not giving you enough gems for your book.

I went on to ask him whether my questions about his father had, perhaps, been too probing, and he assured me there had been no problems:

The least comfortable parts of today's interview are where you are asking me questions that I cannot pull out a decent quality answer to, either because I'm tired, or I haven't thought about it. I feel that you are probing me and I'm giving you shallow answers and that, to me, is uncomfortable. This is really quite painful to me.

David is distressed because he cannot please me. He cannot control himself or be controlled by me and there is no place or peace between these extremes. His fictitious self has failed him; he knows it and he blames himself – even hates himself:

Why am I giving you shallow answers ... I know I'm not particularly bright, and I'm not particularly analytical, and that's possibly why I'm giving you answers that are not as deep as would be useful to you – and useful to me. It's partly because I could be tired; there could be other excuses. But it's uncomfortable to me that you're probing and you're hitting the bottom of the barrel too easily – sorry, that's the wrong analogy – I'm not giving you substantive answers and I'm sorry.

His aim to succeed at everything is doomed to failure, and he inevitably overrates his capacities and does not reckon with his limitations. 'Up to a point', argues Karen Horney in her general account, a person's resilience

gives him a capacity to bounce, but on the other hand repeated failures in enterprises or human relations – rejections – may also crush him altogether. The self-hate and self-contempt, successfully held in abeyance otherwise may then operate in full force. He may go into depressions, psychotic episodes, or even kill himself or (more often), through destructive urges, incur an accident or succumb to an illness. (1991: 195)

Looking back on his career before being seconded to Whitehall, David gave the impression of being comfortably in control with success at every stage leading on inexorably to the next. He made 'the best' and 'most rational' decisions at 'O' level, 'A' level and in choice of subject at university. He embarked on his 'career path' equally systematically. He wanted plenty of money, security and a long-term future. At each stage he was planning the next stage in his mind. The vacation job he did when at university was a logical step to his first job, which, in turn, led him further on. He had, in his words, 'a long-term grand strategy'. During his early years with the international company he did an analysis of part of company policy and 'produced something that said what you should be doing is doing this for the right reasons. If you agree with these reasons, you should dump seven-eighths of what you're doing, which they did.' David's 'right' reasons propelled him on in his search for glory. The company picked him up as a high flier. When a senior colleague told him that there was an opportunity coming up of secondment to the Civil Service, David weighed up the pros and cons. As we have seen above, David thought he knew what was involved and that he had the skills to cope with it: 'Ideally, you want a reasonable amount of overlap, so I look for new jobs that use a lot of my existing experience but give me new experience.' He thought he was in control and he took the plunge. It was, truly, the nightmare of success. Nevertheless, because the situation was so new, David had a great deal of autonomy, and that meant control:

> I like to have an area of responsibility that is pretty well defined. I think it's my nature that I like to know what is in my patch. Having a grip on my patch is important to me. If anything, my problems – interpersonal problems – that I see in this are that I don't convince other people very easily that my patch is gripped. My ideal is for them to simply never notice my patch except when I say to them I need to know this or that.

David wants absolute control and to determine for himself when, if at all, he needs other people. Irritatingly, the Civil Service has its hierarchy. His boss works to an Under Secretary who, in turn, works to the Deputy Secretary, 'So as it actually works out on some issues I can be almost second-guessed, third-guessed and fourth-guessed, which can be immensely frustrating.' David cannot abide being disapproved of in any way: his false self is tied to success. I think he is showing good insight when he reflects on this:

> I feel almost humiliated if people take me to task for something that they think that I've done wrong. It's quite a blow to me frankly, and it

makes my life quite difficult. No doubt you'll want to talk about this at some length. It's very difficult for me when I have clear views of my own about the long-term direction, but am not all that good at justifying precisely why I want to do that and arguing my case all that well, and then when I receive censure because someone disagrees with me, I feel that if I could argue it better, they wouldn't criticize. This causes me to question my long-term aims, and it can make my life really quite difficult because I know what I want to do but I can't make people come along with me, and then I feel humiliated because they tell me if I'm wrong. But, on the other hand, I get immense, quite unnaturally immense, pleasure in people's telling me that I've done a good job. I'm thrown quite a bit from extreme to extreme by this.

Such, in Horney's analysis, is the neurotic obsession with mastery and the parallel self-hate and self-contempt. David's obsession with control can, he recognizes, cause problems:

I think perhaps I exercise a bit too much control. Instead of saying, 'I don't really care what you do as long as the thing kind of gradually goes in the right direction', I exercise a bit too much control. I say, 'I want to know where are we at the end of the point in time, where I expected us to be at this point in time and, if we're not, I won't shatter from the rooftops, but I need to know where we are so that I can know whether we've got a problem.' It's a very mechanical way of running people which actually a lot of people don't like, and is quite unnatural, and can cause problems, and perhaps is overdoing it. But it sure delivers things . . .

David had moments when he seemed to be more aware of his real self:

My ambition is much more of a sort of rounded satisfaction. Ambition and satisfaction is all about doing a good job, having a lot of fun, fun in a sort of gruelling way, and every job to be somehow better than the last one – better in terms of more satisfying . . . I don't look for jobs with power. I look for jobs with satisfaction and I get satisfaction out of fixing things. I get satisfaction out of mechanical things, bolting things together, and I'll get a lot of satisfaction, I think, out of fixing this business.

Clearly, as he acknowledges, the privatization programme stretched him beyond his capacities. Now, managing this subsidiary *is* giving him more satisfaction. He prides himself on breaking down power and status hierarchies:

I talk to everyone by their first name. My door is always open. I go down and I wander round and I talk to people. I break down silly rules. I involve people in the decision making. When we have our executive committee meetings (when all the directors and I have a meeting), I've broken all those up so that instead of having a closed session which is the bosses deciding what to do with the company, a lot of people in the company come in when we're discussing their subject, so they participate in decision-making. I'm breaking down the hierarchy in a way because I believe the company will operate much more effectively as a team rather than a bunch of 'gods' at the top who retain all the power and hand down tablets of stone.

In his late thirties, David was earning £60,000 a year when I last interviewed him early in 1990. He had a big car – a £25,000 Rover, 'very nice, a nice car'. However, despite having a vision of running the company free from his inner conflicts, he is still pressed. His wife is

pissed off that I'm still getting home late. The driving to and from here is ghastly ... I get up at six now and leave at seven to get here at eight. Also I try to leave at six each evening and almost never manage it, so I get home at about eight each night ... I haven't got any pressures, there are no vast national deadlines to meet, so it's really pretty silly frankly. The trouble is there are so many fascinating things to do: and to drive the business at a certain pace I'm making so many deadlines ... I can't tell people they've got to do something by Tuesday and they've done it by Tuesday at five – I can't just bugger off at five-thirty. I have to respond to it and turn it round and get it back out again. That's the honourable response from me to pressing people – that I will play the same game.

I asked David whether he could use his style of work and responsibilities as an excuse to put to his wife to justify his way of life. He would not accept such an excuse and said simply: 'I'm not happy.'

He has got everything he wants but he is not happy because he is caught up in his inner conflict. In his search for glory he is in danger of destroying himself. As Horney put it: 'like any other compulsive drive, the search for glory has the quality of *insatiability*. It must operate as long as the unknown (to himself) forces are driving him. There may be a glow of elation over the favourable reception of some work done, over a victory won, over any sign of recognition or admiration – but it does not last' (1991: 30). The search for glory 'can be like a demonical obsession, almost like a monster, swallowing up the individual who has created it' (p. 31).

Locked into People and Project Goals: the Programmed Path to Glory

The 1980s produced a mass of high-tech companies in university science parks, in the golden circle round London and along the M4 corridor (Massey et al. 1992; Hall et al. 1987). Defence contracts, information technology, space research, communications, robotics were the buzz words. This was a world of rationality, of order, of computer-speak. Offices were small, neat and clean. PCs and work-stations were everywhere. Clever men and women reached success in their twenties. Heavy responsibility was matched with a studenty style of rather gauche enthusiasm in the teams as one project succeeded another. A jovial camaraderie often masked acute anxie-ties and rivalries.

This, evidently was no cosy world but a harsh, competitive struggle: the failure rate of small companies was high. The speed of innovation in software and hardware meant that most had to run to stand still. Defence contracts were large and lucrative but the giants like British Aerospace or Marconi could not take on all aspects of all contracts. Competitive sub-contracting spawned a hierarchy of firms, each feeding off the level above, competing fiercely between themselves and beating off those below.

Knowledge was power, and to allow creativity to flourish organiz-ational structures were flat, with project members competing with each other but with few senior managerial positions as rewards. Effective project managers tended to move to smaller, even more dynamic companies or ventured into the dangerous waters of business start-ups.

This distinctive culture appeared to breed a new model of success. As Ruzicka remarks,

> In an age when men are making computers that rival and even surpass some capabilities of the human being, a converse development is also taking place. Men are themselves becoming more like computers. Many aspects of a person's functioning in today's business and professional world can be more effectively performed if he can function more like a programmed computer. Thus, the more success a

man achieves in his attempts to function objectively, mechanically and predictably, the more he comes to resemble a computer. When he becomes too successful in his attempts to remake his personality in the image of a computer, he does so at the expense of losing his individuality along the way. The men who suffer most from this loss are those who rely on him for emotional, human interaction – especially his wife and children. And yet, in the rare movements when he allows himself to be something other than the image he so painstakingly tries to maintain, he perhaps feels the loss most acutely of all. He is not happy. (1973: 1)

Jim Waterfield was a man of this world. He controlled his interviews neatly, treating them rather like an exercise in textual analysis with his CV as the text. 'Good question', he would interject at intervals as the interview progressed. He completely objectified his self. He was a product, still in the development stage perhaps, but being carefully groomed for its launch into a well-prepared niche market for his own company. He spoke jerkily, precisely, in bits one could say, and his clipped, staccato style was perhaps intended to reflect an uncluttered, orderly mind used to sending computer messages from screen to screen. I will let him describe himself:

I lock into people. Sometimes I don't say what people want to hear from me I'm afraid but I tend to be fairly genuine, fairly sincere ... I work fairly hard but only because I get committed to programmes ... I've got a fair degree of patience, I believe, so I have done projects where the actual thing I was supposed to do was less than interesting, but as long as the major objective that I've got in any particular phase is of interest or of importance to me, then actually I have a fair degree of patience and application.

I'm afraid sometimes people look at my managerial decisions and they ask me to explain why I believe such and such is right ... I used to worry whether I should be able to analyse everything ... I've learnt – or I believe I've learnt – that sometimes you just know what's right and what's wrong and, even if it's not quite perfect, I feel that trusting my own judgement has become part of my character. I guess I like challenges, and if I really look back, eighteen months to two years is pretty much what it seems to take to take a job you don't believe you can do and start to get it under some sort of control ... After eighteen months to two years I'm normally looking for some form of change – not necessarily out of the company ...

I'm not one to just get buried in detail. I actually don't mind hacking the detail but I like to understand what is going on around me. I like to have some freedom [but] I'm prepared to sign up to a commitment

and I'm happy to commit to deliver. [I'm] internally driven, yes ...
[that particular] project excited me and I really didn't care too much
what else happened in the world but I really wanted to fly my piece
and say, 'That was mine' ... if you went to that team and said, 'Whose
is that?', everybody knew it was mine. And that matters: a certain
pride ... I like to know what I'm trying to achieve. I used to have a
little joke about people – that you should always try and learn
something every day and achieve something every year, and that's
what I tried to do in the first ten years ... I like to get a target and it's
difficult to set a target in further than two, three or four years. I'm
happy to put in patience, application, effort to keep going towards
such a goal as long as it seems achievable – however much of a long
shot. I have a pride in actually being able to look at any point in my
career and saying, 'My objective in this phase was to gain this kind of
experience, or to develop this kind of equipment or meet that kind of
project', and it's only that that gets the inner momentum going ... if
people come to me and say, 'Thou shalt do this', OK, I don't mind.
There's no arrogance. If I can share the objective, that's OK, but if I
can't share the objective, they're wasting their time ... Typically [the
projects] have been more risky, more challenging, but they're often
just different ... I don't want to do the same thing all the time. I like
to grow a little. You gain out of the experience and if it's going to be
successful doing it that way, then I like to be on successful things.

Jim prepared himself carefully for his route to success. At school
he enjoyed 'the learning experience'. He resisted being a 'physics
and maths person all the way through' which, nevertheless, he
seemed to be, and he was constantly, he says, looking for new
challenges, although he followed the fashion of the 1970s of going
on to read electrical and electronic engineering at university. 'I felt I
learnt a tremendous amount from the exercise.' On graduating he
selected a company making missiles. 'They took on a team of 300
graduates and just fifty experienced guys with us, and in eighteen
months this new team was allowed to play with whatever new
technology it wanted and prove it would meet a certain level of
performance – and we did it.' Such was the age of the new
technology in the early 1970s. However, the political and economic
climate changed rapidly: the whole team was fired. 'But, I didn't fuss
too much. I felt that I'd learnt what I was going to out of the project.
My part of that project worked ... and I'd got a very rounded
experience as a result of it.' This became the pattern for the next ten
to fifteen years. Jim endlessly gained 'good experience', developed
his people skills, and even built himself a new house for his young
family on the way.

The company he worked for at the end of the 1970s wanted him to stay with it, but Jim felt there was a gap in his CV, so he moved on. He inspected his file: 'In analysing what experience I lacked, I didn't feel that I had the consultancy experience ... there were things that I felt I knew how to do but I hadn't really stretched enough ... I was attracted by the idea of doing some consultancy for a while in order to work out where there were opportunities.' In the early 1980s he moved, as he put it, from hardware to software and joined a major British company that he felt would be 'a good springboard'. Having made the jump, he had immediate doubts. He felt that he had been over-sold important aspects about his new company and he became 'very uneasy about what could or couldn't be achieved'. However, it was imperative to him that his CV should not suffer. 'I decided I must find something which I could write up on my CV in two to two and a half years' time.' He had, as he said, to make the company do something for him. 'I couldn't just put dates on a CV. That's not good enough ... [In] two and a half years I had three days' holiday. I was beginning to think I must be a workaholic but I really cared about getting something on the CV in that two and a half year period.' It would be impossible for Jim to face a gap in his CV.

His life, his career, his CV – they all came to the same thing – must show a regular progression through different projects. It is as if Jim is stuck in the mould set in his primary school, where three or four week projects on trains are followed by projects on the weather, dinosaurs or rockets and space. The final products are displayed on the walls of the class room, bear the names of their creators and are sometimes marked. Another project is achieved. The CV has begun.

He now has his own start-up:

> This is the third time I've been through a starter business kind of phase in terms of creating an identity in the market place, adapting whatever business development strategy you've got, being involved with projects to make sure they work – because that's my reputation. If they don't work then my reputation is damaged and I don't want to see that because that's what pays my wages.

This is a crucial and significant shift. During the first phase, as Jim put it, he was pushing up his learning curve; his second phase was project packing on his CV; and now he is simply marketing himself. It was very hard to find out what Jim actually did during his working day – a problem that I commonly found among the successful. Again, let him describe his work in his own words:

> In terms of what I do – the phone rings a lot in our business. My slot involves communication – not just with our staff but also with clients, so I spend a lot of time talking to them. Typically in a day the phone is always going so it's very difficult to get two hours uninterrupted . . . Training staff, because typically I would dive in and actually decide what goes on in a project as well as get people like Mark up to speed, and stuff like that . . . Phones are going a lot. I bid on many of the jobs that we do.

He carried on talking, continuously and fluently until I interrupted him in despair. He was supposed to be taking me through a typical working day and I had not got him past nine o'clock when the phone was ringing. Does he ever stop for a coffee, has he a secretary? Yes he has seven or eight cups a day – far too much. But who needs a secretary?

> We do our own typing. We sit in front of the computer. I'm writing proposals, I do a lot of proposal work, I'm writing study reports . . . I've always been close to the numbers side as well so in a typical day I've always had to worry about what's on the spreadsheet, looking at performance on projects, and that's probably been true in most of my jobs since I was twenty-five. I like to commit to project goals so, in a typical day, I try to get people locked into that same thing . . . I see myself as a bit of a troubleshooter. I like to think that when any of the team is in trouble, I can dive in and say something meaningful.

The truth appears to be that Jim spends most of the day in the office on the phone and this carries on to at least seven and often later. He has a personal computer at home and does the firm's accounting at weekends. He rarely reads. He's even given up reading the paper on Sundays. How then, I asked, does he keep in touch with technological developments in his highly complex specialized field? 'Good question – it must be the case that one doesn't. I read whatever I need to get through projects . . . reports and the like.'

I spent much of the second interview exploring with Jim the specialist niche that his four-person firm was expanding into, and discovered to my amazement that, while I had problems in working out what his firm did, the clients he worked for had problems too:

> One of the problems with specialist niche areas, if you wish, is that they do take a while either to cultivate or keep cultivated so there

certainly is a high marketing overhead in what we do. It's very often the case that the client can't write a very formal statement of work for you, so it's fairly opportunistic. Given a problem that they will find difficult to write down and describe for a contractor they don't know, they will often pick somebody that they do know because they know they have a reasonable rapport, they have an understanding of the problem already, and also because they're aware ... as well as tramping the corridors just to keep in touch with individuals, you also have to keep up to speed. You have to be involved in conferences, you have to keep in touch with people so that you're aware of what the current programme problems are – and it's that awareness that actually sells.

Jim phoned me up after the second interview in some anxiety lest I reveal the highly specialized area in which he worked, which in this case does make it difficult for me to explain precisely what his firm is all about. Basically, he and his colleagues prepare proposals for funding agencies which, if successful, they may either do themselves or sub-contract. Jim has cultivated the right contacts – by locking into them – and has the experience and, as he constantly emphasized, the commitment – as well, of course, as technical expertise. There's a tricky balance between using reputation to get contracts and having to sub-contract a proportion of the work because of overload. I originally contacted Jim since the company he had previously worked for had a very high reputation and I was seeking someone who was a clear success in the world of high-technology and advanced software. I was recommended to Jim as a high flier. I was a little taken aback to discover that while he was clearly highly technically proficient – and it would be wrong to underestimate that – the main product was himself. 'So', I said, 'You yourself are a product?' – 'Yes,' he replied, 'and I get sold as such as well, of course ... Do I consciously work on selling myself for things? Yes, to a percentage of my time.' In this world of contracting and projects, everyone seems to look at what they do in terms of percentages of their time.

Jim was one of the most difficult of the successful people I interviewed to get close to in any way. Finding out what his firm actually did was hard enough, but finding out more about Jim than was set out on his CV was seemingly impossible during the three or four hours of interview time. He had a 'strong family background, very much at ease, very happy childhood'. People would look at his family and say 'always happy'. He has a younger sister who is a nurse – 'very strong family ties'. His wife knew the kind of life she would lead when she married him, and after twenty years she apparently knows that 'she'll see me when she sees me' in the evenings. Earlier in his career, 'there was one particular year when I worked just about every weekend'. He has been on family holidays with his wife and two children but his family does not expect a holiday: 'If we can fit a holiday in, then great. If we don't, then we still do things in the summer.' His wife never takes the children on holiday without him. Just after he started up his new company he and his co-director decided they needed to rethink their strategy so they set up a working holiday in the south of France with their wives and his children. Luckily the weather was good so 'it was a genuine holiday rather than work'.

In no way does his family suffer, so he says, from the pressure of his work. 'It is true that I feel my children are used to the fact that I'm not there.' However, he and his wife recognize the problem, and he makes sure that he spends some 'quality time' with them. I wondered when he actually finds time for this quality time, given his lateness in returning in the evening and his work at weekends. He acknowledges that this probably means that his children 'stay up far too late' with his fourteen-year-old daughter rarely sleeping before eleven or twelve o'clock at night. 'How do you think she sees you?' – 'Mad, crazy.' – 'But what kind of father has she got?' – 'I hope that they know that he cares ... I think that most people that know us see us as a tight, close family.'

His wife is endlessly loyal and supportive: 'She knows that I tend to get committed to things. She knows that I'm happier diving into things like that and her normal response to me is, well it's whatever makes you happy.' All Jim's responses were so clean, clear and problem-free that I felt I should try and see if there were any cracks in the picture window. But he never had rows with his wife. He can't remember the last time he lost his temper and he said he rarely feels sad, although 'the things that make me sad are people issues – my father died three years ago: that had a big effect'. Indeed Jim has consciously struggled to master his emotions and feelings, believing that letting fly, as he put it, would not achieve anything. I accused him of protecting himself, of defending himself from vulnerabilities. What I meant was that if he revealed his true feelings to people he might sometimes get hurt or appear less strong, and that he was afraid of this.

Jim did not quite take the point. Apparently people had said to him that his emphasis on linking with people might lead him to put their interests before his own:

> then it costs you something, it hurts somehow and, typically, people
> see it as making yourself vulnerable because of a bond or link with
> other individuals. So, typically, people assess me as having much more
> of those personal links and personal dependencies almost than they
> expect and yet I've presented to you a position where I'm defended
> somehow.

It is perhaps significant that 'people' judge his natal family, judge
the quality of his own family life and now negatively judge his
'linking with people'. Perhaps he protests too much that linking with
people does not make him vulnerable. 'I'm lucky', he says, 'that I
have really strong links with people ... I don't see that sort of
friendship as an undue risk.' But he does imply that it is something
of a risk.

I asked him whether he ever talked about his feelings to friends
or colleagues – perhaps in response to problems they shared with
him. Certainly, he agreed, people had come to him with problems.
'And again, people think that's a waste of my time, but actually I'm
prepared to pay that sort of price for being close to people.' So,
despite what 'people' say or think Jim will take something of a risk,
pay something of a price because he has decided to lock into people
on his road to success. Jim has no worries, he loses no sleep. At
forty he is full of bounce and confidence in the success of his
business, and largely defeated my attempt to probe the doubts and
anxieties of the human condition. 'Personal life? I genuinely feel
very lucky ... I don't apologize for the fact that I'm all right with
life. I genuinely don't feel that I'm losing out in any particular way.'

The interview ended then and Jim showed me out. I felt very
strongly a certain tension, anxiety and indeed hostility coming from
him as we went down the stairs. I hurried away with considerable
relief and I had great difficulty at the time in accounting for my
feelings.

Neurotic Pride and the Struggle for Mastery

One of Horney's developments from Freud was in her formulation
of the search for glory and the way that people attempt to resolve
their inner conflicts through the concept of an idealized image. She
saw this created image as a monster that prevented the individual
from realizing his or her full potentialities. Instead of facing difficult-

ies and fulfilling potentialities, he or she was diverted by the need to actualize the idealized self. The central inner conflict, according to Horney, is the conflict between the pride system, supporting the idealized self, and the real self. Freud could not see the psychological importance of the search for glory, since for him the factors in the expansive drives which he observed were 'really' derivatives of infantile libidinal drives. But for Horney, 'the inner dictates are an expression of the individual's unconscious drive to make himself over into something he is not (a godlike, perfect being), and he hates himself for not being able to do so' (1991: 374).

As I said earlier, I am in no position to judge what the circumstances might have been that led David and Jim to a compulsive search for glory. Nor am I competent to explore in any detail their measures to reduce tension. Both attempt to create inner peace by controlling feelings from the real self that might disrupt the structure. An automatic control system is put in place which holds back the individual not only from acting on impulse or in expressing feelings easily but from the impulses and feelings themselves. Horney claimed that: 'If through alienation from self and psychic fragmentation a feeling of organic unity is lacking, some artificial control system is necessary to hold together the discrepant parts of ourselves' (p. 181).

This control may be called dignity, pride, stoicism, wearing a mask, being realistic, unsentimental and so on. Some may even recognize their controls and wish they could let go. David, for example, recognized that his wife could explore what he called 'interpersonal issues', whereas he confessed to having 'a problem explaining things sometimes'. He feels that he can communicate with his wife but 'there are a lot of people who always get the wrong end of the stick'. For David people are either on or off: they understand or they do not and he himself has what he calls 'tunnel vision'.

Both David and Jim use their minds to distance themselves from themselves in the name of what they would call objectivity. As onlookers they no longer become part of their inner struggles. Thus, mind comes to be opposed to feelings and the self. Tensions are released, conflicts covered up and some unity may be maintained, but the costs to the development of the real self are great. By compartmentalizing, conflicting currents are disconnected and Jim and David no longer experience conflict as conflict. Jim in particular seems to come close to Horney's '"well adapted" automaton'. He feels, thinks, does, believes what is considered appropriate or right in given circumstances. This emotional deadness, the walking zombie has also been discussed by Fromm. What Horney calls shallow living, Fromm calls a defect. Such people do not have symptoms such as anxiety or depression. 'The impression is in short that they do not suffer from disturbances but that they lack something' (Horney 1991: 288; Fromm 1944: 380–4). I had a very strong feeling of this in relation to Jim: David seemed still to be able to make contact with his real self.

I did not look for people who seemed to need psychotherapy. Some of the successful people I interviewed seemed to be well in touch with themselves and not especially neurotic. However, as I have tried to indicate in this chapter, the search for glory can be a dangerously false monster for some. It is certainly a powerful force in the creation of *fin-de-siècle* anxieties.

6

Success-led or Anxiety-driven?

Reflexive intellectuals fare no better in coping with the confusions and ambiguities of the late twentieth century than do the more traditional or conventional managers in industry. Novelists took the lead in exploring the changing *Zeitgeist* with varying degrees of skill and perception. One of the most interesting and, perhaps, partly autobiographical novels to explore these dilemmas is *Daniel Martin* by John Fowles. The following passage illustrates one particular source of anxiety and unease:

I certainly could not call Barney a failure in worldly terms; yet something of that also hung about him – indeed has continued to hang around all my Oxford generation. As with Ken Tynan, so many others, I certainly can't except myself, destiny then pointed to far higher places than the ones actually achieved. Perhaps we were too self-conscious, too aware of one another and what was expected of us, too scared of seeming pretentious; and then, in the 1950s, we were fatally undercut and isolated by the whole working-class, anti-university shift in the English theatre and the novel. Tynan's famous rave for *Look Back in Anger* was also a kind of epitaph over *our* hopes and ambitions – over the framework of middle-class tradition and culture that we had all been willy-nilly confined in. All this reduced us to watching and bitching; to satire; to climbing on whatever cultural or professional bandwagon came to hand, accepting the fool's gold of instant success. That is why so many became journalists, critics, media men, producers and directors; grew so scared of their past and their social class, and never recovered. (1977: 113)

This theme is explored by other novelists such as Frederic Raphael in *The Glittering Prizes* (1976) or Margaret Drabble in *The Ice Age* (1978). These novels tend to focus on those from more established middle class backgrounds coming to terms with new values, new uncertainties and new moral dilemmas.

In this chapter I want to view these new opportunities and ambiguities through the eyes of someone without a secure middle-class background. Is success more unequivocal when a sharper contrast with family of origin is possible? Are the signs clearer for members of the rising reflexive élite than for those feeling under-mined or betrayed? In order to discuss these issues, I will explore in some detail the case of John Maltby, who, when I first interviewed him in 1990, was a television producer in one of the largest of the ITV companies. He was then forty-six. His father was a skilled manual worker, son of a Catholic immigrant from Eastern Europe who had settled in Scotland. His mother was the daughter of a carpenter-joiner.

As a boy, torn between the Catholicism of his father and the Protestantism of his mother, John was probably more conscious of his marginality. He got a scholarship from the local Irish Catholic school, where he described himself as an 'anxious, detached little boy' and entered the local grammar school at the age of eleven.

> It was a little mock public school in a town where at least two-thirds of the pupils had working-class fathers; they weren't even allowed to play football – they played outside the school and were given detention for it – they had to play rugby. It was a class war, I tell you, before your very eyes. There were these people trying to impose values on us, which a lot of us just couldn't understand. So I struggled with it, trying to be a good boy (like my mum wanted a good boy) until I got to sixteen and then several things happened to me really. I got so weary of my sense of singularity and my anxiety that I just about threw out all my old values. I began swearing and cursing. I discovered two great things that changed me – one was masturbation and one was evolutionary theory – truly! I just got emotionally exhausted, doing this wonderful thing, then having to go in and tell the priest about it every time, promising not to do it again. That just emotionally exhausted me. And, secondly, when we learned about evolution at school when I was fourteen or fifteen, I swear it was like a bolt of light to me, it just made such beautiful, elegant sense. Goodbye to all this claptrap nonsense of a sort of cosmic post office where you applied to St Aloysius, who was a good friend of the Virgin Mary, who put in a word for you with Jesus Christ, who'd created tigers on this day and

whales on another day . . . All of a sudden it was great. Truly, I'm not romanticizing it. I thought this is beautiful, I love it. In fact, I got a strong sense of the beauty of an idea, the symmetry, the elegance. The fact that not only did it explain everything, it didn't explain anything away, it just gave you lots of fascinating questions. I do think evolution is a most wonderful, beautiful idea. So I thought, well, stuff all that Catholic nonsense. Also I was beginning to feel my muscle and, at sixteen, I did become one of the lads by entirely putting to one side my own quirky individuality and saying fuck and shit and bugger like the rest of them, and dumping the church. I was at last one of the lads and I liked it.

This new-found confidence helped John to be the first one in his entire family not only to pass the 11 + but also to get good A levels and to go to university. Referring to that period of his life, he said, 'I was a huge success.' He went on to get a first class degree in psychology and, riding the tide of history, in 1965 he was offered an assistant lectureship as soon as he graduated.

John was well on the way to becoming one of those who would alarm, if not depose, the Oxbridge cultural élite:

In my early twenties I was still full of myself. I'd got this first class honours degree, I was a university teacher; my parents thought I was Jesus Christ on earth; I was incredibly, horrifically cocky. I took to hanging around with people who worked at the local television station – researchers and young producers – and I appeared on some local studio programmes being a stroppy, aggressive, clever young man.

Clearly the humdrum world of a junior lecturer's job could not compete with the glamour of television, and so John exchanged 'laying down the law in lectures' for being not much more than a tea boy. This collapse of his success trajectory caused him serious emotional and psychic distress resulting in a kind of breakdown:

For the next six to nine months I was first of all very anxious and then depressed – I had the real Plath's *The Bell Jar*. I was cut off from people; I was disoriented; I was exhausted. I was already married; I'd had the university job and suddenly I was just exhausted. My TV career was in the doldrums for about a year.

John took some years to recover from the turmoil of that period: he moved away to a remote area, recognizing his own anxieties and trying to come to terms with the complexities and confusions of his identity and aspirations. The details need not detain us. John eventually came back to London and became what most people would describe as a successful producer, eventually making programmes on a variety of educational and documentary topics all over the world.

Yet John Maltby is still very unsure of himself: 'I don't think I ever really found out the real job I should be doing and I don't think I'm a success.' John has a deep insecurity and anxiety about his own capacities, alternating between cynical detachment and enthusiastic commitment. Highly articulate and self-aware, he can strip himself of false-consciousness one moment and then allow himself to be enveloped with the glamour of television the next. This is a complex and subtle issue, made the more complicated by John's idiosyncratic marginality and anxieties and the peculiar fragilities of the world of television which he has in some small way helped to shape, as it, in turn, has shaped him.

On the one hand John can feel strong and powerful:

> We really fancy ourselves . . . we see ourselves as an élite, as kings of creation. All those beliefs that people have that broadcasters think they're the bee's knees and they can pop in and out of other people's lives as they feel like it – they're absolutely true! Maybe we're due for a bad fall as a result of our hubris.

John's fear of the consequences of hubris means that he can never be secure in his success: he is watching, analysing, doubting and mocking. His auto-critic can be devastating:

> I think we're wicked and we're naughty but we pay a price because we don't ever stay properly with anything and we get blasé, and that's worst of all. I mean, I don't like the current affairs world and the news world when people say, 'Oh, it's another dead baby story' . . . and they can get like that, those people. I believe their emotional responses can become corroded and eroded. Not that I've ever seen a TV programme or a book or anything that actually properly shows how emotionally depraved the people who work in TV can become.
>
> I interviewed a chap recently with terrible burns and at one and the same time (you must be able to imagine this) I'm saying to him, 'Tell me about how it felt when you woke up and realized that your face was all burnt', because I know that's what people who watch TV, or me if I watch TV, want to know. I want to know how the bloke feels. And I'm asking this man to expose himself publicly to people and reveal his innermost feelings to people and, to the extent that he does

that, a cold, reptilian part of my temperament is saying, 'Got that, good one, that's great, I can cut that with so-and-so', etc. At the same time the real me is saying, 'That's really awful.' As I say, I will often, and I know other people do this, I have done interviews where I have cried. Really, I'm not being histrionic, I'll get really upset because I'm meeting a real person who's got a real problem, and yet that little reptilian part of my brain is thinking, 'Got that, that's really good, we can use that.' And I know that comes out in a cliché ... but it's true. It's a daily thing, you know, but you're not necessarily exploiting people. Often people want to tell you about how they feel about everything and give intimate details. You have to slow them down, you have to say, 'No I don't really think you should expose yourself that much.' I'm not sure that that conventional idea of the producer's exploitation versus the subject's need for privacy is actually true. You're negotiating, you see. The person comes to you, and they have certain needs and wishes. I mean, a classic example (and this happens to me, and it worries me) is that we'll do a programme and you'll interview someone for three-quarters of an hour, looking for a few key phrases and so on, and that person wants to give you three-quarters of an hour of stuff. It's their life, for God's sake. It's like me talking to you. If you were me, and I were you, I might take thirty-five seconds of all this, of me saying, 'It's the greatest job in the world' ... and the rest ... bin it! I do that all the time. I do all that, and take forty-five seconds out of it.

It is too simple to dismiss John as a mere cynic – or at least one must consider more carefully what the role of the contemporary cynic might be:

The modern mass cynic loses his individual sting and spares himself the risk of exposure. He has long since ceased to subject his eccentricity to the attention and mockery of others. The man with the clear 'evil eye' has disappeared in the crowd; anonymity now becomes the large space for the cynical deviation: the modern cynic is an integrated asocial character whose deep-seated lack of illusions is a match for that of any hippy. He does not regard his own clear, evil gaze as a personal defect or as an amoral quirk to be privately justified. Instinctively he no longer understands his way of life as something evil, but as part of a collective, realistic view of things ... This is the stance of people who realize that the times of naïveté are gone.

Psychologically the contemporary cynic can be understood as a borderline melancholic; he is able to keep his depressive symptoms under control and remains more or less capable of work ... cynics are not dumb, and every now and then they certainly see the nothingness to which everything leads. Their spiritual make-up has become elastic enough to make the constant doubt about their own pursuits part of their quest for survival . . . cynicism is *enlightened false consciousness*. It is the modernized, unhappy consciousness, at which Enlightenment has simultaneously laboured successfully and in vain. (Sloterdijk 1984: 192)

John Maltby is not at ease with his success:

I have a perpetual dream which is that I'm still at school or university or something and I suddenly realize that all the others are years younger than me and they've been working for their exams and I haven't. In my dream I realize that I've been wasting my time, that they've been really getting on with it and I've just been fooling around, and I suspect that reflects an unconscious feeling that I have that deep down I haven't achieved whatever I thought I was going to achieve when I was a university teacher or even a student.

Those who want to be dismissive would see John Maltby as an archetypal member of the chattering classes. He is a creative communicator; he is a television producer; he is a writer and has published several books that go with his programmes. He loves communicating and he wants to carry the stigmata of creative people – 'That's why I wear a black leather jacket.' His peers see themselves as 'commando leaders'. They talk about being 'at the cutting edge'. Academics may be despised for a mere commitment to the truth. John has to have more than that: not only must he tell the truth, 'but it must be interesting and snappy and diverting and make people leave their tellies on and not switch over. Because of my academic background I can take big fat books and reports that frighten many of my colleagues and pull out what I think are the guts of it. I'm very proud of that.'

In a memorable phrase John argued that 'you've got to be success-led, not anxiety-driven'. So what does he mean by being success-led? To be success-led requires two key abilities, he argues: you have to be brave and you have to be playful, that way you will try things on that you are not quite sure of. He has to play a game with his Controller: what are his prejudices? How can they be worked round, negotiated, circumvented? He is not sure whether he has been co-opted into the consensus. Like many professionals and creative people in the 1990s he is not sure how far he is constrained and his autonomy limited by others and how far these are self-imposed restrictions, resulting from the absorption of the organizational culture and values that surround him. He is playing, having fun, and also trying to be brave, to stick out for what he believes he must do.

He can never relax:

> You asked me before what my fears are. I'm living with them. I'm forty-six years old in a business where the proper age for a producer is in his thirties. I'm around the age at which it's OK to be a Controller but I'm old to be a producer actually. I couldn't get to be a Controller myself. I'm not tough enough; I'm not aggressive enough; I'm not narrow minded enough. I see Controllers as rather narrow, decisive, aggressive people.

John is in an endless battle with himself: it is his own approval that he seeks and he knows in his heart when he has done well – 'You can smell it: it's good; it's classy; it's got edge.' He claims that 'The really good people in telly are obsessed with what they do', and it is those people that he wants both to be like and to approve of what he is doing. The rewards from his peers provide a great source of gratification for him: 'My hidden audience is people like me, as it were. People who know about the business, my peers, the producers who know all the difficulties and know what I've pulled off.'

Despite his determination to be success-led and not anxiety-driven, John feels marginalized and apart from what he calls the 'middle-class professional gravy train'. Some of his colleagues have a more selfless devotion to their careers and to hard work and discipline, whereas John feels something of a dilettante by comparison. He lacks what he calls 'real ambition. I think the worst thing you can inherit from a working-class background is a very limited horizon. You don't set out to be a Controller or something like that. About as big as I could imagine was a producer.'

Having recognized that he may have settled for less than he could have achieved, he then justifies this as the best of all possible worlds:

> There's something obsessive about my style of work, this business is a bit like primary school projects: it's one of the nearest things to staying as a child that you're allowed I think. It's play . . . you make this *object*. I'd like to say this. Television production meets a lot of the criteria for the perfect job . . . you get a group of you together, it's like a hunting group. You set off on a specific project, it takes so much time, it's got so much resources, and it has a result which either succeeds or fails. Then you have a little rest, then you start all over again, maybe with a new group of people, with a new topic, and so on. *And* you get to plunder the world! You can meet all the best experts, you've got

expenses to facilitate you getting anywhere and doing anything. I get
to go in and film all kinds of people and talk to them about the most
interesting parts of their lives, then I come out again. I mean, isn't that
a rich and varied life?

But hardly has he settled for a rich and varied life, than off he
swings again, anxiously recognizing that he is 'not quite a proper
current affairs producer – probably because I was corrupted by too
much academic life'. His superiors recognize this potential failing
and urge him to 'keep it glam John, keep it punchy'. This, he says, is
seen as his weakness – he has a tendency to be too analytic. Maybe
he would have done better at the BBC but he feels that he was
handicapped by his working-class background. 'Middle-class people
call it a chip: maybe it's just an excuse.' Nevertheless, he believes
strongly that:

When you come from a thoroughly working-class background, a
middle-class 'career' is just a kind of anthropological journey. I mean,
I think by rights if it wasn't for being a bit bright, I should be back
where my dad is. That's a key point – all this is a bit of a game. That's
why I have this lingering feeling that I've never actually taken a proper
grip on a career.

Just when the sociologist hears echoes of research done in the
1960s on 'career anchorage', where people measured their progress
up hierarchies not so much by the point they have reached but by
the distance they have travelled from the point where they started
(Tansky and Dubin 1965: 725–35), so John Maltby shifts his ground
once more. It is almost as if he feels uncomfortable with any neat
sociological or psychological packaging. He is always quick to see
alternative explanations and to play with these before moving on.
About to become a victim to marginalization he quickly shifts tack:
'Maybe my marginality is a resource . . . I pride myself on not being
an Englishman, the son of an Englishman who did a job like mine. I
mean, I am the product of historical forces.' And having shifted
from victim to the self-sufficient individual making piratical raids on
the comfortable establishment, he switches, yet again, cued in by the
mention of 'historical forces':

My grandfather went to Scotland for economic reasons; my father was
pushed down into England for economic reasons because of the
Depression. I was pushed into where I was because of the 1944
Education Act. I got to be a university lecturer because of the

expansion of universities in 1965. I got to do television because the ITV system was started. I feel myself literally floating like a cork along historic and economic trends.

So John leaps from psychology to sociology to Marxist theories of history with dizzy abandon.

His analogy of being like a cork on the current of history became real when, a year or so after I interviewed him, he was made redundant as a result of substantial industrial restructuring. The company he worked for lost its franchise but John had already gone. Old areas of employment were lost but far more new ones were opened up. Most of those who left the company found work in jobs that did not exist a few years earlier. As John later explained, 'many of us do extremely portable jobs. To be made redundant has quite different meanings for us than it might have to an academic, for example.' But John enjoyed his cork analogy. He could not resist adding, 'This cork floats, remember?'

All this talk of class and economic trends encourages John to digress on his historic role as communicator to the working class:

The conflict within me is between the razzmatazz and show business versus the feeling, the excitement, that was given to me by my education – that there was such a thing as revelation: the truth! And the conflict for me is the fact that most television is deeply cynical and doesn't really believe that ordinary working people can experience revelation. And so one of the things that I've failed properly to do (but it was a fantasy of mine) was that I thought, through television, I would be able to communicate with working-class people like me, from my origins. I remember this great rush of power and confidence that I got when I went to university, this feeling of being the subject instead of the object, because so many working-class people are dominated by the feeling of being at the receiving end of things. They talk big and they talk aggressive but they have no real confidence at all, because the world is so complicated and they often can't make out what all these clever-dick, middle-class people are talking about. And I had this hope that somehow, through telly, you would say to them, 'It's a con.' I never did it, I was suborned. But I'm trying to say I think that I'm naive, liberal and lefty (vaguely lefty, but not properly lefty because working-class people don't make very good left-wingers really, by and large, except if they're miners), but that kind of sentiment produces the sort of wishy-washy liberal like me that you often get in television.

John Maltby is playing with roles, playing with his multi-faceted identity that is his strength, in the struggle to be detached, street-wise and cynically committed. He surely is a type that is as much created by the television age as has helped to create it. He admits that he would expect me to find it 'ridiculous how much people's success depends on the moment-to-moment extrovert ability to have a kind of wit and detachment. One of the qualities that all people who work in television prize themselves on is that they are sophisti-cated; they're informed, and they're quick and subtle and aware of nuance.' He sees himself being the person he describes. He enjoys playing and, as he says, people who enjoy playing and who are 'perhaps rather detached and sceptical people are drawn to it'.

Being a television producer is an obsession; a form of compulsion. John Maltby claims that it is a closed world. Those who work in television have friends who work in television who entertain each other when all they talk about is their careers. Home life, he claims, without a partner in the same business, is not real – it is marginal, irrelevant and quite often solitary. 'It's amazing how many of us are divorced or separated or never got married in the first place and live quite happily on our own.' There is only one way to work in television, he claims. That is where the real life is: 'That's your real life and your obsession.'

The idea that in television you have to be success-led and not anxiety-driven is an important one. 'You've got to assume you're going to succeed.' If you do not do something more creative, a little better than last time, there are young ambitious people pressing on your back. Discussing such issues seems to make John nervous – the fear of hubris again. He points out that because he does features programmes, he does not feel that he is 'working at the front line'; that would make him vulnerable – to be shot at, injured. Perhaps he wants the success without the risks?

As a graduate of a distinguished civic university he readily concedes that 'the Oxbridge of television is to work on one of the important pioneering programmes like *Panorama* or *This Week* or *World in Action*. This is where you get your Master's degree'. He claims for a PhD, to carry on the analogy, you do substantial documentaries – 'that's the real success':

> my Controller here, he's a success, for example. He's a success at several levels because he's produced programmes out of his own genuine concern for the way the world is, and he has taken on the Establishment, when it was wrong, and made it tell the truth. And

that's a very real form of success and that has been reflected in the kind of programmes he's been allowed to make, the budgets he's been allowed to control, and his present position as Controller. I'm actually much happier that he, who's the same age as I am, is my boss and not the other way round. He deserves to be because he's shown a kind of drive and commitment and integrity. Success is two or three things at once. In this business I honestly do believe that if you work really hard, if you're really brave, if you're really creative, if you're really committed, it shows on the screen. When it shows on the screen, people can recognize it. They say, 'Who's that chap who did that? Let's give him some more money, let's give him some more time.'

John Maltby enjoys talking, enjoys communicating, enjoys exploring his motives, his ambivalences and his contradictions. He knows what I am up to, he can play a character in a novel by Malcolm Bradbury, he can adopt the stance of the author of an article in *Theory and Society*, he can take over my role as interviewer, asking himself further, more penetrating and revealing, questions. He can take reflexivity and play with it, deconstruct it, analyse it, distance himself from it and second-guess the interpretation that I am putting on what he is saying. He can draw on the experiences of his biography, of all the probing depth interviewing he has done, of all the sociology and psychology that he has read. He enjoys his own flow of talk; he runs with it; throws it and catches it; distances himself from it and embraces it. Part of his success, perhaps, is simply the experience of being able to discuss what he is doing with such skill, versatility and style. He laughs, mocks and revels in what he is doing.

By and large I play according to the rules but I am not certain who is setting them. Sometimes I get a clue. I explored his relationship with his father and it seemed highly relevant and significant for explaining his attitudes and behaviour, but John saw the limits of the interview. 'We're going far too deep – you can't use this, you know. Here we are talking about work and I'm telling you my soul. I enjoy it but you shouldn't use it.' John, inevitably, has been in therapy: 'I found it great, I found it really useful – like this conversation.'

The sociologist and apparent interviewer perforce becomes an amateur analyst because, to a degree, the role is put upon him by the way John responds. He is used to free-associating. The leaps in self-analysis that I have been discussing are well practised and well rehearsed. He has worked through his ambivalences with his analyst and I am just getting excerpts like listening to some *Pick of the Week* programme where he runs a short piece and then provides the commentary:

> I am not so much anomic, but what I learned very early as a working-class child was that the kind of detachment I had, that sense of standing a little aside from the others, was actually a very valuable tool because it enabled you to study how people did things and learn from it.

So how do I know who is interviewing whom? Is he interviewing a sociologist who thinks he is at work interviewing him? Am I sure that I am taking the lead or is it he? Some of the best material he gave me was prompted by his own questions which were often better than mine. I set the agenda in one sense but my agenda – encouraging him to talk about himself and his motives and ideas about success – is also *his* agenda and he is more practised at discussing himself than I am: 'You see I love communicating: I love explaining to you or anyone else how I feel, how I see the world. What I best of all love is telling several million people something about the world. Partly this is due to insecurity, but also this tremendous urge to communicate.'

I was tempted to let John Maltby flow on in this chapter, unedited, to be true to my source; to present his transcript as a historical document; to abnegate responsibility for analysis. That would make him the author of the chapter. However, John is not able to see himself in the context of all the other material in this book. It is my judgement about what he says that will sway the reader. But maybe the unedited transcripts should be available to scholars in years to come. Should the final decision be with the author or the respondent and which is which and when should it be taken?

John has said many times that he gets strength from his detachment. But he also claims that the current affairs world is very much a male pack. How does the loner fit into male pack values?

> I've watched people trying to push into the pack. They get hazed for a long time and then, if they don't stand up and show a certain amount of edge, they get squeezed out the other side. I've actually seen someone driven to a nervous breakdown by pack members because, if you work in current affairs, you have to show that you are very sophisticated, very informed, very 'on the ball', very tough and a natural pack member – and I'm not. And that's one of the reasons I don't work in current affairs and can't. Features and documentary

people tend to be a little gentler; they're a bit more quirky, I fit better into this world.

John Maltby insists that he is success-led and not anxiety-driven but his insistence does not remove the ambiguities and contradictions. He explained on a number of occasions that co-ordinating the resources involved in producing a programme is a very stressful operation:

> You can do everything right and it still comes out wrong. It's like baking a cake: you put all the right bits in and do the best you can – and it tastes wrong; it looks wrong; it hasn't hit the spot. No one quite knows exactly what it is you have to do to really produce something that's successful. I've had stress symptoms; I've had chest pains; I've had neck pains . . .

Since success is such a slippery and ephemeral notion it is understandable that, despite John's protestations and denials, he must, to a degree, be anxiety-driven as well as success-led. It's the combination, as he recognizes, of being both sensitive and perceptive and also simultaneously, tough-minded and stable. The ability to handle the reversals, shocks, defeats and frustrations inherent in the work is very hard to acquire.

However, true to form, whenever he muses on the internal sociopsychodynamics of the situations, he almost immediately reacts by swinging back to seeing himself as the victim of external circumstances that are producing universal, not particularistic, structures of stress. Like university professors, consultants in the Health Service and many others, he sees himself to be 'in an environment in which we feel ourselves increasingly to be controlled by financial people and scientific managers who haven't come through the business as we have' who don't understand in detail what the work is really all about. 'We are in a historical period where we can be squeezed till the pips squeak, we really are, and the pips, in the end, are stress.' The story is increasingly familiar and is repeated in a slightly different form by the managers discussed in chapter 3. Perhaps more than other professionals, John is aware of the generation behind him.

> TV is a young man's business in all sorts of ways. I think young people *should* do it because it's a fast track . . . But . . . I'm reluctant to leave this place. It's full of extraordinary people: wonderful, potty, talented,

able, neurotic people … it's just such a wonderful job … I like the sense of being at the centre of things, of being where things matter.

Yet while he loves being at the centre of things, he also holds a fantasy of running away, becoming the Controller of a provincial radio station and escaping from the pressure and stress he both loves and hates. Throughout the interviews he veers between the two extremes of being a big fish in a small pond or a modest-sized fish in the sea of London:

> I haven't actually solved the personal problem of feeling that, instead of being this watchful, fluent, careful individual who sees how other people do things, and then copies it a bit, and builds on it, what I've never done (I'm really enjoying this bit), I've never said, 'Fuck you all, this is me, and this may not be the most effective way to do things in the view of the world, but it's how I've finally decided to be and therefore I'm doing things this way because I won that battle and I actually stood up to those people, or that situation, and said that's what I'm going to do.' So, in a sense, I'm slightly embarrassed by my own success because I fear it's the success of compromise, it's the success of being realistic and in a sense, for example (I'm making this up but) I'd rather be a failed major movie producer, or even a failed current affairs producer, than what I am, which is a reasonably successful features producer. So I'm at odds with my own nature, with the deference of the working class. The only way I could get out of it was by being a chameleon and modelling myself on these middle-class people and so on. But what I haven't completed in my growing up, either as a person or at work, is saying, I've learned enough – now I will be *me*. The trouble is, I'll probably go to my grave feeling that tomorrow I'll start being me.

Discussion

'The self in modern society is frail, brittle, fractured, fragmented – such a conception is probably the pre-eminent outlook in current discussion of the self and modernity' (Giddens 1991: 169). For others, writing in post-structuralist mode, the self simply disappears 'the only subject is a decentred subject, which finds its identity in the fragments of language or discourse' (p. 170). Giddens takes issue with popular discussions of narcissism such as those by Sennett and Lasch, who argue that people withdraw from wider environments and seek their personal identity in the private sphere. Yet this is precisely the opposite of John Maltby's world, where 'the private' is little more than a lodging house in which to take basic rest and refreshment before returning to the 'real' world of image making. Giddens draws on Stacey's account of 'recombinant families' in California to suggest that the claim that people are withdrawing from the wider social world is overstated (Giddens 1991: 176–7; Stacey 1990).

In much of his recent work Giddens highlights both broad forces of globalization and detailed discussions of the transformation of intimacy (1992), and says less about the self and identity-forming importance of work and employment at an intermediate level. There is an almost complete absence of any discussion of work in *Modernity and Self-Identity* (1991), and this is to ignore much of considerable sociological interest and importance. John Maltby illustrates very well the dynamics and tensions of success-led and anxiety-driven ways of life as sources of self-identity. The process is made up of multiple ambiguities and contradictions, as this chapter has demonstrated. John can and does go anywhere in the world to interview world leaders and distinguished scientists when gathering material for his programmes. He lives easily in a global environment. His base in London, in which I conducted one of the interviews, is a small and unpretentious flat. His work is his life. The central confusion which he is continually dancing around is the problem of success. He is acutely aware of its nuances and contradictions. To call on Sloterdijk once more: 'to be intelligent and to perform one's work in spite of it, that is unhappy consciousness in its modernized form, ill with Enlightenment ... Counter enlightenment ... banks on the fact that everyone who has something to lose comes to terms privately with his unhappy consciousness or engulfs it with "engagements".' (1984: 194). John Maltby, in these terms is a key type in late modernity; there is much he does not want to lose. His compulsive desire to explore his dilemmas appears as 'a nakedness which no longer has an unmasking effect ... the neo-cynical accommodation to the giver has an aura of plaintiveness; it no longer is self-confidently naked' (p. 194). John's cynicism is a kind of mournful detachment [*Abgeklärtheit*], internalizing its knowledge instead of drawing on it for criticism and change. We began the chapter with the disillusioned Oxbridge generation retreating into satire. John Maltby has led us full circle in his struggles with himself and success. We can now see why 'the great offensives of cynical impudence have become a rarity; ill-humour has taken their place and there is no energy left for sarcasm' (p. 194).

Coda

Since this chapter was drafted John Maltby's career has moved him on to a new upward spiral. He is the producer of an outstandingly successful programme at peak viewing time. He has read what I have written about him and it is surely appropriate and in the spirit of post-modern reflexive ethnography that he should have the last word – about himself and about me, the interpreter.

Well there I am, a modern modish monster, a borderline melancholic and castrated cynic, endlessly articulate, yet so reflexive and self-reflective that I disappear entirely up my own facile insights. Well, there you go, I can't argue with that!

Well I can actually. I know you'll agree that what we are increasingly obliged to realize is that there is no final truth. For a start, we are all far more deeply imbedded in our local times and culture than we can possibly appreciate. We are all types now, and our attempts to live meaningfully in the world are all typical.

Our understanding of the world is as vulnerable to typing as our standing in it. As fast as we can articulate any kind of genuine insight it begins to lose its force as others examine and characterize it. Perhaps the only remedy is to move on constantly, changing viewpoints, discarding certainties as fast as we come to them. In the meantime we each try to put something useful into the world, according to our station . . .

You have, of course, made what you wanted of our discussions. I don't quite know what it is! But I should tell you that as academic talks to media man he also reveals a little bit about the hopes and fears of his own tribe. There are one or two clues hidden in your commentaries about traditions and assumptions deeply, and perhaps invisibly, interwoven into academic culture which aren't there in mine.

As I said at the beginning, my lot clearly come over to you as kinds of butterflies, likeable, but in the end deeply compromised. I don't mind. As I said in the interview, I would probably cut me down to a few thirty-second sound bites . . .

7

Working for Self-identity

We live in a time when the very private experience of having a personal identity to discover, a personal destiny to fulfil has become a subversive political force of major proportions.

Theodore Roszak: *Person-Planet*, 1979

The individualized everyday culture of the West is simply a culture of built-up knowledge and self-confidence: more and higher education, as well as better jobs and opportunities to earn money, in which people no longer just obey. Individuals still communicate in and play along with the old forms and institutions, but they also withdraw from them, with at least part of their existence, their identity, their commitment and their courage. Their withdrawal, however, is not just a withdrawal but at the same time an emigration to new niches of activity and identity. The latter seem so unclear and inconsistent not least because this inner immigration often takes place half-heartedly, with one foot, so to speak, while the [other] foot is still firmly planted in the old order.

Ulrich Beck: *Reflexive Modernization*, 1994

Because we cannot but orient ourselves to the good, and thus determine our place relative to it we must inescapably understand our lives in narrative form.

Charles Taylor: *Sources of the Self*, 1989

It is a commonly held view among sociologists and philosophers, that the creation of self-identity is problematic, something which has to be achieved in a never ending process of reflexivity and life decision-making.[1] An adolescent typically tries on different identities and is perhaps more able to go one way or the other before educational experience, sexual partners and jobs determine the roles and relationships that fix his or her identity. Yet these grid-references to the self are no longer so clearly established in the 1990s. Men can no longer confidently expect to be 'breadwinners' supporting 'their' families; women no longer want or can afford to be 'just a housewife'. How to be masculine or how to be feminine has become difficult and problematic. Simple stereotypes of macho men and fluffy, simpering women are increasingly recognized as being jokey roles, in the same way that some people adopt mocking regional or class accents to distance themselves from situations and circumstances that might reveal insecurity and anxiety. The ways in which people act adopted identities are cued in from the increasingly complex role-models in television soap operas. People can now play being other people: there is a large cast of parts as available options, depending on one's position in the life course or nature of employment. Men and women may shift their gender identity or even their gender orientation quite dramatically. The collapse of 'lifelong' marriages, 'lifelong' careers, fixed and focused sexualities and so much else, implies that new identities often need to be forged around new jobs and new partners.

Distinctive masculinities and feminities are still tied to different occupations: the sing-song announcements of the air hostess are matched by the calm and measured reassurances of 'your captain speaking'. Miners, midwives and car salesmen have their distinctive gender-linked occupational identities. Occupation and class cultures provided useful anxiety-reducing props in the past, as men in particular received collective and solidaristic support for their styles of action. While it is true, as perceptive writers from Loane to Steedman have demonstrated, that men and women did not always follow conventional scripts, nevertheless the scripts were always there to fall back on (Loane 1908; 1910)[2].

If men were expected to lead lives segregated from women's world and work, then those men who wanted to be more loving partners and caring fathers had to conceal this behaviour from peers and naive researchers with inflexible research instruments. Conventional answers from available scripts were easily supplied. Conjugal couples instinctively maintained the subterfuge or deceit. In a world of low social and spatial mobility and without the contemporary mass media of communication, the number of available scripts was necessarily limited. People acted out what was expected from them in their station in life. This does not, of course, imply an over-determined world of passive dupes. There were infinite flexibilities in being a carpenter, a lawyer or a fishwife. However, the general tendency was for the carpenter to stay in work and be a carpenter all his life. The lawyer may not have replicated completely his stereotype in a Mozart or Donizetti opera but he had a recognizably unchanging script. Their scripts carried them through. Women had their social worlds and social values confirmed and reinforced by other women. Part of the modernist project from the period of the Enlightenment was to support the separation of spheres and thus avoid gender-identity induced anxieties.

Despite these apparent greater certainties about identity in the past, there is plenty of evidence to suggest that perceptive individuals from all levels of society questioned, resisted and resented the limitations of established and conventional scripts in local communities of place and occupation. While not wishing to minimize the anxieties and tensions in coming to terms with identity in the period between the Norman conquest and the late eighteenth century, we can see that these anxieties were resolved in a different context. The Diary of Ralph Josselin in the seventeenth century indicates that he had his worries but these were less about his identity than about the appalling hazards of everyday life (MacFarlane 1970: 170–1). Mac-farlane notes that the Diary 'provides a unique description of the way in which a man might squeeze through the Restoration attempts to induce conformity', and he got the impression that 'Josselin remained in a protracted state of insecurity because of his noncon-formity' (p. 28). These were early stirrings. As Calhoun remarks: 'In the Protestant Reformation perhaps most importantly, but through-out the early modern era, a revolution in thinking gave individual identity new moral and social weight. It became increasingly an object of personal struggle not merely a premise of action' (1994: 2).

Part of the conventional wisdom of the sociological tradition is that there was a shift from a world based on status to one based on contract; from mechanical to organic solidarity as the basis of social cohesion; from *gemeinschaftlich* values to *gesellschaftlich* values; from ascriptive social positioning to achieved social positioning, and so on (Nisbet 1966; Parsons 1953). This modernist, emancipatory trajectory of progress has been so heavily criticized, mocked and lampooned by many working in a framework they describe as being post-modern, or, more cautiously, late modern, that newcomers to the debate might feel that it is unnecessary to make any effort to understand this sociological tradition simply in order to know what it is that has to be discarded.

Leaving aside the false trails provided by the dichotomizers and social evolutionists of the last two hundred years (Nisbet 1966), it is nevertheless clear that many labels, scripts and narratives that served as boundary markers for identity construction in the past have come to the end of their useful lives. The collectivist solidarities of working-class unionism have failed to deliver and working-class pride has been undermined by de-skilling, political attacks and employers' divisive strategies. The rhetoric of revolution has worked most effectively in the former communist world, where consumerism and freedom to travel proved to have potent force. As the empires of class and ideology collapsed, new sources of identity based on gender, religion, ethnicity and nationalism rose up to fill the vacuum.

We need to know who we are. We need roots. The social co-ordinates of family and kinship, frequently linked to place, have been largely, but not completely destroyed. The same applies to family businesses and similar dynastic enterprises. If we cannot be sure of our gender identities, our jobs, our life course pattern, and how enduring our present set of relationships may be, then evidently we are alone in constructing our self-identity in our own way. This is the issue Giddens addresses in his magisterial introduction to the topic:

> Self-identity is a reflexive achievement. The narrative of self-identity has to be shaped, altered and reflexively sustained in relation to rapidly changing circumstances of social life, on a local and global scale . . . Only if the person is able to develop an inner authenticity – a framework of basic trust by means of which the life span can be understood as a unity against the backdrop of shifting social events – can this be attained. A reflexively ordered narrative of self-identity provides the means of giving coherence to the finite life span, given changing external circumstances. (Giddens 1991: 215)

This is the text which this chapter will unpack and expand.

The core notion is that of a 'reflexively-ordered narrative'. However, those such as Giddens, who theorize about the conditions of late modernity, have developed their ideas on a very modest empirical base. There has been a curious disregard and neglect of the life-story tradition of social-historical and sociological research, which has developed most significantly over the past quarter-century. Oral historians and those sociologists interested in auto/ biography have now provided an increasingly rich ethnographic base to give the empirical evidence for more abstract theoretical assertions. In this chapter I draw on four case studies to explore in some depth how self-identities are accomplished among those who may appear to be successful participants in the late modern world. My main concern is not to question whether or not they are successful in the worldly sense, but to explore how far such apparent worldly successes can be transformed into personal successes in reflexively ordering their individual self-identities. Clearly the material presented in relation to other cases in previous chapters bears directly on this question, and readers are sure to see connections for themselves. However, here I am going to discuss two men – a general and a vice-chancellor and two women – a university lecturer and an artist. The women were in their thirties when I interviewed them, so that their 'success' was inevitably less than that of the men, although it is unlikely that they will become as conventionally successful as the two older men when they reach a similar age. Each of these four people exemplifies in a distinctive way the iterative interaction between the ontological narratives of actors – the way they make sense of their personal lives, defining what they should do in the context of whom they think they are – and the meta-narratives of the historical conjuncture in which they live – the end years of the Thatcher government and the collapse of the Berlin wall and all that followed from that. The main theme is the interrelations between the public and private.

Sir Richard O'Dowd – known universally as Dick-O – was a man whose personal identity fused with his public identity and who revelled in the new managerial power that the 1980s brought some academics. The opportunity to act as an Almighty, shifting and shuffling individuals and departments to achieve a more 'rational' pattern suited Sir Richard perfectly. He was truly a History Man (Bradbury 1977). Laura Miller was a feminist academic in a Midland polytechnic soon to become a fully-fledged university. Her identity as a researcher and writer was at odds with the management's style. The basic pressure she had to face was the overriding demand to get more 'bums on seats' doing useful courses for policemen, public sector junior managers and the like. Faced with the dilemma of the job coming between her and her work Laura engaged in what the business schools call 'intrapreneurship' – she arranged to subcontract her job in order to get on with the work.

Laura's strategy was paralleled by Martha Kelly, who was an artist but also earned her living as an Education and Information Officer for a major national gallery in Scotland. Martha, like Laura, had to cope with both her work and her job, but in Martha's case she did both and was consequently frantically overworked, although always cheerful, with a sharp and perceptive sense of humour and a quick way with words. She, too, had to get 'bums on seats' to listen to her lectures on aspects of the art in the gallery's collection. She also had to perform bureaucratic functions at odds with her flamboyant artistic style.

Finally, General McAlpine was a man whose ontological narrative had for centuries fitted well with the metanarrative of the need to defend our lovely land. He came from a military background and he never considered being anything else but a soldier. He was like a thoroughbred shooting dog or sheep dog who knows exactly what to do, as it were, in its bones. Sadly for General McAlpine, when I interviewed him peace was breaking out all over. The end of the Cold War made a lot of his rhetoric appear archaic and he was being turned into a military accountant – much against his will. He was a little sad that he had, as it were, been stabbed in the back by the meta-narrative of the day, but he consoled himself by nipping off for a bit of bird-watching at lunch time at the nearby reservoir.

In presenting these four cases I have mentioned only two forms – ontological and metanarratives: two further forms – public and conceptual narratives – will emerge as I discuss each person in turn. I hope to create images in the reader's mind of the complex interweaving of different forms of narrative producing distinctive tensions of self-identity in the 1990s. If the reader already knew these people as well as I do, I could move quickly between them in my narrative, making comparisons and contrasts. Maybe if I were writing a novel or a play I could interweave them as characters, and the reader or audience would come to some understanding of their complex identities by, as it were, seeing them in action. I am stuck with having to present information serially, and in that ordering I am introducing bias, interpretation, values and all the rest of it but, I hope, in a creative way. (The problem of writing culture causes anthropologists much pain: writing cases is just as painful. One just has to suffer and struggle through.[3])

Sir Richard O'Dowd

Sir Richard is undoubtedly successful: his comments on higher education appear regularly in the press. He is a fluent speaker and has thought through his own career and road to success carefully,

since he frequently seeks to justify to himself the broad policy
decisions that he makes for others by what he himself has achieved.
Unlike most of my other respondents Sir Richard (I cannot bring
myself to use his nickname of Dick-O) talked to me as an equal.[4]
We arranged to meet in London after one of the regular meetings
that brought him to town. As with all my respondents I asked him
to introduce himself. In what follows I am concerned less with the
specific details of his account but more with style and form of his
narrative.

As with most respondents, Sir Richard used the co-ordinates of
family, locality and class to introduce his narrative. He stressed the
lowly social origins of his parents, their religious non-conformity and
their liberal/labour politics: he feels he was given strong parental
encouragements to 'get on':

> Neither of my parents had any form of higher education but they
> strongly supported it for me ... passed the 11+, went to a good
> city grammar school with a high proportion of university entrants and
> was strongly supported both parentally and in school terms, especially
> the latter, because my parents belonged to the generation who felt
> that when a professional adviser at school, particularly the head
> teacher, said 'do X', you did X and the parents didn't intervene. I
> suppose the thing I gained most from my parents was a degree of self-
> confidence which has stood me in good stead ever since. The belief
> that, if you had opinions, you should be prepared to articulate them,
> both orally and in writing we were encouraged to do that from a very
> early age. For example, I was public speaking at political meetings
> from the age of thirteen or fourteen in ways that I have since learnt
> are totally abnormal, but which seemed to me to be perfectly normal
> at the time.

He went up to Oxbridge as the classic upwardly mobile grammar
school boy. Ill at ease initially because of cultural unfamiliarities but
very quickly recognizing that he was clever enough to beat the more
self-assured undergraduates with a public school background, he
emerged with a first class degree. He was advised to pursue a career
as a university teacher and for that he needed a PhD. He completed
his doctorate in two and a half years, most of which time he was
earning extra money teaching twenty-one hours a week. He married
his girlfriend from his home town during the first year of his
postgraduate work and, as he describes it, their identities fused. In
the mornings he did his extra teaching:

And then one came home, one wrote one's PhD in the afternoon and Beryl typed it in the evenings, day after day after day, and that's how we did it. And we admit, looking back, we missed lots of opportunities. I mean, we didn't go out; we didn't go to the theatre; we didn't go to concerts. In that sense there is a loss, no doubt. But in terms of actually doing a PhD in the set time, it was simple.

Sir Richard looks back with considerable pride on his capacity to achieve his goals in a direct, no-nonsense way. By his early twenties he was a university lecturer, a senior lecturer in his mid-twenties and by his late twenties he was a professor and head of his department. His description of himself makes him sound like a kind of machine that is wasting itself if it does not work at full capacity. As a newly appointed lecturer he felt he was grossly under-employed – rather ominously, in the light of what he was to become – equating his job with the numbers of hours teaching he was expected to do. Most young lecturers would happily spend their time extending and deepening their knowledge of their subject, but Sir Richard found such a job 'unutterably boring'. In addition to his research he took on 'God knows how many jobs on the side because I was absolutely bored stiff. I just couldn't see how this was a full-time job.' I asked him how far these extra jobs were necessary to augment his modest salary when he was starting up married life. He said that he had indeed felt obliged to double his salary in the first four or five years of his career by these means, but he went on to emphasize: 'I can't be bored for more than five seconds and I had to do more work.' This compulsion to do more work is a crucial ingredient in Sir Richard's identity and self-image.[5]

Some of Sir Richard's early moonlighting activity involved running specialist summer courses requiring entrepreneurial ability which he found most enjoyable. A very strong element in his personal, ontological narrative is his need to be independent:

One of the beauties of this profession – even at the top, even as vice-chancellor, is that in effect since I was eighteen – well, really all my life because my parents encouraged us to be very independent – I have never really been answerable to anybody else . . . every, every day of my life I have decided what to do, in what order and in what priority, and because I got promoted very young and I've had a secretary since I was twenty-six or twenty-seven really, I feel I've been uniquely privileged.

It is because of this strong theme in Sir Richard's personal narrative that he had little difficulty in reconciling 'Thatcherite values and the values of the collegium' in order to justify the ease with which he fitted in with the managerial style of the 1980s. He used a form of metanarrative to describe how his identity moulded his job as much as his job moulded his identity. He believes that the 1960s and 1970s were aberrant in the level of privileges given to academic staff – a time when resources came before students.

Sir Richard's self-image seems to be of an effectively operating machine on the fast track. Very few people are promoted to the top of the academic hierarchy in their twenties and he had no reason ever to lack confidence, as he readily acknowledges. He likes analysing what he does and his ontological identity in terms of his 'nature'. For example, he likes to treat his secretary or PA well and gives them the highest possible status – 'and that's always paid off. I mean, it's partly my nature but partly calculated. If you treat people really well you get magic service out of them.' He knows he is on the fast track and it is the movement rather than the being that appeals to him. 'Beryl always teases me for never ever enjoying the present, always looking on the next stage. I tend not to think about what I have achieved or what I did yesterday, but what's the challenge for tomorrow?'

How does he account for this particular trait? It comes from his family background, he claims. He sees his father and brothers as having a 'restless urging'. He accepts that he has simply inherited this O'Dowd trait. A crucial aspect of his identity comes from what he describes as his 'big weakness ... I need to be loved or liked ... I like to wander about my empire and know that people are not saying, "That bastard's walking past", but say, "Hi, Dick". I like that. I like that very much.'

What was the secret of Sir Richard's success? How did a very able academic, good at passing examinations and writing a thesis become a highly successful manager? Partly, he claims it was luck. He moved to an unfashionable university that was struggling to survive, lured by the chance of a senior lectureship at an age when most academics would be fortunate in getting their first job as an assistant lecturer: 'It could have been a disaster ... it could, because of social pressure, which I'm very conscious of now but was much less conscious of as a rather – although politically I think I was really quite sophisticated – I think socially I was very naive and maybe still am ...'

However, because he had come to a large department with forty lecturers – there was only one professor who vetoed all attempts to add further professors – (a department that size would normally have four or five professors), Dick O'Dowd was on the spot and got accelerated promotion. When the other professor left, he found himself with fifty staff, ten secretaries and a huge budget. He had found a way to use up his formidable energy. When his university was the victim of ferocious cuts, his vice-chancellor came to him and said: 'go and earn a fortune'. Dick O'Dowd responded brilliantly to the challenge: 'It turned out to be staggeringly easy and we went from nothing to £300,000–£400,000 a year in non-UGC income . . . by every trick in the book. I was very proud of that, and we saved the department.'

This success later helped him to be appointed a pro-vice-chancellor. Soon after this his vice-chancellor was running a campaign to get more representation on the University Grants Committee from outside the charmed circle of Oxbridge, London, and four or five other universities. So when a vacancy came up the chairman of the Committee phoned up Dick's vice-chancellor for suggestions. Richard's name was put forward once they had 'checked out that I was a good Oxbridge man, that I do know, a good Oxbridge man. Oxbridge has stood me in good stead actually at various points.'

Thus, Richard found himself on a committee concerned with streamlining part of Britain's university system: he became, in his words, a political bureaucrat. Under the circumstances of the time he was given 'a free hand to bribe VCs and to bribe individuals, and I thought that was marvellous, because I could go to an individual and say: "I will get you a place in a research university if you tell me you're willing to move" and I could go to two VCs and say: "You won't lose", and "You will gain".'

This period of dirigiste planning came to an abrupt end and Sir Richard was outraged. 'I'm a real interventionist.' His goal was to reconcile enterprise with planning, and he described the retreat from such planning as 'grotesque'. Sir Richard did not wait until the system he enjoyed operating changed, but moved on to be a vice-chancellor when there were still rather few people with his experience and managerial talent available: 'During the 1970s I manufactured change in order to satisfy myself. During the 1980s I've never had to manufacture change. The change has been, in fact, almost too fast at times.'

Sir Richard's compulsive working style has its costs. At one stage, when he claimed he was 'easily' increasing the income of his department, he also suffered. 'I can say to you truthfully now that for three months or so I felt physically dreadful as well as mentally shattered . . . I went "funny" and – I've never told anybody this – I became physically impotent, I mean in the sexual sense, for two or three months.' Later when he became vice-chancellor he got another problem:

> I get what I gather is a distended gut, that is I get stomach-ache varying from very mild . . . to an extreme form . . . where it has been unrelievable. One just has to live with it for days on end at times . . . very, very unpleasant . . . . The other thing that gets me very twitchy is that although I work extremely hard and fill every minute, you know, just occasionally you have a day when you literally can't get it all in. You know that it isn't going to work . . . and I find that spoils the whole day. Even if great chunks of the day are very pleasant in substance, the day is spoilt because at some point one is going to be half an hour late for something else.

Sir Richard now runs one of the largest and most prestigious universities in Britain. He prides himself on his approachability, his vision and his political skills. He believes he has a special ability to understand both issues and people and to keep a balance between the two. As he talked about what he was trying to do – 'maintain the best values of collegiality and economic endeavour with increasing managerial pressures' – I felt that his identity was being over-influenced by the metanarratives of political and educational policy. I had an intuitive feeling that in the swirling tides of late modernity, he was no longer on the crest of a wave. He had climbed rapidly to a highly prestigious formal role but his identity did not fit it so well. Like so many people, his identity was becoming, in certain respects, fossilized. I asked him in conclusion, what in his life had given him the greatest pleasure and what gave him the most pride. He did not speak about his family, his meteoric rise up the academic ladder or the prestigious position he now holds. Rather, he referred nostalgically to his period of shuffling people round the higher education system. As he said: 'The mid–80s – I loved it'.

Laura Miller

Laura introduced herself with her name and her age:

> I'm a fairly lively, outgoing person who likes a lot of sports and fresh air and good wine and good company. I'm very committed to my work. It's very important to me that my work's going well, otherwise I feel very depressed generally. And when my work's going well I feel

very animated and lively and inspired and enthusiastic about life in general ... I think what's important is that I feel needed and involved and satisfied from doing my work, and that it gives me a range of activities and a certain degree of flexibility and autonomy.

She sees a danger in having her identity so closely wrapped up in her work, and she tries to get involved in various external activist groups and social clubs to create separate compartments in her life, 'in case something goes ghastly wrong in one compartment [so that] it doesn't sort of contaminate all the rest'. However, Laura is not simply a teacher in higher education, she is primarily a sociologist, which she sees as being 'a way of life. I think, a way of looking at the world. It's a way of living and a way of thinking ... you can never stop work as a sociologist.' Her identity is so suffused with this ontological form of narrative that it is worth allowing her to enlarge on what she means, reflecting as she does initially the interpreter's rather than the legislator's view of the intellectual in late modernity, using Bauman's useful distinction (1987):

To some extent everybody's an amateur sociologist, and I frequently interview people who have very, very perceptive and interesting and sociological observations on the world. So it's Gramsci's idea that some people are organic sociologists, but by studying sociology what you do is ... develop that curiosity in the world in certain kinds of rational ways. You gain a sort of familiarity with certain sorts of methods and procedures and concepts which once you've read them – it's a bit like when you've read certain novels – it changes your perception of reality and you can't ever change it back again. You stop being, I was going to say you stop being naive, nobody's naive really, but it gives you a certain view of the world that you've got really. And it gives you a certain handle on things. It gives you a way of understanding things. And I think it gives you a way of controlling the social world in a way, because by understanding things you can control them and then they are no longer quite so upsetting. And I think that's the appeal, in some ways, of sociology.

Later she develops her position, perhaps inconsistently, to present a legislator's view of her work:

I'd like to think that my work ... and the things I devote myself to, didn't just enhance my own career, but they also made some difference to the world at large, that they made the world a marginally better place ...
    I think what we all would share is a commitment to a sort of human

ethic, the human liberalist ethic, and what I would like to see is that advanced.

It's just that often you *can* see better ways of doing things. With having a kind of sociological background you *do* know a lot about certain social issues and you often *can* see a better way of doing things, given the sort of commitment to human ethics, a commitment to the dignity of human life, and then I think if you can see a better way of doing it you should say so.

Laura's life is burdened by the fact that at the time of our interviews she had very little control over what she did. Her line managers instructed her to do eighteen lectures a week on five different degree courses

and they don't like putting on new courses unless they are ones bringing in money ... under the new funding structure. If it's ... going to be the bums on the seats that brings in the money to the department you could get away with [a new] course, if you could argue that it would actually bring in students. But I don't think a course on Modernity would ever get away with that.

Links with outside agencies are held to be so important to the polytechnic that, she feels, intellectual integrity is compromised. Students without formal academic qualifications are allowed to proceed, she claims, even if they are not up to standard, simply because they bring in the money. (When explaining this to me she became anxious and nervous and I had to reassure her that I was not connected with any kind of academic KGB.)

This public narrative, providing a rationale for her unwilling dishonesty, created stress and anxiety for Laura who had difficulty in fitting her job to her ideals. She claimed that work is central because it provides her with a meaning in life, yet she has a deep disquiet about whether what she is obliged to do is actually worthwhile. She is always doubting whether she is doing a good job, and this anxiety comes from a lack of compatibility between the ontological and public forms of narrative in constructing her identity:

You construct your own goals and your achievements are measured in some ways by your own internal standards as well as by those around you. And so there's always a lot of uncertainty. You're never sure if you've achieved those standards or those standards are right or what you're doing is worthwhile, and there's a lot of tension between what you're wanting to do and what's required of you by various sorts of rules and regulations. And so I think that can lead to a lot of burn-out and depression.

Laura knows that some academics treat their work simply as a job (and are increasingly encouraged to do so) and cease to think about it when they leave their offices. She simply cannot do that. Work for her has 'always been much more tied up with my sense of self-worth and my existential existence I suppose – my existential sense of who I am in the world.'

Probably because Laura Miller is a sociologist she is able to articulate her ontological narrative of who she is trying to be more clearly than many but this insecurity and uncertainty is widely reported amongst the caring professions generally (Pahl 1994). Not only is she more conscious of her own reflexivity she, as a good sociologist in the terms she described above, can use this self-awareness to turn the ambiguity and uncertainty in her work to her own purposes. She manages to get the space in which she feels she can accomplish her own work in her own idiosyncratic and individualistic way. She recognizes that many jobs would not give her that scope so she accepts the self-doubts, anxieties and insecurities that go with her style of work because, she says, that suits her personality type.

Despite being a much-respected feminist, Laura does not make much of gender issues in her forms of narrative. For her it is the oppressive managerial style of controlling and of determining the social relations of student production that is her greatest burden. Her struggle for autonomy and identity has its costs: she has to work very hard indeed. In summer she gets up at five-thirty and does her 'real work' at home between six and eight-thirty. She then has breakfast and goes into work when, as she says, teaching starts and 'there's a sort of gallop through the day'. A combination of lectures and seminars means:

I have to whip out the lecture notes just before the lecture and read them through, and try and read them the best I can, and put them away again and go on to the seminar, and try and think about who's supposed to be giving a seminar paper and what it might be about, and what comments I might have on it ... I don't normally finish until about seven o'clock in the evening. In the evening I tend to put away all the lecture notes and try and prepare some stuff for the next day so I have a clear desk and then the next day I can come in and start again.

I asked Laura whether she had a compulsion to fill her life with work and she readily agreed. She fills her life with a great variety of other activities because she enjoys physical exercise and is an extremely attractive and sociable person who makes friends easily and flourishes on sociability. She has had various relationships over the years but now, in her late thirties, her pattern of serial monogamous relationships is likely to remain the dominant style of her life. It does permit her long periods free from any other obligations than those which she imposes on herself in connection with her work. Laura is endlessly curious, endlessly energetic and seemingly always ready to take on even more voluntary work outside employment: 'I don't like anything to be too safe, you know. If I take risks then I feel I'm putting myself on the line slightly and it's partly an incentive to myself to make me work that much more . . . So it's partly like a sort of goad to myself really. And it's also a way of doing more.'

She acknowledges that there may be a certain amount of egoism in it but that is not significant in her personal narrative account. She claims that she does not care if her name is associated with whatever the project happens to be, and that advancing her career by advancing her name is of little significance to her: 'It's more wanting to be involved in something that's important, something that changes the world, ideas taking shape and ideas actually influencing people and ideas changing opinions. It's more wanting to be involved in that process and wanting to be at the centre of some sort of intellectual life, rather than a straightforward egotism.'

If Laura limited herself to the work she has to do she would be bored and frustrated. She taps her formidable resources of energy to do what she calls 'additional work' in the hope that she can contribute in 'a more global way to the profession itself and to the role of sociology in the world'. She gets her sense of identity and personal self-worth from making what she perceives to be a contribution to the society she is living in. She would not get a sense of achievement from merely doing the heavy burden of teaching that she is paid to do.

The problem for Laura is that her managers do not know what she does: 'They are just managers, that's all they are and it's a long time since they did any academic work – in fact a lot of them have never done any academic work really, have they?' Her identity emerges by battling with a line management which, as she sees it, is making it more difficult for her to have the identity she wants: 'As far as I can see, the sort of management we're ending up with has *not* been enabling – the purpose of it is not to enable: it's to control;

it's to reduce the power of the professionals and it's to reduce their autonomy and it's to reduce their status.'

Here Laura slips easily into public and conceptual modes of narrative to show how her project of reflexivity is caught in a struggle for power between professionals with whom she identifies and managers whom she distrusts. She recognizes that some professionals did abuse the *laissez-faire* world of the 1960s and 1970s. When she was appointed as a junior lecturer she saw some of her seniors getting large salaries (viewed from her position) for doing very little – 'The more incompetent you are, the less teaching you have to do and they do no research, they do very little administration; they do bugger-all really.' So Laura, perhaps unwillingly, recognizes that Mrs Thatcher had a point: there was a need for reform. 'But I don't think the spirit of it is right at the moment at all: the spirit is not to be enabling, to allow people to do their jobs better at all. It's to control them and to de-skill them really.' This increasing managerial control was causing Laura serious problems: student intakes in her institution rose by 30 per cent that year with no extra staff. Her eighteen hours' teaching is sure to increase and she just will not be able to teach in the way she wants to teach. She will not have the time to do research. 'It's evident to me that I'm not going to be able to pursue the sort of career I want to pursue . . . so I've got to find some way round it.'

It did not take Laura long to work out a way to beat the system. She quickly devised a strategy of applying for research grants: 'Instead of employing researchers, as you would normally do, they employ me to do research and they employ a teacher to do my teaching – which I suppose means teaching is being deskilled.' She has effectively devised a new strategy of professionalism for the self-employed:

> I've got various plans for setting up a research unit which could then have its own funds, be more or less autonomous, and employ people. And would employ me among other things. And I could then accumulate equipment and resources, like, for example, a laser printer and a decent computer so you could do beautiful reports. This is the idea partly! And then more or less declare UDI in some ways, have your own little institutional unit, your own little niche. So I'm not over-burdened with teaching, I have a team of people working around it in various ways, and its own budget, its own equipment, and then I'm in quite a good negotiating position, you see, within the hierarchy, because in fact although they're trying to make us teach all those hours, they also want to encourage research. And I think possibly if I

play my cards right, I could be in quite a good position if I manage to build that up. And I've not done it because they've given me anything, I've done it entirely because I've managed to bring in money from outside. That's my long-term strategy!

The clever thing about this strategy is that it has the independence of self-employment combined with the security of full-time employment – 'and that is a nice balance you see'. Yet however successful Laura is in getting these research grants, she still feels insecure and uncertain:

> I have to go out and write another book, and I have to go out and get another research grant, and I have to go out and do more and more to prove that I'm actually a worthwhile person – to myself – to prove my own internal standards that I can do it, that I'm as good as the next person . . . there's always this insecurity plaguing me in the background . . . it drives me on a lot.

Laura knows that she is not driven in the same way by her hobbies and her other interests because she has not defined them as the main source of her identity. She has created for herself a pit of *Angst* into which she is determined to jump. But Laura has a personal ontological project which is focused on her identity as a sociologist, and she finds the more she does the more she is able to do. 'I'd rather pack in as much as I can really. You don't know how long you're going to live, do you, really?'

Perhaps an important clue to Laura's compulsion is her relationship to her mother, who had been downwardly mobile socially and who had very high aspirations for her daughter:

> I suppose I internalized her standards in some ways. It was all built around despising the people around us on the estate: she said, 'Look at all these people; that's how you'll end up if you don't work hard. Look at the state they're in; you wouldn't want to end up like that would you?' We were in some ways taught a sort of contempt for all the people around us . . . so while they might go out and play . . . you know, we don't want to end up like them. So it's very isolating in a way.

Laura imitated her mother's accent in recalling her childhood pressures, and I was struck by the similarities between her mother's attitudes to their neighbours and Laura's attitudes to her idle colleagues.

Now Laura recognizes that she has a problem. She has a PhD and a lecturing post, so where does she go next? 'I've achieved the height of my parents' ambition.' I asked her if she really wanted success:

> I think I have a sort of fear of success. I always sabotage my chances at the last moment.... I feel I won't be able to live up to it if I get there and yet, at the same time, I want to prove myself capable of doing the responsible job. And I persuade myself I can do it in order to make myself do it.

I have been able to observe Laura's progress since I first interviewed her in 1989. She has been dramatically successful in getting research grants and her books have ensured her an international reputation. Though she has been encouraged to apply for chairs in prestigious universities in Britain and elsewhere, she has had some experience of being an academic administrator and she sees how her self-identity would change if she accepted a more senior appointment. Having come to terms with herself, partly perhaps because she is so articulately reflexive, she is confident in her own identity as a sociologist and knows she has many academic and personal admirers. She still works fiendishly hard and has done much to influence the teaching of feminist sociology internationally. Some might argue that she has reached a glass ceiling because she is not a full professor. Yet Laura has positively chosen not to run up the career escalator. She has worked out her identity in relation to her family, her colleagues, her lovers, her friends and fellow sociologists, and she has discarded the putative identity of settling down with a partner and having children. Her security is in her accumulated cultural capital and her friends. She has not surrounded herself with possessions and become possessed by them. The death of her mother gave her some financial security, and it seems that Laura's personal strategy has been a success. When she said she was afraid of success she meant she was afraid of a kind of masculine model of career success. She has created her own style of success based on reflexivity and self-awareness which eludes many people. By coming to terms with her distinctive self-identity she is, perhaps, the History Woman of the 1990s.

Martha Kelly

Martha is a reluctant and subversive civil servant, a grade E curator in a public art gallery, and for that she gets what she calls her bread. But she is also a very accomplished artist who exhibits in London and prominent galleries and has been featured in the quality Sunday newspapers. She has a rock-solid identity as an artist, which she fights to preserve in a less than sympathetic environment:

> I think that making pictures is the best thing to do in the whole of the world you know. I mean I think it's better than driving cars or flying planes or being a farmer, or, you know. I think that being an artist is a very special calling and I actually feel that it's much more special than being an optician or a sociology professor.

However, her job involves putting together exhibitions, lecturing, teaching drawing to schoolchildren and generally being an imaginative communicator of the visual arts. Martha has immense energy and enthusiasm and her job is to transfer this enthusiasm to the general public. However, like Laura, she finds that while her bosses say they want her to be committed to creativity and artistic expression, in fact she believes her boss 'just wants me to teach all the time – as many people as I can. What they call bums on seats. It doesn't really matter too much about the quality as long as you're talking to the masses ... you know; you've got to get the punters in.'

The pressures on Martha are such that she does not feel satisfied because she is prevented from doing the job for which she has the talent and ability. She does not get the time to do the job according to her own standards:

> Sometimes I just think it's really nice because I really enjoy putting images together, and I think sometimes you can feel an audience and they're there with you and they understand. But it's very rare. And I never really have time to research what I'm talking about. So it's lots of recycled stuff. So it's actually really boring. I very rarely get that thing when I just think, 'This is great.'
>
> Yes, I think that I'm knowledgeable enough and sensitive enough with my material in order to make certain visual conclusions and interesting juxtapositions and good, sort of like, thematic links which I am ... I mean, I think I have a talent in that way because I'm an artist, I know how to see about that. And so it's not too difficult for me to do

that. But I can do it and it is successful in that way. I used to approach [giving a lecture] like making a piece of art. It's not: it's just fodder. And I feel hurt that it is just fodder.

Martha speaks rather like those I used to meet and talk with in Czechoslovakia and Russia in the 1960s and 1970s. She is consciously and humorously subversive. Her life is a struggle between her integrity and the insensitive and bumbling – even if well-meaning – people who employ her. Instead of communism she is fighting a rather crude commercial outlook. 'Fuck them . . . do you want art or do you want commerce? . . . they are not aware enough of the balance between commerce and art – the integrity of art and how commerce works with it. I mean it's actually a very, very tricky balance . . . very few people have that right. I think it's a very difficult thing to know about.'

She speaks of the government in the same way as my East European friends spoke of the Party:

> Government is affecting policies . . . major art galleries, national collections have been obliged to open their doors to entertainment functions and they do this to make money. So the works in the galleries are there as like a pretty backdrop to canapés and champagne and what not, and I feel as an artist very angry that these places are used as restaurants and bars . . . it's like you need a venue for an Event. You know, it might be the launching of a new knicker line or something for Marks and Spencer . . . And I just think that is shit.

Martha's ambition is to have one of her pictures in the London Tate Gallery. Given her success so far, this is not an unrealistic expectation. When I interviewed her she had one of her pictures on tour with the Arts Council, and I have since admired one of her pictures on view in a prestigious exhibition on the South Bank. She is unquestionably very talented but she must pose problems for her unimaginative boss who lives in middle-class respectability in Corstorphine. He is responsible for the annual staff appraisal on Martha. Her account of this expresses much about her 'reflexive project of the self' (which, of course, she would dismiss as so much shit):

> Every year we have a little interview and you get what we call a box marking! It's like you get a tick from teacher. You either get a gold star or you get a 'seven and a half out of ten – improve your writing' or else you get a 'five' or else you get a smack. And I always get 'seven and a half out of ten – improve your writing' . . .

I ask Martha to say more about the writing that she has to improve:

> Basically I think I'm a very difficult customer. He has a hard time . . .
> I think I'm too *exigente* as they would say in French. Too fucking
> difficult. I'm not normal enough, you know. I mean on the one hand
> he wanted me to come and work here because I was obviously an
> artist and I was showing my work and I was a teacher and I was
> involved and I did committee work and, you know, I also looked nice
> round the dinner table, that sort of stuff. On the other hand I'm not
> Miss Normal and I am also very powerfully addicted to certain aspects
> of what I consider to be proper in terms of art and how you go about
> the whole business. So I'm awkward and cussid and stubborn and
> determined.

Her boss knows nothing about art and, as she perceptively
remarks,

> Because I am so involved, he feels inadequate and that's the worst
> possible combination . . . And it's also reinforced by the genders . . .
> the age and the physical whatever we are, you know . . . it's like classic;
> it's terrible . . .
> I have asked him when I have my job appraisal, 'What should I do
> in order to get ten out of ten?' Because I'm a single woman and I do
> want promotion and I do need more money. And if he cannot tell me
> which direction I'm meant to improve in, how can I possibly do it?
> And he cannot remember from last year which bits I ought to improve
> and which bits . . . you know . . . Because I'm not – well I'm growing
> my hair actually, so that I think that when I have long brown hair I
> might be very straight and boring and I might get there!

Martha thinks that being married would make it easier for
someone in her position – 'It gives stability and credibility. I think a
single woman is actually quite threatening if she is attractive and
well dressed, as well as being intelligent and successful.' However,
she admits that the organization for which she works finds it hard to
accommodate someone of her verve and style. As she says, 'It's very
boring; very right-wing.' Unlike Laura, she says that she found her
work easier when she had boyfriends around. 'Little support systems
you know. Helpful. You can discuss things with them.' Martha
recognizes that her boss considers her 'really weird' but then that is
the way she wants to be. Perhaps much of her artistic creativity flows
from her oppositional stance.

Martha works hard, very hard, but her goal is to work less hard.

All her so-called holidays are taken up with her art work or promoting her art by setting up her work at exhibitions. When she is doing her art work she usually works a ten-hour day non-stop. She has virtually lost her private life, apart from keeping in touch with old friends. Paradoxically, her fierce commitment to her artistic identity prevents her from having boyfriends which, she admits, did make her life more fun but her dominant self prevents her from accommodating a partnership:

> It's very tricky really because the people that I enjoy spending time with most, that I love best, are artists, right. And artists are very – if they are interested in doing anything at all – are very competitive individuals who are real show-offs and if you have a combination of a competitive show-off who's also a man, who is then maybe somebody that I would like to be with, it's rather difficult, because you have a double competition, a double show-off situation. It's just bad news really.

However hard I try, Martha refused to be drawn into justifying her obsession with her art – 'I've always wanted to do it . . . there's no justification. I couldn't give a toss about justifying it. I just do it.' What's more, she knows her work is good and she is in no way dependent on the opinion of peers or patrons:

> I've got the right feeling for it. I just know what I'm up to. I don't even think. I cannot define it . . . we have language and we have writing and we have all that stuff and this is not occurring in those ways. This occurs in another fashion. It's to do with texture; it's to do with magic. And that's another space.

An important part of Martha's identity is that she positively enjoys being subversive and that she tries to subvert in a way she thinks is funny. If her formal bureaucratic iron cage was not there to oppress her and for her to rail against, she would surely find an alternative.

Perhaps the most striking thing about my interviews with Martha is that each time she quickly slipped into an oppositional role with me, using me as a foil to express her identity in her characteristic way. I tried to explore the roots of her subversive self-image by asking about her school, her family background and so forth. Unlike all my other respondents, she resisted this fiercely. She accused me of asking psychological questions in seeking the roots of her revolt. She was sent off to a convent school between the ages of eleven and sixteen. Her response to my modest psychoanalytic probings was characteristic.

> There are individuals who have certain life patterns, and if you look at your life pattern you see the same things again and again. And it's very tragic to be a child and to be sent off, you know. I mean it's difficult. And if the main reason for being sent off is to have a good education you feel utterly frustrated by the whole business ... There is a sort of let-out clause and either you go and do it publicly and do tantrums and shit on the teacher or whatever, or else you toe the line, try your best, and yes, I mean there must be, there is a streak of character ... I mean, you'd have to go back into my family tree to find out which are the loonies and which are the ones that taught themselves, in order to find out the rest of that story. Obviously it influences my life-style now.

Having drawn Martha into talking about her childhood, I asked her in the second interview whether she was afraid of failure in any way:

> Yes, of course I am! I'm afraid of all sorts of failings. I'm especially afraid if people don't like me when I want them to like me. I think that's my main downfall. I'm afraid this interview is so very deep, digs quite deeply into parts of my psyche which I just don't want to share with you, whom I don't know well enough to want to share them, and that's to do with privacy ... I mean I don't like people digging too deeply into certain aspects of my life because I think I'm quite a private person. Although I'm very sort of outgoing and voluminous [*sic*] you know, like that. But I'm, terribly lucky because I've been very ambitious so far and I've not failed on things that are very, very risky. So I mean that links up to part of my character that is very dare-devil ...
>
> After all, most people live their lives quite happily without having to shove all their stuff all over other people's walls and asking other people to come and either join in or look, you know. So, I mean that's quite scary. But I think ... I get quite a lot of kicks out of being scary, you know, and frightening myself.

Clearly Martha has alternative narratives to account for her self-identity and she had consistently presented one particular narrative in our first interview. Since that first interview had been long and wide-ranging, this says much about the efficacy of sociological interviews as instruments for exploring the identities of late modernity! Martha's hidden identities could not be discovered by most

sociological research methods. She was too well practised in presenting her confident subversive, mocking persona. I therefore challenged her to consider how she does construct her identity for other
people. She replied that would begin by saying she was an artist first
and foremost and then describe what that work involved:

> I also earn my bread and butter at the gallery, which is terribly
> interesting, but it's quite painful because I have to go there every day
> and find it quite a struggle. And I live in a really nice place and I've
> got a bicycle and, you know, I've got a nice life. I'm a lucky woman.
> That's about it really.

The problem with interviewing Martha is that she enjoys playing
with her identities – 'I do show off sometimes outrageously – but I
also find that people find it quite difficult to co-ordinate the various
aspects of myself. So if I'm being *really* showing off I will ... sort of
like throw lots of what might be divergent information about myself
– just to confuse people.'

Unlike Laura, Martha probably would like to marry and have
children, despite all the problems that this would be likely to create.
However, she recognizes that marriage to another artist would not
work but it is with artists that she socializes most of the time. If she
was a mother she could continue to be an artist: 'If you are
determined enough you will produce, and if you are used to
production there's no earthly reason why you should stop. I mean I
can't ever imagine retiring.' Nor can she imagine that any husband
could cope with her volatile temperament. In the end she thinks
husband and children would leave her: 'And then I'll just get on
with the painting ... I think the major problem about kids and
husbands and that stuff is to do with financial independence. I have
been my own mistress for a very long time and I don't like anybody
encroaching on that at all.'

Despite her pose of scattiness Martha is an exceptionally organized and efficient person who juggles two jobs:

> Artists, especially today, have to be completely tuned up, otherwise
> they miss the boat. I know very successful artists who are completely
> organized in terms of how they operate ... It is to do with the
> advertising production – deadlines, statements, press releases, press
> photos ... I mean, just forget about looking out of the window for
> inspiration. It's a very devastating story in the late 1980s ... it's a sort
> of professionalism.

I asked her whether she thought she was a professional: 'Yes, I am now.'

Martha experimented with the narratives of her identity as we shadow-boxed around the interviews. She revealed and she withdrew. She mocked and she was deadly serious. She laughed and she was angry. She has to fight for her identity and she has to be highly organized and highly professional – even if these seem to conflict with the magic of creation. As she recognizes, 'Life's a struggle.' Her ambition is to be employed less in order to work more.

General McAlpine

I am rather a traditional officer, insofar as my father was in the Army ... An elder brother having escaped to the Navy, number two was destined to follow in father's footsteps and I've never regretted that ... I went to Sandhurst at a time when Sandhurst was a two-year officer training course and from there I was commissioned into my regiment, stationed abroad ... After two years I was agreeably surprised to find myself selected to go to Oxford University to read an in-service degree for three years, which I much enjoyed. I returned to my regiment and then followed, I suppose, the expected pattern of promotion on time coupled with merit. Then, at the age of twenty-nine, I sat the Staff College entrance examination to go to the Army Staff College ... On the conclusion of the year's course I then returned to my regiment. I say my regiment because having joined one particular regiment that becomes your family and sort of backbone throughout your career.

The General was well protected against career anxiety. At every stage in his life promotions arrived on schedule. The narrative of his identity is easy for him to tell. He did a succession of tours of duty, generally lasting two years, until he was finally selected to command his own regiment which was a two and a half year appointment, before moving to a staff appointment at the Ministry of Defence at the tail-end of the Falklands conflict – 'a very interesting time to be there. Unfortunately, I only did that for a year because I was picked up for promotion again – I was given the command of a brigade in Germany.' There is no need to mention each step in his career, as every two years or so he moved, before ending up as a general with the United Kingdom Land Forces. 'Each has been a real challenge and at no time have I felt that I've gone sideways.'

Career choice – and to a large degree personal identity – have been taken care of by others for the General. 'There never was a moment when I thought: "I don't want to be a soldier", or, "Do I want to be a soldier any longer?" ... if you are an ordinary general staff officer you tend to be told: "This is what you're going to be doing next", and your choice then is either, "Well, I don't want to do it", or, "Thank you very much".'

Our interviews were very cordial but I find it hard to be as informal in referring to the General as I can be with the others. He was obviously in uniform and that seemed to emphasize a distance between us. I therefore find it easier to refer to him simply as General M, and readers may learn from that something about me as well as something about my respondent. Maybe lingering indoctrination from National Service still has power!

General M's life is managed by the military secretary and his staff, who plan the careers of all officers. Everyone is assessed. Everyone in the Army is reported on once a year and this forms the basis of his or her career development. Indeed, the two main factors that attracted General M to the Army were steady advancement and the excitement of doing a job which did not primarily involve sitting in an office. Ironically, the steady advancement ensured that he more quickly found himself behind a desk, although he does not quite see it that way:

> It was always assumed by my mother and father that I was going to join the Army and I didn't disagree with that. So there was an element of, right, the thinking has already been done, as it were, and I perhaps wasn't a party to it; I merely acquiesced ... I look back and don't regret coming into the Army.

He was completely prepared for his passive role in relation to his self-identity.

Nevertheless, General M has not been able to avoid the public and metanarratives of his profession and the times in which he is living. In sharp contrast to all his previous socialization and training, he is having to face a new management strategy associated with the introduction of a budgeting system. General M is now a budget holder of £25 million and has to sit behind a desk. Even if everything is going well, he has to consider how he can make his resources go further by doing things more cheaply and/or more efficiently. Until very recently,

Generals and commanders had no budgetary accountability and were concerned neither with inputs nor outputs really. They were simply interested in training.

Some of my colleagues say: 'I joined the Army be to a soldier. I didn't join the Army to run a budget. If I wanted to do that I would have gone to an office in London.' I think there is a fear that of course gradually we are all being pushed around, that we can't afford to do this, you haven't got the resources to do that. Hitherto, I suppose, one's got round that by getting on the end of a telephone and persuading somebody up the line that actually the exercise you are trying to plan – or the activities if you want – is so important that you must have the resources. One hasn't had to worry that it's actually meant somebody else has gone short. Now, of course, that will become much more difficult. And I think from that point of view, there is the worry that some people will feel that accountants are spoiling this, or the accountants are saying, 'You're not getting value for money. Therefore you can't do it.'

As generals become managers the Army has to do considerable re-thinking on its training programme. Financial training and financial management training is not what putative generals expect to be taught in staff college. It will also affect the Army's pattern of recruitment. As General M remarked, 'The attraction to "go anywhere, do anything, have gun, will travel and shoot people" sort of approach to Army recruiting would have to change.' However, he went on to admit that what he calls 'the straightforward basic infantry men with rifles on the end' are hardest to recruit now.

So how does General M handle the Army's new 'enemy within' – the accountants? How will the accountants measure the effectiveness of General M's brigade without a bit of fighting to see whether they would win?

No number of statistics will tell you that – whether they've all done their annual firing, done their swimming test, done everything else. Only I will actually tell you whether they are an effective brigade . . . . The accountants will come back and say, 'How are we going to measure this, General McAlpine?' Well, I would say that I hold an exercise for them. I would like to hold an exercise for them every year and then I will put them through a test. They will carry out a series of manoeuvres and exercises and then I will be able to tell whether they are effective and there won't necessarily be anybody shooting at them – although, of course, nowadays, with simulators and all that sort of thing, you can have force on force exercises with people shooting each other using lasers and that sort of thing. So that is how we would get round that.

General M's role is becoming much more concerned with 'getting round' the managerial imperatives, much in the same style as that pursued by Laura Miller. What General M likes being is a soldier boss. I asked him to give me an example of something where his skilled soldier's eye could spot some trouble in the effectiveness of the fighting unit of which he was in command. He gave me a recent example where he judged the standard of the training on the ranges to be 'unacceptably low'. Given that he claimed he was now using soldier's, not accountant's, skills, I asked him on what criteria he came to this skilled judgement. 'I suppose it was a fairly straight-forward one on firing – I mean they weren't hitting the target.' The General used his experience and authority to address one of the instructors and he explained that he said:

> Look this is not good enough. How are you going to put this right? At the moment we are just wasting ammunition firing away down there. These chaps have not got the techniques right. They don't know what they're doing. So how are you going to put that right? And they said, 'Right, we're going to have to go back and do some revision . . .' I said OK, right, get on with it!

Later on the General will expect to be invited back to the range 'to see the polished product'.

Now evidently it is important for generals in a peacetime Army to make sure that they have 'polished products' – that is, soldiers who can more or less shoot straight and so forth. However, the real problem, as General M readily recognized, is to keep up morale, which basically means that it is necessary to be alert and effective because one day the shooting may be for real. Unless there is a prospect of actually fighting, it is hard to encourage people to take all the preparation and discipline seriously. If generals start to think seriously about 'doing it cheaper' it might be more cost-effective to have little wars from time to time simply to keep everyone on their toes. Paying generals large salaries to go round like spin doctors keeping up the chaps' morale may not be so efficient and effective, even if they can organize tests or exercises from time to time.

Paradoxically, even when a bit of real war did take place at his garrison, General M could do nothing about it. The IRA blew up a car with one of his senior NCOs in it who was badly injured.

However, because the car was parked outside an Army house at the edge of the garrison it became a police matter and the Army had nothing to do. So if an increasingly armed police force becomes completely responsible for internal law and order and, perhaps directly accountable to the Home Office, where does that leave the Army? What kind of anxiety does that provoke for General M? He certainly seems to regret that 'the chances of being shot at were a great deal higher' when he was a junior officer than they are now. Tours to Northern Ireland are useful since they introduce 'adrenalin to a great extent ... so there is still some adrenalin which flows, but as one becomes more restricted to the United Kingdom and this sort of job, it certainly isn't the same'.

Yet General M is flexible. If policemen are doing soldiers' jobs then he can get more interested in policemens' work:

> One of the most attractive things perhaps about this sort of a job is that there are many outlets ... if I wanted to I could spend every day either visiting troops on the ground or civil authorities, policemen, whatever. And I actually do enjoy – I go off and spend half an hour or forty minutes talking to a Chief Constable about – well it may not be about military home defence – it will inevitably turn out to be talking about acid house parties. But, I mean, I do thoroughly enjoy that.

General M enjoys his flexibility and autonomy even if the job is not quite what he expected. 'I'm a very keen bird-watcher and I couldn't actually be in a better place and on a number of occasions, if I take an hour off for lunch, I don't actually go and have lunch. I take a pair of binoculars and pop down to the reservoir and spend half an hour looking at birds ... ' Given his background and what he calls 'moulding' this slightly deviant activity is probably more adventurous than it sounds. Since General M was seemingly as straight as an arrow, I simply asked him how he thought others perceived him, how did he feel he presented his identity. He said he would like people to say: 'Well, here's a chap who is fairly sort of straight, sensible, honest-looking, honest-behaving, a man with integrity ... a chap who is perhaps very straightforward.'

Compared with the rampant reflexivity evidenced by Laura and Maggie, General M seemed like a man from a bygone era. And in many ways he is. I tried for some hours to find some anxiety, some insecurity, but in vain. Yet I felt we were talking as freely and openly as with any of my respondents. In one of my own previous identities I had been an officer, and for a time had worked with the RAF equivalent of General M. I could speak his language, and engage in an informal dialogue. When I was asking about his soldiers who could not shoot straight he might well have noticed my tongue in my cheek but he continued to respond with a kind of boyish amiability. He was due to retire shortly, in his early fifties, so I encouraged him to fantasize about possible new ways of changing his identity. He found it very hard to imagine himself differently: 'Maybe when I retire, I'll make a conscious effort not to put a tie on to go to the pub, or something like that.'

A Sociological Excursus on Identity

The way sociologists understand and analyse identity has changed dramatically since the mid–1960s. In an article that seemed ahead of its time when it was published in 1966, Peter Berger referred to what he described as the 'successfully socialized individual' as someone who '"knows who he is". He feels accordingly. He can conduct himself "spontaneously", because the firmly internalized cognitive and emotive structures make it unnecessary or even impossible for him to reflect upon alternative possibilities of conduct' (1966: 107). The individual recognizes her identity in socially defined terms and these definitions turn into social reality through the way people live in society. Such is the social construction of reality. Berger accepts as uncontentious what is now seen as highly problematic. 'Every society', he claims, 'contains a repertoire of identities that is part of the "objective knowledge" of its members' (p. 107). It may be that Berger is in fact referring to roles rather than identities. Society has broad expectations about doctors, engine drivers, fathers and grand-mothers. However there may be as many different father roles as there are fathers and, if a certain fraction of the radical Right in Britain had their way, almost everyone would end up as a budget holder – including children handling their pocket money. Berger recognized that in the process of socialization the child appropriates the world in which he is located 'in the same process in which he appropriates his identity – a moral universe as he identifies himself as a "good baby", a sexual universe as a "little boy", a class universe as a "little gentleman" and so on' (p. 112).

Debate at that time centred on the way people negotiated their roles in a more flexible way in response to the expectations of others. Confusions and contradictions arising from incompatibilities between different roles in a role set or in playing the same role simultaneously to different audiences were the focus of attention. The development of understanding by sociologists was more apparent than real at this time, although dissenting voices were becoming more common. Ralph Dahrendorf wrote ironically of *Homo Sociologicus* (1973) and Dennis Wrong explored the 'Oversocialized Conception of Man in Sociology' (1977: 31–54). In retrospect the debates of a quarter century ago, which at the time seemed so exciting, now appear curiously rigid and archaic. This was partly, perhaps, because Freud had made extraordinarily little impact on sociology during the first half of the century, in so far as Parsons and his colleagues incorporated a rather limited view of Freud in their grand synthesis *Towards a General Theory of Action* (Parsons and Shils 1951), and partly because sociologists were anxious to stake out their own terrain with the dominant paradigm of structural-functionalism which emerged in mid-century. Those such as George Homans who were most offended by the social determinism of his Harvard colleagues (1961) developed a rather idiosyncratic behaviourist psychology which was a long way from the psychoanalytical approach of Karen Horney or Melanie Klein on which others could have drawn, had they been so minded.

It has been argued that Paul Ricoeur was intellectually important in making the move on from the notion of the individual to the notion of identity, although few English-speaking scholars recognized this for a time. For Ricoeur identity is a continual process of construction through successive stages as we redefine the distinction between 'I' and 'not-I' (see Le Rider 1993: 39–45). In the fashionable vocabulary of the time the modern crisis involved the deconstruction of previous solid identities and the reconstruction of new stabilities. The problem is how that should be done. Since Berger was right to emphasize the endless iteration between self and society – later developed by Giddens into the notion of structuration – the condition of late modernity makes it peculiarly difficult for individuals to find the social co-ordinates round which they can draw their maps of self-identities. Changes in love, kin and friendship relations and changes in the way employment is structured and distributed give rise to substantial anxieties in contemporary society (see chapter 8). The traditional frameworks and role-models are in constant flux. Young men do not want to end up being unemployed like their fathers, but many do not see clearly a way of avoiding it. Young women are uncertain about the balance between different forms of work, between being single or being married, being a full-time mother or a full-time worker or some combination of the two. And even those in employment are unsure how they should play their roles so that they may 'be' the person that they feel they are – that is, to enable their social roles and their personal identities to become increasingly congruent.

Ricoeur's notion that the constitution of identity is essentially a narrative operation was particularly seminal. Others had come up with a similar idea. Thus Alasdair MacIntyre in *After Virtue* suggests that 'Narrative history of a certain kind turns out to be the basic and essential genre for the characterisation of human actions' (1981: 194). There has to be a story; there has to be a script. 'Deprive children of stories', MacIntyre remarks, 'and you leave them unscripted, anxious stutterers in their actions as in their words' (p. 201). People identify with what they say about themselves and what other people say about them. 'He is, to quote Wilhelm Schapp (a disciple of Husserl), "in Geschichten verstrickt", "ensnared in stories" and "the self itself has no qualities: all the qualities reside in the stories"' (Le Rider 1993: 40).

But the stories are not easy to tell. Some parts are well-scripted, others are developed in an *ad hoc* or *ad lib* way. Faced with a sudden bereavement or the unexpected loss of employment, we may need guidance or counselling to cope with unfamiliar feelings and the need to come to terms with a new identity. Traditional *rites de passage* may be forgotten or inappropriate:

> In the light of psychoanalysis, the feeling every subject has of its own identity becomes an endless, unpredictable interplay of conscious and unconscious identities: identity projected into the future and identity fed on remembrance; identity of family, group or national membership and identity of rejected memberships; identity of 'normality' and identity conferred by life (sex, race, age etc); and the aspiration to negate and transcend all these limitations. The psychoanalytic approach also confirms that as regards the destiny of the subject, identification fantasies can supplant 'real' identity to such an extent that the opposition between reality and fantasy is meaningless in any attempts to understand a personality. (Le Rider 1993: 43)

The project of individuals in the condition of late modernity is to resist being labelled by a single characteristic such as gender, class, locality, religion or ethnicity. Those who insist on religious solidarities, as in Northern Ireland, or extreme identities, as in the area of former Yugoslavia, are held to be unacceptable role-models for the majority. 'I am because of who I am' is a more acceptable model than: 'I am who I am because I was born to this family in this village'. But if people are resisting over-determining fictions based on class and gender or whatever, they are obliged to construct new fictions. A woman is not simply 'a lone parent'. She is rich or poor; she is an avid reader of contemporary fiction or she never reads a book; she is an employed person with friends and colleagues or she is lonely and embittered; her mother is round the corner full of material and psychic support or she is completely estranged from all her family; she is Princess Diana or she is not. The permutations are endless.

One of the problems that eluded sociologists in the 1960s and 1970s is that their focus on self, roles and identity did not do much to incorporate changing power relations – or, simply, history – into their analysis. While they might have accommodated the iteratively produced self – particularly those symbolic interactionists, who emphasized the 'looking-glass self' and taking the role of the others – few had Erving Goffman's range of subtlety and even he was less than explicit about his theoretical stance.[6] Paradoxically, the new emphasis on narrative as the process that constructs and re-constructs identity, which emerged in the 1980s, came just at the time when historians such as Hayden White were reacting strongly against theoretical historical narratives and were exposing the missing or tacit metatheories of traditional history (1973). However, the oral historians and sociologists who were using the concept of narrative had rather different things in mind from what the historians were jettisoning with some embarrassment. Narrative and narrativity are recognized as concepts of social epistemology and social ontology. These concepts enable us to constitute our social identities and help us to recognize that we are generally not able to control our social narratives. The contemporary approach to narrative has become more technically refined – and therefore complicated:

> Narratives are *constellations of relationships* (connected parts) embedded in *time and space*, constituted by *causal emplotment*. Unlike the attempt to produce meaning by placing an event in a specified category, narrativity precludes sense-making of a singular isolated phenomenon. Narrativity demands that we discern the meaning of any single event only in temporal and spatial relationship to other events. Indeed the chief characteristic of narrative is that it renders understanding only by connecting (however unstably) parts to a constructed configuration or a social network (however incoherent or unrealizable)

composed of symbolic, institutional and material practices. (Somers
and Gibson 1994: 59)

Plot is the syntax of narrative: emplotment implies that there must
be a selective appropriation in constructing narratives since the
range of possible social and personal experiences is virtually limitless. Somers and Gibson in their helpful discussion of these matters
distinguish four discussions of narrativity; as follows:

Ontological narratives

These narratives define who we are, which thus enables us to know
what to do. 'This "doing" will in turn produce new narratives and
hence new action; the relationship between narrative and ontology
is processual and mutually constitutive. Both are conditions of the
other; neither act *a priori*' (Somers and Gibson 1994: 61). To have
some clear sense of self-identity we need to see our lives as more
than a series of disconnected and unique events, so our ontological
narratives process these events into episodes and plots. We have
these various personal scripts and we act as we do in relation to how
a particular script is going. This may mean that we act inconsistently
or are obliged to act with duplicity in order that one script is not
undermined by another. Or we may find a particular script or
narrative so hard to sustain that it has to be abandoned. It may
conflict with another more rewarding script, or we may be confronted with impossible to sustain inconsistencies. The point is that
ontological narratives help us to grow into and become our self-
identity. Of course, there is nothing new in emphasizing the subjective orientation to social action, and the problem of meaning has
vexed sociologists for most of the century. The element that is
distinctive to the current discussion is the construction of a narrative
in our own words, whether spoken in justificatory accounts that
gradually coalesce into a consistent script, or in autobiographies and
diaries which typically reconstruct thoughts and actions in a favourable light.

So how do people construct these stories and where do they come
from? Sometimes stories are complete fabrications. When I spent
some years studying the Isle of Sheppey in Kent I was struck by the
dramatic tales of heroism and drama some of the young men told in
pubs. To begin with I believed these stories of stealing fast cars,
racing policemen down the motorway and similar, often illegal,

daring exploits. However, I came to understand that these private stories were invented to provide some excitement and drama in an extremely dull and boring life. There would be the odd true story in the local newspapers from time to time and this would add credence to the fabrications. Since things *like* the stories did happen from time to time, why should the one being recounted in the pub not also be true? It would spoil the general feeling of male camaraderie and bonding to suggest that it was a pack of lies. It was more rewarding for all concerned to play up as audience to the narrator. After a time, I suspect that the story-tellers believed their own stories. Thus myths are born and perpetuated.

However, for most people, their narratives are largely true, and they are ways of making sense of the events of their lives and coming to terms with what they have to do and what they want to do. Stories are mutually supported and sustained through interpersonal webs of relationships. Ontological narratives are not essentialist scripts, although there is a case of recognizing the recurrence of distinctive scripts from one generation to another in certain families (see e.g. P. Thompson 1990). More typically, it is the process of reflexivity that selects significant events and circumstances and weaves these into an ontological narrative. But inevitably, we are not free-floating atoms. Time, place and social structure put limits on the scripts that are open for us to devise.

Public narratives

These narratives extend beyond the individual and may reflect everything from cultural stereotypes, like the grammar school boy who made good through scholarships and hard work (the Horatio Alger syndrome) to narratives about the family ('Our family has never gone far from the land'; 'We've always been very musical', and so on). Family scripts may relate closely to occupational communities or particular places ('There's always been Hardakers round here and even if they leave, they always get drawn back'). Some families have historical fictions that serve to justify contemporary traits. Stories of travel and adventure or military and naval exploits serve to justify traits of character amongst contemporaries. Individuals can fall back on these narratives when seeking justifications for particular acts or experiences.

Conceptual narratives

These have, perhaps, become increasingly common as people have recognized more clearly how larger political and economic forces can dramatically change their lives. The Great Depression of the inter-war period affected much of the working class very deeply. Now obsessive concern with financial accounting makes many more of the middle class vulnerable. The Comfortable Class is becoming the Anxious Class and may be short of conceptual narratives to account for their plight. They can talk of 'market forces' and 'down-sizing of organizations' but this leads to a degree of cognitive dissonance when it is the Party of the Right, traditionally committed to preserving privilege, which is now espousing the forces that are leading to their contemporary anxieties. Many middle-class people in Britain referred to Thatcherism as a shorthand for a kind of conceptual narrative which involves putting a cost on work and activities which were purportedly well done in the past as much out of professional pride and responsibility and altruism as straight financial gain. This has led many people to question what success – both personal and collective – is. The old conceptual narratives of class and career are being replaced by more shifting and problematic narratives based on gender, and more elusive qualities of style and presentation.

Metanarrativity

These master-narratives related to such issues as America's changing world role and the rise of Japan, Britain's role in Europe and the debate about Europeanization. The collapse of communism and the apparent triumph of liberalism have led to some doubts about appropriate metanarratives. While the announcement of the End of History has evidently been premature, there is uncertainty about the outlines of contemporary metanarratives. Some refer to post-Ford-ism, globalization and post-modernism as significant metanarratives. Others find these labels confusing, over-simplifying or vacuous. Politicians struggle to supply 'the vision thing' which is surely a symptom of the lost metanarrative. These metanarratives should provide the framework into which conceptual narratives can fit. There is a disjunction in the 1990s between these two forms of narrative, which it is the job of sociologists to attempt to bring together. Those such as Bauman, Giddens, Kumar, Urry and others who are advancing substantially in this enterprise, have nevertheless been less successful in disseminating their work to a wider critical audience among politicians and opinion-formers.[7] This may be a reflection of the anti-intellectualism in British society. However, it is not clear that in Italy or Russia intellectuals are any closer to a wider informed public.

Conclusions

In this chapter, we have considered four reflexively ordered narratives which may now be considered in the light of the sociological issues just outlined. First, of course, these are people who are successful in terms of their employment and career. Certainly I asked them about family, friends and other interests but, as they all said, they did not have time to do much but work. Sir Richard and Laura both rise early and work late. The General seems to have the lightest load. The two men have supportive wives who entertain and provide social back-up. The General has the further advantage of staff to run his Army residence. Laura and Martha have not the time for much private life, although I suspect both would enjoy having supportive 'wives'. Because of this dominance of career, the narrative of my cases focus on two main aspects of their identities – either, in the case of the men, how they got where they were, or, in the case of the women, how the job gets in the way of the work that most fulfils them.

All four, significantly, are embattled with unsympathetic 'accountants' or bureaucrats or line managers who are perceived as being less enablers than interferers. The job is not what they expect. Martha and Laura are oppressed by the 'bums on seats' syndrome – as also is Sir Richard, if at one stage removed. General M is rather like a steam engine enthusiast faced with the arrival of diesel or electric locomotives. It may be cheaper and more efficient but it is not really proper rail travel. The Cold War provided the *raison d'être* of his existence. Certainly the Troubles in Ireland helped with the adrenalin flow but it is not like having real enemies. So all the narratives have an element of nostalgia – a wistful memory of a time when the job and the work were satisfactorily more happily fused; when efficiency, personal fulfilment, professional integrity and altruistic concern came together in a pleasing balance.

Now the job involves 'getting round' the managerial directives for General McAlpine, using 'every trick in the book' for Sir Richard, being creatively subversive for Martha, and by 'intrapreneuring' and setting up her independent research unit for Laura. So all four were skilled in developing devious strategies to create, preserve and enhance their self-identities. They were all aware of areas of constraint and areas of manoeuvrability. Apart from the General, who provides an excellent example of someone living life as fate, they were covering up anxieties and insecurities. Perhaps Sir Richard had been too lucky and, having gone rather far rather fast, was showing signs of strain. Sir Richard has certainly had the most worldly success; the General was looking forward to an exciting final posting abroad at his last interview, but the outbreak of peace led to its cancellation and ruined the culmination of his career. Laura has her independence, has ten books to her name and more are on the way. Martha has gone half-time, achieving the success of partial disengagement from employment.

What then, is the source of the ontological narrative? Where do these people get the idea of their true selves expressed through their work? It is not simply the job or the occupation which makes them, since they are all to a lesser or greater extent fighting the job in order to do their work. Martha is committed to the magic of creativity as a vocation. Her imagination and quirkiness stand out from the others. Laura, as a fellow sociologist, was too eager to provide the account she thought she knew I expected. To some extent she reflected me back to myself – or what she thought was me. The General was unsure what was expected of him, but having said he would do the job for me, he adopted the straightforward stance of getting on with it directly and without any attempt to hide or cover up. He knew he needed soldiers who could shoot straight and he could not see the surreal element in the story he told. He had been moulded not to be reflexive. His was not to reason why . . . He had always wanted to be a soldier and 'everyone knows' what soldiers do. He may have trouble ahead in retirement.

Giddens's approach to self-identity is, perhaps, too fluid and flexible. His assertion that 'self-identity today is a reflexive achievement' (1991: 215) implies too great an autonomy on the part of actors. In this book I am considering people who are among the most successful in our society. Even such people find themselves seriously constrained by the agents of the political programme set up in the 1980s. The project which began as being apparently empowering and liberating became dominating in the 1990s. The narratives of these men and women and the others who are described in some detail elsewhere in this book are not limited to working out private reflexive projects. Public, conceptual and metanarratives are there strongly, if not oppressively. The tension between the public and the private may be increasing, as managerialism spreads ever more widely. Those running the gallery in which Martha works imagine that they are being more open and more accountable, 'giving the taxpayer what she wants'. Cocktail parties in the gallery are paid for by those who are wealthy. The artist rails. But is Martha's resentment different from her predecessors (who would more likely be male) railing against their Florentine patrons? Perhaps some of the tensions of late modernity are more traditional than some observers imagine.

8

From Hoccleve's Complaint to the Anxious Class

Anxiety is the dizziness of freedom

Kierkegaard

Anxiety is how we handle stress
Rollo May: *The Meaning of Anxiety*, 1977

What to do? How to act? Who to be? These are focal questions
for everyone living in circumstances of late modernity
Anthony Giddens: *Modernity and Self Identity*, 1991

Is there something special and novel about contemporary society
that generates unprecedented unease, insecurity and anxiety? The
idea that we live in an Age of Anxiety, to take the title of Auden's
poem,[1] carries with it the assumption that at some previous time
insecurities, doubts and anxieties were less prevalent. Life then was
more secure and stable; social roles were more predictable, the
stages of the life course were more likely to be clearly specified, and
what people expected to happen in their lives generally turned out
to be the case, unless disease or disaster struck. Writing in a more
popular context, Giddens has claimed that:

> in the increasingly global cosmopolitan world which is the context of
> our daily activities, we all have to construct our lives more actively
> than ever was the case before. Even without the corroding effects of
> markets, traditions and pre-established habits lose their hold. The
> result is a mixture of emancipation and anxiety, fuelled by new sorts

of uncertainties. To put things simply, our lives are less and less lived as fate.[2]

Those who implicitly or explicitly subscribe to such a stable and reassuring past, whether it be termed 'fate' or 'tradition', have to make a number of assumptions.[3] Politicians and moral entrepreneurs who hold up some tranquil and law-abiding golden age as the reassuring benchmark of the good society to which we should now return, frequently allow their rhetoric to encourage them to ignore even a superficial historical understanding and certain sociological commonplaces. It may be helpful to set out some of the assumptions in such golden-ageism (from which, I regret, not all sociologists are exempt):

1 The historically secure, less anxious society must, perforce, be stable, with relatively little social mobility either upwards or downwards. This implies that the political, military, legal, ecclesiastical and other élites emerged from a very narrow stratum and were, to a degree, self-recruiting. Those men, and traditionally they *were* men, who were expected to reach high office by way of their privileged package of socialization, education and, later, inheritance, buttressed their economic advantage with strategies of social exclusion. Clubs, leisure pursuits, intermarriage and a general cultural style coalesced into an invisible protective cocoon to deter and defeat potential interlopers. Peeling off this cocoon has perhaps caused new anxieties in contemporary society, but these are, in general, accepted as preferable to the inefficiencies and lack of meritocratic advantage of the old order.

2 The universal and fundamental existential questions about the meaning of life, including anxiety about death, the creation of a separate sense of self apart from one's parents and the coming to terms with other people whom one can never really understand, were either suppressed or were handled effectively in non-anxious-making ways. When discussing these issues Giddens and others appear to reify the idea of 'tradition' which, in Giddens's words, 'offers an organising medium of social life specifically geared to ontological precepts' (1991: 48). So, in this previous, putatively golden and less anxious age, answers to these difficult fundamental questions were provided by 'tradition', which it may be not entirely unfair to unpack as ignorance and servitude, an unquestioning adherence to fundamental religious or magical systems of meaning and explanation, and as providing little

opportunity to move mentally or physically from pre-ordained patterns of thinking and patterns of livelihood.

3 Roles based on age, sex and marital status are assumed to have been clear and unproblematic. Doubts about gender identity and sexual orientation, about the suitability of one's marital partner and of 'acting one's age', were, it is assumed, readily resolvable. If this meant that whiskery old women who lived on their own after the deaths of their husbands and who enjoyed the company of cats might have to be burnt as witches, so be it. (At least it must have reassured those who felt that you cannot buck tradition.)

4 Innovation, creativity and eccentricity were hard to accommodate within traditional society. The minority of dissidents or intellectuals were in danger of being stoned as heretics, crucified or made to suffer in many ingeniously nasty ways. This, again, was part of the price to pay for the putative psychic security that some appear to associate with tradition. A brilliant and astonishingly detailed account of the endemic anxieties of a previous age is provided by MacDonald's analysis of the remarkable medical records of Richard Napier, who was rector of Great Linford in north Buckinghamshire. He practised astrological medicine there from 1597 until 1634. 'He treated tens of thousands of patients for every kind of malady and became a famous healer at a time when it was not unusual for clergymen to be physicians as well' (MacDonald 1981: 20). Napier left detailed case notes about his patients. There were 2039 cases of mental disorders in Napier's practice. The sex ratio of Napier's mentally disturbed patients was much the same as for a modern medical practice (p. 36).

MacDonald does much to dispel the cosy view of 'tradition' with its so-called ready-made answers to people's personal troubles:

> Seventeenth-century villages bore no relation to the peaceable kingdoms anxious urbanities imagine made up 'the world we have lost'. Criminal records abound with evidence that hatred, fear and violence were endemic in rural England before the Industrial Revolution, and many witchcraft accusations were simply extensions of personal hatreds and family feuds ... Rustic hamlets were relentlessly intimate, and it was impossible to avoid people whom one hated or feared. (p. 109)

The deep feelings and tensions of this harsh world created general and widespread anxiety. The nuclear family was both the source of great anxiety and also a possible source of consolation.

It is unnecessary to labour the point by developing further examples of the fallacies associated with the idea of tradition. Nevertheless, the growth of social and spatial mobility, the recognition of the importance of the unconscious and the other great insights of psychoanalysis, the emancipation of women and the social recognition of children, the acceptance of cultural, ethnic and religious diversity, have all helped to create a distinctively modern society. Whether such things are causes or consequences of 'economic' development continues to vex, if not cause anxiety, to scholars who prefer neat 'economic' or 'cultural' explanations rather than a messy model of multiple and variable causation. Arguments about, for example, the relative importance of kinship and capitalism in supporting or hindering social and economic change are likely never to be finally resolved.

Since the eighteenth century social and economic analysts have shown how societies changed through the expansion of the middle class. New economic and cultural opportunities provided new economic roles and while these were typically filled from below, the number of large landowners who became bankers and industrialists is of equal sociological interest. However, the obsession with vertical mobility may mean that lateral mobility is neglected. It would be sociologically naive to imagine that the impetus and incentive for upward social mobility is spread randomly in the population. The great motivator of social mobility is, of course, not absolute but relative deprivation. Those born to mothers who have slipped down the social scale are more highly motivated to regain the social position from which they feel they have fallen. The opportunity to enhance one's social ranking, often to a relatively minor extent, is both a prime stimulant for social change and one of the fundamental sociological sources of unease and anxiety, driven, since the desire is generally fuelled by relative deprivation, if not social envy.

By using the notion of 'tradition' uncritically, it may be forgotten, despite the consistent reminders of anthropologists, that 'there is, of course, no society, anywhere, without prestige' (Davis 1977: 89). Prestige, or social honour, will exist even in a society of equals and, as Peristiany argues, under such conditions, 'to attain the respect of one's fellows may be as high as honour can point' (Peristiany, 1965: 23). However, Davis disputes this, arguing that 'honour stratification invites equals to quarrel' (Davis 1977: 98), so that disputes about honour occur most frequently in the undifferentiated ('equal') middle ranges of communities (p. 101). The idea that anxiety was less prevalent in so-called traditional society is hard to sustain. Prestige and honour have to be struggled for: they cannot be confidently predicted and controlled. Other people's judgements can be swayed by one's enemies. New enemies may be unwittingly created by the emotional weakness or powerful passions of one's daughters or the hot-headedness or cowardice of one's sons. Quite apart from the insecurities occasioned by the vagaries of the weather, Mediterranean peasant life was seemingly in a permanent state of anxiety due to the power of one's neighbours to bestow or withhold respect. 'Characteristically, location in a particular position implies an assertion of a particular moral worth and, equally characteristic the process of location implies a judgement made by other people, usually neighbours' (p. 77).

Those who insist on the importance of fatalism and the consequently reduced anxiety in 'traditional society' surely must have a hard time in sustaining their case in the light of the available evidence. However, assumptions about tradition are, of course, difficult to refute with the kind of empirical material that is available for contemporary society – to which we shall return later. To claim that downward social mobility is *sui genesis* more likely to cause insecurity and anxiety than the unpredictability of maintaining honour in traditional society is hard either to refute or to confirm. However, what does seem to be true is that the sense of anxiety as expressed in the word 'thoght' has existed in English from about the year 1220 (Seymour 1981: 116. n.7). Since some readers may be forgiven for imagining that Freud discovered anxiety, the early expression of anxiety in traditional society deserves to be explored. Either anxiety is part of the human condition – indeed, it is perhaps what makes us truly human – or it may be viewed in a more limited way as a peculiar affliction mainly of the middle class that takes its form in particular ways at particular times. If it is the latter, then it is hardly possible to argue for distinctive features of post-modernity as the source of new and original psycho-social disturbances. If, as Giddens implies, the symptoms of anorexia nervosa and bulimia are a response to the strains and tensions afflicting women in *late* modernity (1991: 103–8), he would presumably relate the neuroses and obsessions of late nineteenth-century Vienna to the strains of *emergent* modernity (Le Rider 1993), and the visionary experiences of Anna Trapnall and 'women prophets' in the seventeenth century to the strains of *early* modernity (Mack 1992). I have no objection to such *ad hoc* ways of relating public issues to private troubles. I find it much more difficult to make the stark contrast between 'high modernity' and 'tradition' when discussing anxiety.

The problem is compounded by the fact that there is no clear psychoanalytic consensus on the precise nature of anxiety, as Rollo May lucidly indicates (1977). Even Freud's seemingly straight-forward model has been disputed, and Freud himself changed his views over his lifetime. Initially Freud focused on the *mechanism* that produced anxiety. An individual who experiences real fear represses it and this produces neurotic anxiety which, in turn, produces symptom formation as a solution to the anxiety. Hence, this attempt to explain anxiety is in terms of *instincts*, whereas others, including Kierkegaard, saw the conflicts as being fundamen-tally ethical. O. H. Mowrer, for example, relates anxiety to people's distinctive problems of exercising social responsibility. For Mowrer, the social dilemma, out of which deep anxiety arises, is rooted in infancy: the child cannot escape from the situation producing anxiety, since the anxious child is dependent upon his parents as well as fearing them. The fear of punishment and of the withdrawal of love and approval from significant others is repressed, and this leads to neurotic anxiety arising out of guilt and immaturity. For Mowrer, anxiety is conceived as the attempted return of the repressed, and represents a striving on the part of the total person-ality towards a re-establishment of unity, harmony and health. Anxiety is both necessary and normal. Indeed in Freud's later thinking he accepted that it was innate but still related it to an instinct – namely that of self-preservation.

It is not necessary to explore all the variations in the psychological approaches to anxiety, but it is significant that May's final conclusion is that anxiety, while being part of the human condition, nevertheless can become more acute under given circumstances, particularly, he argues, where the condition of social values is chaotic. This may both cause and exacerbate anxiety. He goes on to conclude: 'The burden of anxiety falls most heavily on the middle class, caught as its members are between difficult standards of behaviour and the awareness that the values supporting the standards are defunct' (1977: 359).

Contemporary middle-class patterns of child-rearing which are based on permissiveness may be deeply intrusive and manipulative, and Barbara Ehrenreich has captured the situation very vividly:

> The middle-class permissive relationship becomes a ceaseless, intense dialogue: 'Do you want this or that? Now or later? Or maybe

something else?' – a dialogue extending, in some cases, right down to which morsels of food on a plate will be eaten and in what order. No statement is ever final ('You can't have that now'); everything can be renegotiated ('Well maybe you can have it if you're good'). If this is permissiveness, then the secret of it is that 'permission' must be won, or at least fought over, minute by minute; and the kind of personality that results is not likely to be easygoing but profoundly insecure and desperate to please.

The child of authoritarian parents can at least withdraw into fantasies of freedom or revenge, but the child of overly permissive parents has little inner space to retreat to. All of its whims have been noted and addressed, even if not always indulged. It has learned to expect from its parents not only security and affection but the pleasure of instant response and approval. By the age of three or four it has, more likely than not, become addicted to approval, or at least to attention, and has no sure sense of itself when the attention is momentarily withdrawn. (1990: 907[4])

However, since 'traditionally' working-class parents have been more 'permissive' and middle-class parents more 'strict' in their commitment to deferred gratification (Newson and Newson 1965), it is not very convincing to argue that anxiety is more acute now solely because of changing patterns of child-rearing. Why should permissiveness produce anxiety in one class but not in another? The answer, surely, is the further middle-class expectation that children should succeed, get on, move up and so forth. But do achievement and success create anxiety or are they responses to it?

Anxiety was not discovered by Freud, although he certainly made our understanding of it greater. Nor is anxiety a peculiar symptom of late modernity, which follows from the insecurities of 'Risk Society', the seductions of consumer capitalism and the renegotiation of new divisions of labour.[5] Anxiety is part of the human condition. However, more people are more reflexive now than at any time in history – but this is only a matter of degree. There is clearly a distinction here between reflexive individuals and a reflexive society, which is not always clearly acknowledged. A reflexive individual may grapple with the ambiguities and uncertainties of the human condition in a traditional society, where most people accept their fate for want of any education or institutional encouragement to imagine otherwise. However, by contrast, those who adhere to fundamentalist or traditional values can quite well coexist in contemporary reflexive society. Those, such as Ernest Gellner, for example, who have explored the impact of traditional Islamic fundamentalism in contemporary society have been largely ignored by those stressing the novelty of reflexive modernization. By making an overly sharp contrast between the dominant style of social organization and the over-arching structuring of people's beliefs and values, some sociologists may have been guilty of forgetting the deep-rooted nature of anxieties which, to be sure, take different forms in different contexts. There is nothing wrong in discussing the social origins of the distinctive forms of anxiety that emerge in the contemporary context, as long as this does not slip into over-general statements about the origins of anxiety *tout court*.[6]

Reflexivity existed in a complex way in the past, even if it did not extend very widely. The problem is to get empirical evidence. In a largely illiterate population one cannot be sure how people talked over their mead, cider or ale. Some insight into pre-modern reflexivity and anxiety can be found in the poems of Thomas Hoccleve (1368/9–1426). He lived in what Stephen Medcalf has termed an 'edgy generation' (1981: 128). At that time 'thought' meant 'worry' or 'anxiety' as well as 'thinking'. In present-day jargon Hoccleve was heavily into exploring the self as a reflexive project and he recognized the dangers of introspectively induced depression. In the opening stanzas to the Prologue to *The Regiment of Princes* the poet lies tossing on his bed unable to sleep: 'Musyng upon the restelesse besynesse/Wyche that this troubly worlde hath ay on honde'.[7] He meditates on the capriciousness of Fortune and the purposelessness of striving for worldly success – perhaps there will be peace only in his death, he thinks in despair. Thinking about the insecurity of his 'smale lyflode' (way of life) 'Thought layde on me full many a hevy lode'.[8] Somebody with nothing to lose might be able to avoid the wiles of Fortune yet if he was poor and sick, where would he be then?

> Allas, where ys this worldes stabylnesse?
> Heer up, heer down; here honour, here reprefe
> Now hool, now seke; nowe bountee, now myschyf

And so the poor poet tosses and worries in his bed:

> So longe a nyght felte I never none,
> As was that same to my jugement.
> Whoso that thoughty is, is wo-bygan.
> The thoghtful whyght ys vessel of turment;
> Ther ys no grefe to hym equipollent.

He graveth deppest of sekenesses all.
Full wo is hym that in suche thought is falle.[9]

It is surely especially hard for someone to suffer from an anxiety without a Freud or a Kierkegaard to reassure him that 'anxiety is normal'. The poet wants to be alone; he sees no point in striving; he finds the burden of anxiety too great to bear: he longs for death.[10] The poet, or Hoccleve, goes out next day and finds an old man in the fields to whom he pours out his worries. The old man urges Hoccleve not to think too much: only the proud think that they can rationalize their faith. Is it too fanciful to see here the debate between tradition and modernity in the fourteenth century? Medcalf does not reject such a notion completely. He recognizes that Hoccelve's inner debates and apparent autobiographical account implied a real inner life of reflexivity. How that emerged out of medieval conventions which could not apparently accommodate such feelings and anxieties remains unresolved. Medcalf comments: 'This poet, with all this doubt about the meaning of life, does not suggest that the gap runs between man and the world, between intelligible spirit or self and unintelligible object or matter: he thinks of an unintelligible but still seamless world with a gap between it and its creator' (1981: 150).

In an astonishing passage in Hoccleve's *Complaint* the poet appears to be describing his recovery from a nervous breakdown or severe depression. His career had not been progressing well and he walked the streets of Westminster in confusion and distress. In a Goffmanesque way he grasps that if he is seen in his present state his presentation of self will give him away. If, on the other hand, he turns into a recluse people may judge him even more odd. 'O Lord', he exclaims, 'So my spirit was resteless'.[11]

In a burst of what contemporary cultural theorists might call post-modern insight, Hoccleve, in the early years of the fifteenth century, is prompted by the coming of Autumn to recognize:

That stablenesse in this worlde is there non.
There is no thing but chaunge and variaunce.
How welthy a man be, or well begon,
Endure it shall not: he shal it forgon.
Deth under fote shall him thrist adown:
That is every wightes conclusioun,
Which for to waive is no mannes might,
How riche he be, strong, lusty, fresh and gay.[12]

For those misguidedly imagining that the late twentieth century is a time of a striking contrast with 'tradition', more understanding of the strains and social tensions of previous times would seem to be necessary. Langland's *Piers Plowman* is a vivid and vigorous attempt to explore and to respond to the contemporary condition of England in the fourteenth century. This was a period of great cultural transformation, and Langland supported a 'traditional' mode of social organization that was being corrupted and subverted by market-centred relations, and which led to considerable social unrest and, ultimately, the Peasants' Revolt of 1381. This was not a tranquil period. Societies were 'riven by intense competitiveness: by the struggle for honour and worship, status and precedence, power and wealth' (Jones 1983, quoted in Aers 1988: 9). In David Aers detailed study of Margery Kempe's Diary, written in the early years of the fifteenth century, he makes it clear how the élite in such market communities as King's Lynn in Norfolk were 'driven by the desire for economic success, for political power and social recognition' (1988: 75). Aers claims that Kempe was not the hysterical neurotic of much previous commentary but rather, that she showed a remarkably 'modern' response to the pervasiveness of the cash nexus and an oppressive patriarchy. She lived in a society obsessed by display and aggressively competitive conspicuous consumption. Aers refers to Kempe as having 'a compulsive discontent, a haunting anxiety which seeks alleviation from the very processes that stimulate it' (p. 79). Kempe shows a great inner turmoil in her writing which was 'the guilty product of her own struggles for an identity which would enable a relative autonomy in relation to priest, husband and others. The cost of this individual struggle is a terrifying isolation combined with immense aggression against her husband, her community and the self formed by conflicting tendencies within it' (p. 85). This produced a guilt and hatred of herself: she bit her hand so that a scar remained all her life; she tore her skin with her nails and thought of taking her life on many occasions. There seems to be much in common here with contemporary accounts of women such as Sylvia Plath (Rose 1991), Marilyn Monroe (McCann 1988) or even Princess Diana (Morton 1992).

From Anxious People to an Anxious Class

In the last few years sociologists have begun to document what I shall refer to as Hoccleve's Complaint among the middle class in America and Britain. In 1988 Katherine Newman provided useful documentation in *Falling from Grace: The Experience of Downward Mobility in the American Middle Class*, and a couple of years later Barbara Ehrenreich's *Fear of Falling* (1990) was published. Drawing on the University of Michigan's longitudinal panel data, Newman shows how a fifth of the families in the top quintile fell into the lowest three quintiles during the 1970s. She calls the experience of people who lose their 'proper' place in the world 'falling from grace', and notes that while there are ritual ways of celebrating the rags-to-riches syndrome, there is no cultural support for downward mobility. 'After success' in America is to become identity-challenged:

> Despite its various outcomes, managerial downward mobility gener-
> ates a floating, ambiguous, liminal condition that can be as permanent
> as that of the disabled ... To be a downwardly mobile executive is
> first to discover that you are not as good a person as you thought you
> were and then to end up not sure who or what you are. Uncertainty
> over self-identity eclipses the damage of self-blame. (Newman 1988:
> 93–4)

The economic context of this change, dubbed by Harrison and Bluestone as *The Great U-Turn* (1988), has been well documented. No longer was the American middle class on an escalator of economic advancement. Changes in the employment and housing markets have created widespread actual and relative economic decline to which American culture finds it hard to accommodate. The idea that there will always be more opportunity for the next generation dies hard and the optimism of the limitless frontier lives on. However, generational moods are notoriously slippery notions to handle, and the injunction to 'go West, young man' may quickly change in meaning from going West to find fame and fortune to going West to a more laid-back and meaningful life-style (whether in California or in Devon). Newman's claim that 'intergenerational downward mobility is causing broad-based cultural confusion' (1991: 125) may be becoming out of date as the younger generation reacts against the stability and career-led success of the generation above it. However, clear answers to this and similar questions must await the results of longitudinal panel data focusing on attitudes and values.[13]

Perhaps the Americans have moved too rapidly from characterizing the middle class as 'the contented class' to seeing it as an 'anxious class'. The 'fear of falling' may not be so strongly engrained in the younger generation. The following statement by Ehrenreich may not be so applicable to the under thirty-fives in the late 1990s: 'In the middle class there is another anxiety: a fear of inner weakness, of growing soft, of failing to strive, of losing discipline and will. Even the affluence that is so often the goal of all this striving becomes a threat, for it holds out the possibility of hedonism and self-indulgence, (1990: 15).

This is one reason for the preoccupation of the middle class with child-rearing: credentialism is a fine strategy of social exclusion when there is a small, largely self-recruiting middle class. It is much more awkward when it becomes a barrier for the children of a much enlarged middle mass to surmount. As Ehrenreich pithily puts it: 'The barriers that the middle class erected to protect itself make it painfully difficult to reproduce itself' (p. 83). So the dilemma that middle-class parents face is how to match up their liberal concern that the children should 'be themselves' and be relaxed and uninhibited, with the clear need for deferred gratification in the great race for credentials. How to combine discipline with permissiveness in child rearing is one distinctive *fin-de-siècle* source of Hoccleve's complaint. As Ehrenreich goes on to say:

> Viewed from outside and 'below', then, the professional middle class has simply become a more impregnable fortress. Once only men had had to scale its walls, devoting their youth and young adulthood to preparation and apprenticeship. Women could drift in on the strength of their charm or of so slight a credential as a bachelor's degree in French literature or art history. Today, however, almost no one gets in – male or female – without submitting to the same discipline and passing the same tests that were originally designed to exclude intruders from below. (p. 220)

So the middle class in America and Britain are facing a situation of living after success in the 1990s. The middle class has come 'dangerously close to adopting the presumed wantonness of the poor – that is, the actual wantonness of the very rich' (p. 231).

Reflections on the British middle class by popular commentators were, until well into the 1990s, relatively muted in Britain. This may

be partly due to the domination of the British press by the Conserv-
ative-supporting Murdoch media empire, but also because the more
radical elements in British society appear to have been overwhelmed
by the triumphalism of the wealth-creating managerialism of the
1980s. Whingeing against 'Thatcherism' by disaffected people in the
National Health Service or higher education had, to a large extent,
bored itself into sullen acquiescence through repetition. However,
as the Conservative Party lurched rather aimlessly in its economic
and social policy under John Major in 1993 and 1994, more strident
middle-class protest appeared. In the summer of 1994, for example,
the *Sunday Times* ran a feature on 'The Lost Tribe'.[14] This was
based on a representative quota sample of 894 adults aged eighteen
and over at fifty-three constituency sampling points throughout
Britain. The sub-heading announced: 'Bruised, battered, bewildered
– Britain's middle classes have never had it so bad'. This is a far cry
from the exultant delight in insolently parading wealth which
appeared to be the dominating motif a few years earlier (see above,
pp. 23-4):

> In John Major's Britain ... the middle classes are experiencing a crisis
> of uncertainty and insecurity. They are being squeezed with higher
> taxes by their natural party of government, and they are unhappy
> about it. They are unsure of their jobs, the value of their houses, the
> quality of their children's education and standards of health care.
> Worse still, they are staring at a prospect hitherto unthinkable – that
> the quality of life for the next generation may actually be worse than
> their own.[15]

The Mori poll conducted for the *Sunday Times* confirmed 'a deep
unease' which was greatest among the middle-aged middle class –
those between the ages of thirty-five and fifty-four. The survey was
focused on managerial, professional, administrative and clerical
workers and, of those in employment, 35 per cent were concerned
that they would experience redundancy over the next twelve months.
For a quarter of the families redundancy had been a recent experience. The recession of 1990–2 did for the middle mass what was
done to the manual workers in Britain a decade earlier. As the
Sunday Times report remarked: 'the comfortable life is over. The
middle classes are working longer hours, without extra financial
reward, just to hold on to their job.' Anxieties were expressed about
the quality of education and the National Health Service. The
middle classes are ambivalent about the effects of the radical

conservatism of the 1980s. While 43 per cent still felt that the reforms had been good for Britain, 37 per cent believed that free market ideas have undermined British industries and destroyed the spirit of working together in the country's interests.[16] The report of the survey was illustrated by three journalistic case studies of solid middle class families. These were headed respectively: 'Now life is a struggle', 'Our insecure selfish society' and 'The price we paid for success'.

The themes outlined in America in the middle and late 1980s are now being described for Britain. The parallels appear close. A piece similar to that published in the *Sunday Times* appeared in the *Guardian* six weeks later: 'Britain's middle classes have found that the market economy intended for the working classes has come to their own door with a vengeance ... Talk of "no more jobs for life" and of accepting lower living standards was for the lower orders and not them.'[17] The new jobs for Britain's middle classes – and this primarily means their children – will be overwhelmingly part-time, self-employed or fixed contract.

The *Guardian* and the *Sunday Times* are, in this respect, united. 'The freedom promised by markets has created new swathes of anxiety that did not exist before.'[18] The middle class in Britain, as in America, is falling from grace, but their so-called anxieties are not simply based on the fear of redundancy, less generous pensions and downward mobility for their children. The endless renegotiation of divisions of labour and gender roles provides a further source of what is somewhat loosely termed 'stress'. To this we now turn.

In September 1994 the first results of the British Household Panel Study (BHPS), a major longtitudinal study of a panel of households, was published by the Economic and Social Research Council's Research Centre on Micro-Social Change at the University of Essex (Buck et al. 1994). This was an important event, since it enables us to recognize much more accurately a dynamic picture of social change in contemporary British society than had been hitherto possible from serial 'snapshot' studies of different samples, however frequently they were taken. The Essex study is the only complete national sample of life histories of British adults and the report on *Changing Households* provides information on about 10,000 British people interviewed during the Septembers of 1990 and 1992 in some 5000 households.

Given the large amount of conjecture and speculation concerning real or imputed changes in the society of the 1990s, it is not surprising that there was considerable journalistic interest in the findings that were reported. National newspapers carried stories referring to an 'age of turbulence',[19] and the 'worries of everyday life getting worse'.[20] 'Britain has entered an age of anxiety', noted *The Times*, 'with increasing insecurity over jobs, homes and relationships'.[21]

The report confirmed that there is a clear trend towards increasing 'flexibilization' of men and women's employment. Rather than categorizing women as being simply employed full-time, part-time or not at all, the report showed that there was a recent and unequivocal growth in the category of 'multiple employment statuses per year'. This category includes 'cases where women move between employment status (e.g. from part to full-time, or from self-employment to employment or between employment and unemployment) in the course of a calendar year' (Buck 1994: 52). This turbulence is found even when the researchers control for switching during the year of birth of a child by looking only at women whose youngest child is more than one year old. Increasingly women's employment growth has been associated with 'irregular' jobs providing 'discontinuous employment'. Men's jobs, too, are increasingly outside the old core category of full-time continuous employment. There is more self-employment among men: 'as economies become more and more dependent on specialised human capital and the specific know-how of very highly skilled workers, so a growing proportion of the workforce seeks to maximise its earnings by becoming independent consultants rather than waged employees' (Buck 1994: 59). Many small businesses fail and many consultants barely make a living, but there seems little doubt that the secure career of the male breadwinner is in decline. In a survey of members of the Institute of Management it was shown that job changes due to organizational restructuring grew from 10 per cent of the sample in the period from 1980 to 1988 to 25 per cent in 1992. The delayering of organizations has led both to redundancies and an increase in sideways or downwards moves – from 7 per cent during 1980–2 to 15 per cent in 1992 (Inkson and Coe 1993). A recent pamphlet attempting to summarize the available statistical and survey data quoted the American Labor Secretary Robert Reich, who suggested that one consequence of these shifts is to feminize the language of work:

> The qualities that used to be associated with women's work – flexibility, adaptability, service and teamwork – are now being demanded of men. Discontinuous and uncertain work is becoming far more widespread. Moreover, as security increasingly comes from employability in a fluid labour market, rather than from having a permanent job,

women appear to be better prepared, culturally and psychologically. (quoted in Wilkinson 1994: 13)

Another Institute of Management report claimed that in 1993 women were twice as likely to resign as men. Women managers and directors in the UK's largest organizations fell from a peak of 10.2 per cent in 1993 to 9.5 per cent in 1994. This is the first fall in twenty-one years of the previous steady growth of women's employment at this level.[22] While women may be turning their backs on corporate careers, they may also now be pioneering a new style of holding longitudinal job portfolios, which is likely to include a period of child-rearing, part-time employment, self-employment and so on. One of the most acute analyses of women's feelings and attitudes towards employment is provided by Rosalind Coward's vivid and controversial study (1992). She quotes one of her respondents as saying that the ethos at work and especially the competitiveness 'makes her sick' and goes on to comment:

> She doesn't have the necessary devotion to her self-advancement to make her identify with the institution and its aims, nor can she invest part of herself (as she sees it) in the company. She also has a strong sense of the shallowness of the ethos. She finds it hard to believe that people can take the ethos seriously, while at the same time she is deeply affected by it and resents not having got on as well as male contemporaries. This 'duality' was a repeated refrain. (p. 34)

Coward goes on to argue, rather unfashionably essentialistically, that 'when women feel jealous themselves, and particularly when they feel jealous of other women, they often suffer much greater personal discomfort than men. Paradoxically, women find it peculiarly disillusioning when another woman adopts male values and then succeeds. And that is the point at which they feel they would be happy to escape' (p. 40). Not only does Coward explore women's jealousies – both in employment and as mothers – but also argues, following the insights of Melanie Klein, that envy is stronger in women than in men. Coward claims that a crucial element in understanding women's greater propensity for envy arises out of their relationships with their mothers. Unlike boys, girls do not have to distance and differentiate themselves from their mothers and they retain a rivalry and hostility towards – and from – their own mothers and sisters. 'This means that competitiveness is rarely able to develop in a pure form for women, but is always seen as a destructive attack' (p. 44).

These confusions about envy and jealousy produce anxieties for contemporary women and underlying these anxieties are feelings of guilt. Summarizing the results of nearly 150 qualitative interviews Coward concludes: 'I didn't find much evidence for the existence of the confident "have it all" women of the 1990s. Instead I found women trying to find a way of living that held their guilt at bay' (p. 105). In Klein's classic essay 'Love, Guilt and Reparation' she traces the origins of women's guilt to the satisfactions and dissatisfactions in the infant's relation to her mother and her breast. The infant gets comfort and gratification, but also experiences frustration and is made to feel rage when the mother and her breast, or the equivalent, is not there or disappears too soon. This is a crude simplification of a complex argument which Klein summarizes in her essay on the theory of anxiety and guilt – 'guilt is inextricably bound up with anxiety (more exactly, with a specific form of it, depressive anxiety)' (1988: 38). The implication of Klein's approach is that people have to learn to live with ambivalence and ambiguity: they have to live with and accommodate to their aggressive and hostile feelings with their capacity to give and receive love and make reparation.

The crucial question at issue is whether in our culture, at this particular historical conjuncture, there is something about changing patterns of work and employment in the context of the renegotiation of gender relations which is creating particular problems for women. We shall return to what may be the implications for men later. Coward certainly claims that there are, and there are indications in contemporary feminist theories of similar problems. Denise Riley has discussed the category of 'women' as an 'unstable category' in history (Riley 1988: 5, quoted in Barrett and Phillips 1992: 8), and Michèle Barrett and Anne Phillips suggest that 'feminists have moved ... from notions of a female identity or the interests of women towards the instability of female identity and the active creation and recreation of women's needs or concerns' (1992: 7). Paradoxically, it would seem that Klein is providing a rationale for arguing that women's 'traditional' role provides a cultural solution to certain anxieties. If it is the case, as she claims, that ambivalence leads to guilt and it is this guilt which then encourages masochistic submission, then women have some very painful self-exploration to do as they are inexorably drawn into or seek employment. Women make up 85 per cent of the part-time work-force and it is in this area that most of the new employment is being created. There are about three-quarters of a million self-employed women in the

UK, and the number is rising. The Institute of Employment Research at the University of Warwick calculated that in the early 1990s women held 38 per cent of professional jobs which are expected to have the highest rate of growth of any occupational group during the 1990s (1993). In many parts of the country there are now large areas where women in employment outnumber men. Even on Merseyside, which until recently had a stereotypical image as an area of strong male manual worker unions, there are now 246 thousand women in employment compared with 230 thousand men.[23] Such differences are not, of course, without historical parallels in certain industries such as pottery or textiles but it is the widespread incidence and growth of such gender differences in economic activity rates that is distinctive in the 1990s.

Unfortunately the *Changing Households* report has very little information on the *meanings* for the people concerned of the social and economic statistical data that is presented. However, there was one question which required respondents to say what had been important to them or their family in the previous year: 'This might be things you've done, or things that have been of interest or concern. Just whatever comes to mind as important to *you*.' Faced with this invitation, 37 per cent of the men and 46 per cent of the women mentioned family events. These were mentioned more frequently than matters relating to employment, the next most frequently mentioned topic, where the percentages were 27 per cent for the men and 21 per cent for the women. Of course, it may be that the wording of the question could have encouraged respondents to think that events that were individual, personal and private were by their nature family events, and only if employment led to serious changes in personal circumstances, such as being made unemployed, was it worth mentioning them specifically; otherwise jobs were taken for granted like the weather. On the other hand, 'birth and copula-tion, and death', as T. S. Eliot insisted in *Sweeney Agonistes*, are the basic facts that affect everyone but each in a particular and person-ally significant way. Be that as it may, the Essex team interpreted the answer to that question as indicating that 'family events were by far and away regarded as the most important aspect of people's lives over the last year'. They go on to note that, 'in talking about events that mattered, people are almost as likely to talk about something that happened to someone else, as they are to talk about themselves', and, finally, 'men and women have very different views on what really matters in life' (Buck et al. 1994: 263). These conclusions are expressed in strong, if not emotive, language. Unsurprisingly, the authors recognize that 'Freud was right about the importance of love and work' (p. 271).

In order to link the guilt and anxieties associated with employment with those associated with family and kin, we are fortunate in having a recent study of considerable sensitivity and sophistication, based on field research carried out in the late 1980s in Britain (Finch and Mason 1993). Like the Essex researchers, Janet Finch and Jennifer Mason were concerned with the dynamics of social processes and, while their research was partly based on standard social survey methods, they also relied on qualitative research methods and, in particular, the use of the vignette technique (Finch 1987: 105–14). The authors were less concerned with the actual behaviour of their respondents but rather more with the behaviour that was felt to be appropriate – what the respondents felt they ought to do under given circumstances. In exploring appropriate family responsibilities, the authors were surprised to find that gender did not appear to be significant as a variable determining the norms of family and kinship behaviour (Finch and Mason 1993: 17). A highly significant finding of their study was that people did not recognize any clear rules about family and kin responsibilities. Even in the case of parents' responsibility towards their children, questions of 'deservingness' or of 'genuine need' entered into the way responsibilities for adult offspring were negotiated. Essentially people had to learn to balance their responsibilities and, in practice, this must raise all kinds of ambivalences, involving envy, jealousy, guilt and gratitude. Unlike Coward, Finch and Mason do not draw on Klein's insights, which is unfortunate. However, it is possible to infer from their account that they are, indeed, tapping into a source of considerable social anxiety.

Unusually, for sociologists, Finch and Mason do focus on the individual, the particular, and on specific historical circumstances. When discussing the relationships between a particular set of parents and their daughter, for example, they write:

> At the time we interviewed her, Sarah was struggling to redefine the relationship with her parents to take into account their apparent need to be more dependent on her. This is a situation which no doubt many daughters have to face. Yet we cannot simply understand the situation in this family as 'an example' of the difficulties which both mothers and daughters experience in coming to terms with the dependency of the older generation. The distinctive features of Sarah's struggle were created by the history of *this* relationship – a relationship in which Sarah's mother had come to see herself as 'responsible for' Sarah in a strong sense. (p. 39)

The attempt to create a balance between dependencies – 'the idea of "not becoming beholden" – seems to be a driving force behind the way many people negotiate their relationships with kin' (p. 59). The negotiations involved in relieving such a balance are complex and often precarious. Women seem to be better able to engage effectively in such negotiations than men. Through these various negotiations people are being constructed and reconstructed as moral beings – as reliable sons, caring sisters, responsible fathers and similar roles. People get more committed to these moral identities over time, and failure to maintain consistency can cause much anxiety. The single question in the Essex panel study revealed many tips of sociological icebergs requiring fuller description and analysis. The most important event for one elderly couple was negative – 'The family doesn't visit us much. There has been a lot of friction. They keep asking "Have you made a will?"'' (Buck et al. 1994: 276).

Finch and Mason conclude that in the late 1980s, 'women are more likely than men to *need* to develop sets of reciprocal commitments with relatives because they are still more likely to be allocated the major responsibility for the care of children and the management of a home' (1993: 176). Furthermore, the authors suggest that, in contrast to men, they are unlikely to have had a consistent record of employment in well-paid jobs to provide financial independence. The problem is now not limited to women. Men also need to build up reciprocal commitments in a more turbulent social and economic environment, and they may not have the skills or experience which their partner or the absent mother of their children have already accumulated. We return to this in the final chapter.

Finch and Mason do not explore in any depth the problems and anxieties created by high levels of divorce, serial monogamy and the growth of stepchildren. In the United States it has been estimated that between 60 and 75 per cent of all children are born to a single parent or will lose a parent to divorce. The average length of time in a single-parent household is about six years, so that more than a quarter of all American children are now likely to acquire a stepparent before reaching the age of eighteen: 'Overall it seems likely that close to 15 per cent of all children will go through at least two family disruptions by late adolescence. This estimate includes only recorded marriages. If cohabitational unions were included the figure would be significantly larger' (Furstenberg 1990: 383–4).

There seems little dispute that divorce is generally an extremely stressful event for children, if not for their parents, and some recent evidence suggests that the long-term effects of marital disruption may have been underestimated (p. 393). Furstenberg mentions on a number of occasions, in his review of the effects of divorce, that there are few longitudinal studies to provide good evidence on the long-term effect of divorce on children and, in particular, to trace out children's transition from one marriage to the next. He suggests that 'the ambiguity of family norms may help explain why bonds between stepparents and their children are weaker and sometimes fraught with conflict' (p. 396).

The British Household Panel Survey showed that in a single year at the beginning of the 1990s 3 per cent of children experienced either the arrival of a stepparent or the return of a natural parent. More generally it was shown that 14 per cent of wave I households (interviewed in the fourth quarter of 1991) were affected by some sort of change by wave II (interviewed in the fourth quarter of 1992) and 8 per cent were changes occasioned by an event other than the arrival or departure of children. Perhaps of greater significance is the fact that over the period 1990–2 15 per cent of households experienced a significant fall in income. This amount of turbulence in households over a two-year period may not be much less than occurred in, say, the fourteenth century, but because people may have a mistaken notion that modern society is more stable and secure they may feel a sense of relative deprivation.

However, perhaps the most dramatic change affecting family, kin and households is the striking increase in life expectancy. Since 1901 life expectancy at birth has increased from forty-five to seventy-three for men and from forty-nine to seventy-nine for women. A fifty-year-old man now lives on average to seventy-six, compared to sixty-nine in 1901; a fifty-year-old women lives to eighty-one, compared to seventy-one in 1901. The British population in the 1990s is the oldest ever known. Those aged eighty-five and over are expected to increase from half a million in 1981 to 1.1 million in the year 2000, an increase of 37.5 per cent during the 1990s. It has been estimated that Japan will have just under a quarter of its population aged sixty five and over in 2025.[24]

Britain will never have a much younger population than it has now: the ageing of the population is now permanent. This has a number of implications. First, it means that if people marry in their twenties and they do not experience divorce or separation, then they will have a high expectation of being together for sixty or more years. This is a situation without precedent. In the past, mortality took the place of divorce and it was very unlikely that both partners would survive to any great age. 'Traditionally' long-lived marriages were highly exceptional. Hence, it is perhaps not surprising that as people change and develop they may feel that the partner they met in their twenties or thirties is not the same person twenty or thirty years later – an important theme in Giddens (1992). Similarly, their parents are unlikely to be longing for supportive grandparental roles. Those divorcing or separating in their thirties may find their parents going through a similar process. A woman in her early thirties, who might hope for a mother who would help to take care of the children when she returns to employment, may find her mother is setting up a business herself or supporting her redundant husband. And the same pattern occurs for the generation above. With luck, the woman in her early thirties may have a grandmother who is still vigorous in her late seventies to take care of her great grandchildren.

This collapsing of age-stereotypes and the increasing replacement of biological age by social age provides potential for much social turbulence and anxiety. A couple in their early sixties might well have all four of their parents still alive. Their children may have divorced or separated and have remarried acquiring new stepchildren.[25]

A Polemical Excursus

It is important to stress that the one unique and unprecedented element in contemporary family and kinship relationships is the ageing of the population owing to the increased expectation of life. Marriages were short-lived in the past; children had to get used to stepparents; siblings were separated as some travelled or migrated in search of work; families moved around the country, particularly when dependent on particular occupations; war, disease, crop failure, new technologies and the discovery or re-evaluation of natural resources led to massive disruptions and movements of the population. All this turbulence doubtless caused much misery and anxiety. Such is the stuff of the social and economic history of Britain over the past thousand years or more. In fact a very persuasive case could be made that change, disruption, disaster and crises were *traditional* elements in past times. The novelty of the late twentieth century is that, by and large, people do not expect to meet sudden and violent death as part of the hazards of everyday life. When family members migrate to America or Australia they do not necessarily lose contact with those they leave behind. Regular letters can come in a few days; telephoning is becoming progressively cheaper and the cost of air tickets from London to New York is not much more expensive than an ordinary return ticket from London to Aberdeen by train.

There is a school of thought which believes there has been a collapse of the private and of 'family life', often tacitly based on a crude materialistic determinism. The ready availability of microwave ovens and ready-prepared and packaged meals leads, they claim, to a form of eating known as grazing. Snacks are taken erratically during the day. Younger members of households descend from their separate heated and furnished rooms to raid the refrigerator like so many members of a hunting and gathering tribe. Hard-pressed senior females in a flexible-employment-mix stick messages on the fridge door before leaving for the next shift. The home, according to this scenario, becomes a hotel. The chiefs go on a shopping 'expedition' late on Friday, or perhaps on Sunday, and 'stock up' for the week ahead. There are no common meals, no traditional Sunday lunch, no toiling over a hot stove by the resident housewife to feed those who have worked up an appetite kicking a football in the park or walking back from the pub. According to this view, consumer capitalism is destroying family life. Marks and Spencer, Sainsbury, Safeway, Tesco, Gateway and all the others down to Costcutters on the corner are keeping women out of the kitchen where, by implication, they belong. Those foolish enough to hark nostalgically back to 'traditional values' and 'basics' have to reckon with mangles, washboards and possers instead of washing machines, and the massive peeling of potatoes and stringing of beans, instead of frozen chips and beans or boil-in-the-bag rice.

The home evidently is not consistently a hotel, although at certain periods in the life-course it may briefly resemble one in certain respects. There is not a chief cook or resident chamber maid. People are not unattached atoms restlessly moving between pop-music-filled sleeping boxes, Mickey-Mouse jobs and fast-food outlets. There are, of course, strong social pressures to make young people into consuming atoms, since increasingly, town centres are given over to shopping malls or their pale imitations, where the young are strongly encouraged to spend some of the lowest wages in Europe on sugar, alcohol, noise and colour. It is hard for parents to compete with that at home. As the BHPS report put it: 'A woman aged thirty-three comments somewhat ruefully that the main thing to happen [during the year] was "going on holiday as a family, and being together as a family for a change"' (Buck et al. 1994: 278).

The BHPS indicates that young people are more self-centred than their elders and, as I have suggested, they are strongly urged to be so by the way consumer culture focuses on them. However, the strong conclusion from the sample of nearly 10,000 individuals is that people are not isolated islands:

> Their lives are intricately and intrinsically connected to others, both family members living in the same household and family and non-family members living elsewhere ... ties across generations and geographical locations remain strong ... when it comes to the importance of kin, households are remarkably permeable. Mentions of family members who live outside the household outnumber household family mentions by four to three. (Buck et al. 1994: 278)

Families are now much more complex than at any time in the past. As long as we do not make the silly mistake of conflating household with family, it is arguable that the family and family relations are now, in the 1990s, stronger than at any time in the past (Wilson and Pahl 1988: 233–72).

However, the way 'the family' is presented journalistically is substantially at odds with the reality. People read that parents are failing to discipline children, that young men are hooligans or yobs, that mothers put their personal employment and sex lives before their responsibilities to their children, often choosing to live on their own rather than being 'looked after' or 'supported' by a man; that fathers are failing to provide order and stability in the home; that old people are left lonely and uncared for; that promiscuity, divorce, child abuse, and all kinds of perversities and exploitations are rampantly widespread.[26] Foolish and ill-informed politicians refer to non-existent golden ages full of anxiety-free happy families. However, when such people are either personally embarrassed by being caught with their trousers down, or their hand in the till, or are collectively responsible for more redundancies and less social support, then people are understandably confused.

All the scholarly evidence suggests that people worry about their personal social relationships seriously and responsibly (see Finch 1989; Finch and Mason 1993; Gittins 1993). The growth of a mass market for pop-psychology books providing some kind of self-therapy is another kind of evidence (Giddens 1992). Because people are aware of conflicting messages and advice, provided in abundance by the popular mass media, they cannot expect to find easy and unambiguous solutions. They may be worried and anxious by a troubled feeling that they are not living up to standards but they are unsure what such standards are. If they turn to priests, philosophers or more mundane instant sages they will not get clear and unequivocal answers. Life *After Virtue* is not easy (MacIntyre 1981; Bauman 1993; Bauman 1994).

I have concluded this chapter polemically because sociological and philosophical analyses have failed, since 'the world we live in (and help to bring about through our life pursuits) appears to be marked by *fragmentation*, *discontinuity* and *inconsequentiality*' (Bauman 1994: 16). So concludes one of the most esteemed of contemporary sociologists, and certainly most serious commentators would agree with that. Clearly, they would say, we do indeed live in an age of anxiety, and there appears to be plenty of evidence from the BHPS to support that. Nevertheless, about a fifth of respondents claimed that nothing much happened during the year that was worth recording. What was especially important during the year? 'Nothing. I worry a lot, but nothing ever changes' (woman aged seventy-three) (Buck et al. 1994: 274).

There may be signs of a change however. A market research company have drawn on samples of 2,500 people over some twenty years to analyse how values have changed (Wilkinson 1994: 4–6). This is a notoriously slippery area to work in, but it is reported that in the 1990s the value map of British society has shifted. There has been a move away from a concern with the outer trappings of success to values involving empathy, connectedness, emotion, ease and green concerns (p. 7). The leading edge values, it is claimed, are more focused on androgyny, internationalism, complexity and excitement. Overwhelmingly, people are looking for a new kind of *balance*. It is this notion of balance which may be the key to 'after success' and to which we turn in the final chapter.

9

Seeking Balance

... in Communist society, where nobody has one exclusive
sphere of activity but each can become accomplished in any
branch he wishes, society regulates the general production and
thus makes it possible for me to do one thing today and another
tomorrow, to hunt in the morning, fish in the afternoon, rear
cattle in the evening, criticise after dinner, just as I have a mind,
without ever becoming hunter, fisherman, shepherd or critic.

Karl Marx: *The German Ideology*, 1845-6

I seldom know, in any detail, what it is that my friends really do
in their work, because when we meet we talk of other things.
Ironically, I think, I like them better when they are not succeed-
ing, and they me likewise, because there is more space and time
for friends and fun. To put it crudely, they, and I, are less boring
when less successful.

Charles Handy: *The Empty Raincoat*, 1994

The changing patterns of employment that have taken place over
the last two hundred years have created new dilemmas and possibilities which have led to new anxieties and new questions about the
nature of identity and success. Much current discussion of these
questions adopts a very narrow time perspective, generally being
limited to the last half of the twentieth century. However, the roots
of the present situation go back to the eighteenth century and
earlier. Certainly, the large-scale employment of married women
from all social backgrounds for most of their working lives is without
historical precedent and is largely a product of changes in the labour
market over the last thirty years. However, the widespread depen-

dence of all adult household members on employment is a relatively recent phenomenon.

It is perhaps worth reminding ourselves how the ladies and gentlemen of substance enjoyed their success in former times. Before the emergence of industrial capitalism, wealth came largely from the land, and it is interesting to recall how those with wealth and education passed their time. We are more likely to find evidence from the upper levels of society, who were literate and had the time and wit to be self-conscious about their lives. The Fussells' account of the English countrywoman provides examples taken from diaries and other, mostly secondary, sources. They had no shortage of material to draw on. Many grand ladies of the early seventeenth century were spirited and resourceful: 'It was a common possession of great ladies, and was developed by their training and their active partnership with their husbands in the business of life' (Fussell and Fussell 1953: 53). The Fussells draw on a letter written by Dorothy Osborne of Chicksands in Bedfordshire to her lover in 1653. They suggest that the account of her day would have been typical of many country ladies of the time. She got up earlier than she would have preferred and did domestic management until she got bored, when she went into the garden until it grew too hot for comfort, when she would come in to do some embroidery, reading or similar diversion:

> About ten o'clock (this sounds as if it was latish in the day) she thought of making herself ready. When that was done she visited her father in his room and afterwards went to dinner, then the midday meal, and often served so early as eleven o'clock in the morning. She sat in great state with her cousin at a table 'that would hold a great many more'. After dinner they sat and talked, but 'the heat of the day' was spent in reading and working, and about six or seven o'clock she went for a walk on the neighbouring common 'where a great many young wenches (the daughters of small farmers and cottagers) keep sheep and cows and sit in the shade singing of ballads ... '. Dorothy returns home when the cattle are taken in. 'When I have supped, I go into the garden and to the side of a small river that runs by it, where I sit and wish you with me.' (56–7[1])

English country gentlemen concerned themselves with estate management but were also discerning collectors and connoisseurs. Some of the best collections of old master drawings were brought together by English collectors in the late seventeenth and eighteenth centuries. These were not simply trophies brought back from Italy as part of the grand tour. One of the problems in collecting drawings is that they are rarely signed and attribution requires a discerning eye. Many artists such as Cambiaso or Guercino were copied, often very skilfully, and it would have been easy for Italian dealers to pass off competent drawings by contemporaries or by later admirers as being by the traditional masters. The extraordinary fact is that there were so many excellent examples in English collections. Since most collectors had their own distinctive marks, which they stamped on to their drawings, it is possible to trace particular drawings as they passed from one collector to another. Similarly, catalogues of some of the great sales of collections still exist, and it is possible to make very close analysis of the taste of the English gentlemen collectors of the pre-industrial period. Undoubtedly they were cultivated and knowledgeable. Very often they wrote their suggested attributions on the back of the mounts on which they set their drawings. These mounts were often skilfully matched to the drawings with appropriately suitable paper and ink and wash lines.[2]

Creating a fine collection of old master drawings, presenting them well and making plausible attributions and connections with known paintings would require considerable time and effort. Other interests such as exploration and discovery or natural history would require a similar dedication and scholarly commitment. Country houses had well-stocked libraries as well as well-stocked stables. Those who emphasize the stupidity and arrogance of some landowners are telling only part of the story. The civilized English gentleman has not always received the respect and informed understanding that some, at least, deserve. This is partly due to the envy and class antagonism that came with the gross inequalities of industrial capitalism but also to the brasher, wealth-creating style of the ascendant class of industrialists and, later, financiers. Such men were often less cultivated and filled their new Victorians mansions with contemporary paintings by Thomas Sydney Cooper or Alma Tadema and ethnic bric-a-brac from foreign tourism to exotic places.

A detailed sociological discussion of the balanced and satisfying life based on estate management, sport, scholarly and cultural interests, travel and so on enjoyed by certain sections of English landed society in the seventeenth and eighteenth centuries requires a separate book. The disruptions of the Civil War and early industrial capitalism were very great, and all scholars are in debt to Lawrence Stone and others who have done so much to illuminate the social complexities of English landed society.[3] However, without falling into the obvious trap of golden-ageism, it does seem that, for a time at least, some particularly fortunate and highly privileged women and men did live the kind of fulfilling and balanced life that bourgeois romantics like Karl Marx were later to describe in the nineteenth century. It is, of course, understandable that those whom Jane Austen could describe as 'of low origins in trade', had neither the cultural capital nor the time to develop a more balanced life-style based on physical and mental labour. While those sociologists who have an ideological commitment to social mobility would praise the career trajectory of one Margaret Hilda Thatcher from her origins as a provincial grocer's daughter to becoming Prime Minister, it is perhaps a reflection on our times that the best her son can do is get extremely rich on murky dealing and spend his fortune on fast cars and life in Dallas.

The role-models of the established landed gentry have largely disappeared. It is possible to describe three overwhelmingly important themes that developed from the early eighteenth century that are at the root of our current confusions and dilemmas. These in summary form are:

1 the collapse of cross gender business partnerships and the growth of the separation of spheres;
2 the development of a male monopoly in reason, scientific rationality and the public sphere of political life;
3 the idea that a male 'head of household' is the chief earner providing for 'his' dependents from a 'family wage'.

The Separation of Spheres

Women suffered an absolute setback at the end of the seventeenth century from which, perhaps, they have still to recover completely. Alice Clark has shown how, until well into the seventeenth century, women played an active and productive part in various trades (1968). A tradesman and his wife would work as a partnership, with neither being necessarily dependent on the other. However, by the early eighteenth century Daniel Defoe complained that, even in those trades that were 'proper' for women to work in, and even if they were willing to do so, their husbands now prevented them: 'our tradesmen, forsooth, think it an undervaluing of them and to their business, to have their wives seen in their shops'. So the 'lady' was put back to sit in the parlour while the purposeful husband 'strode out to make his mark' in the all-male 'real' world, vastly pleased that his all-male business could not be thought 'less masculine' and therefore 'less considerable' than others (George 1973: 159, quoting from Daniel Defoe's *The Complete English Tradesman*).

Throughout the seventeenth century very many pamphlets, tracts and sermons were published describing and analysing with increasing exactness the specifics of gender roles and relations. 'More particularly', George comments, 'they were asserting male dominance and superiority with an intellectual precision, wholly alien to women-baiting of the medieval past' (p. 159). The contrast between a struggle between rough equals, rather like the distinction between tradesmen and countrymen, now shifted to a characterization of a new ideology of dominance based on the woman-as-dutiful-wife. The supporting justification and rationale behind this ideology was provided by the English Protestant preachers: women were to be chaste, constant, understanding, decent and docile. For the preachers, the regeneration of men had to begin through the appropriate behaviour for males in marriage and family life: a seventeenth-century version of Old Testament patriarchy was developed, whereby authority came from God to the (male) heads of families. Domestic conduct books – published in great quantities – made it clear to women how they should fulfil their docile and subservient roles. 'The confinement of the female to domesticity and the home was crucial to the creation of the godly society for one primary reason – to prevent promiscuity' (George 1973: 166).

All these speeches, sermons and tracts which began in the late sixteenth century and continued for a century or more clearly did not have immediate effect. Women were not so easily subjugated, as the work by Phyllis Mack (1992) and others have shown in their studies of radical feminism in the late seventeenth century. However, as Defoe early in the eighteenth century noted in the *Complete English Tradesman*, the coming of capitalism and the joint stock company led to the final shove in creating the separation of gendered spheres. As George neatly concludes, bourgeois women were

> both pulled, by the given roles of social esteem, and pushed, by men exulting in a newly defined masculine superiority of the private – privatized – concerns for the nuclear family. There they would stay, shut out of a world exploding with individual opportunity by their lack of education and specialized training and by the self-fulfilling prophecy of their 'natural' place and inferiority. (1973: 170)

Masculinity, Reason and Control

While what happened to women in the sixteenth and seventeenth centuries was degrading and demeaning, what happened to men from the early eighteenth century was arguably even more damaging. The 'man's world' that appeared in contrast to the woman's private sphere was one where reason came to dominate emotions, feelings and desires. The language of the emerging political life was that of and for men who would manage and control the polity as they were evidently controlling the economy. The Enlightenment provided the moral legitimacy for capitalism and, as imperialism expanded and flourished in the nineteenth century, white European males defined themselves as the new enlightened heroes bringing the advances of reason and science to a world supposedly void of reason and civilization (Hall 1992). Men like Cecil Rhodes saw their mission in terms of the three Cs – Christianity, Civilization and Commerce. Men who built businesses, factories, bridges, railways and empires were trained to hide their emotions and welcomed the opportunity to be emotionally alone. As Seidler has argued, men lost the capacity to communicate their feelings. Men, he argues, are so used to identifying their interests with the universal interests of others that they are blinded to the tensions and contradictions in their own experience:

> As men, we are so used to exercising control over reason and language that we barely recognize situations when we do this. We are so ready to offer solutions to that situation, assuming that this is what we are being called upon to do, that we rarely learn to listen. Often what our partners want is an experience of being *listened to*, but this can be hard for us to provide. We are so used to using language as a way of proving that we are right, or defending ourselves as men, that we automatically use it to 'solve problems'. We can feel hurt and rejected when our advice is not taken when it was not asked for in the first place. (1994: p. 29)

Seidler writes perceptively about the disabling consequences of the rationalist tradition, disputing Descartes and Kant, who seemed to suggest that thoughts alone are the chief source of dignity and self-respect. Kant is seemingly blind to the importance of the feelings with which we act towards others in our moral lives. For Kant, claims Seidler, 'the motive has to be a rational one if our behaviour is not to be determined by emotions and feelings' (p. 33). Emotional work has been left to women, and men misperceive the importance of how they behave towards others as long as they believe that their motives and intentions are pure. 'But this is to sustain a Kantian tradition within which our motives and intentions are supposedly within our rational control. It is as if the will is a matter of reason alone, but this leaves room for all kinds of self-deception' (p. 33).

In the man's world, power, control and subordination are central. Success in capitalist society is seen as what individual happiness and fulfilment is all about. Following Erich Fromm and Simone Weil, we can recognize men struggling with the insecurities of an ambiguous freedom. In order to achieve wealth and power men had to struggle as individuals, they had to strive for social mobility and to use their talents and abilities to prove themselves as worthy and effective supporters of their dependents. Success could never be taken for granted. 'It always had to be proved, so that if men could take their existence as rational selves for granted, in a way that was never available to women, they could never take their position of success for granted, for this was always at least partly dependent on the conditions of the market' (p. 46).

Women, in the private sphere, were paradoxically protected from these disabling market pressures. Only now, in the late twentieth century, are there clear signs that women are resenting and resisting the disabling masculine mode that dominates political and economic institutions (Coward 1993). Curiously women's lack of expectation of controlling gives them a new power in a world when few have the opportunity to retain control. The loss of control for men may be harder to accommodate. Men learn to dominate by learning to control their own emotions, feelings and desires. Michael Roper has written a brilliant case study of post-Second World War organization men which does much to flesh out these rather general statements. He introduces his analysis by saying:

> The organization men in this study did a lot of 'deep acting' on behalf of the company. They routinely demonstrated their expertise and fascination with technology as clues to the quality of their company's products. When quelling industrial disputes they strove to project a persona of absolute confidence and authority ... Masculinity for the organization men was built on career achievement; they themselves, however, never felt this edifice to be secure. (1994: 3, 13)

Organization men, who may have fitted well into an earlier phase of industrial capitalism, are not so well equipped for the work and family flexibilities that are coming to be the dominant style of the 1990s.

The Breadwinning Head of Household

It is a commonplace to observe that until the last couple of hundred years the basic economic unit was the household in most of Western Europe. There were divisions of labour, to be sure, and specific tasks would be gender or aged-linked in different ways in different contexts. Old men, young children, old women and young women worked together to accomplish the basic tasks of life. The rhythms of the seasons provided a balance between different kinds of work, and seed-sowing, chicken-caring, bird-scaring, hedge-laying, weaving, ale-making and countless other tasks were shared in a mutually supportive and balanced way. This is not to suggest some kind of rural idyll of happy peasants, since evidently harvests failed, people went hungry, and natural calamities combined with the lack of medical knowledge led, in general, to shorter and more painful lives. Nevertheless, those who were obliged to be the new wage-earners of the emerging industrial society in Britain and the USA put up a considerable struggle, as E. P. Thompson and H. G. Gutman have shown (E. P. Thompson 1967: 56–97; Gutman 1973, reprinted in Pahl 1988: 125–37). The traditional work pattern 'was one of alternate bouts of intense labour and of idleness, wherever men were in control of their working lives' (Thompson 1967: 73), and Thompson goes on to wonder whether, since this is still the pattern for artists, writers and perhaps students, it might well be a 'natural' human work rhythm. Thompson did write 'men' and it is unclear whether these putatively natural rhythms applied equally to women who were not artists, writers and the like. Be that as it may, the pre-industrial work rhythms were hard to subdue. Douglas Reid's case study of attitudes to work in Birmingham from 1776 to 1876 provides some illuminating insights. The custom of Saint Monday epitomized the lack of work discipline which carried on into the middle of the nineteenth century in that area:

> The prime supporters of Saint Monday were the better paid. High price rates could provide good wages for skilled men, but they often elected to take a moderate wage and extensive leisure. Tuesdays, and even Wednesdays were sometimes their holidays. For such 'playing

away' followed not merely from weekend drinking but from deeply held traditional attitudes towards a potential surplus of wages: 'the men [are] regulated by the expense of their families and their necessities; it is very well known that they will not go further than necessity prompts them, many of them.' Even the 'lowest class' of workmen who received 'the second rate wages' would try to observe the custom. (Reid 1976: 78–9)

According to Reid, the decline of Saint Monday was more to do with the workers' raised aspirations for housing and travel than with the employers' demand for work discipline. The growth of consumption provided the most effective motor of change. It is unclear whether men and women were equally opposed to the expansion of the work discipline, or whether either or both readily accepted the mores of expanding personal consumption.

The question of the internalization of the work disciplines of industrial capitalism is highly contentious. Industrial conflict, which often seems to relate to the length of tea-breaks or the access to and availability of fringe facilities, may well reflect, at a deeper level, the tensions of resistance. The suggestion that young people do not now have the same commitment to the work ethic that may still be present in their parents may again indicate how easily and quickly work disciplines may be lost if they are not both inculcated at an early age and regularly reinforced. If Reid is correct in claiming that personal consumption was the key element leading to a form of accommodation between capital and labour, then this provides an independent 'cultural' motor for social change. Critics would claim that this so-called independent motor was more a product of the manipulations of the capitalist market. Either way, there is an important issue to explore: if people can develop new cultural practices endogenously, then presumably they can do so again when the pattern of work is once more being restructured and renegotiated. If, on the other hand, they are easily manipulated by capitalist commercial interests, they may be equally easily manipulated by more progressive and altruistic interventions.

In a widely quoted article on the family wage, Hilary Land has noted that 'the British social security and income tax systems have ... been firmly based on the concept of the male breadwinner and dependent housewife and mother since their inception' (1980: 72). There has been substantial debate on the origins of the family wage and the degree to which it was imposed on an unwilling working class by a well-meaning middle class, anxious to protect over-worked women, or whether it was self-imposed by a working-class patriarchy or some combination of these and other factors, such as middle-class prurience provoked by working-class women exposing themselves in the course of their heavy labour in the mines or as blacksmiths (see e.g. Humphries 1977: 241–58). The detailed reasons for the emergence of the ideology and the extent of its effective penetration need not detain us. However, its roots go deep, and the idea that men sacrifice themselves or 'do it all for their families' has done much to develop a distinctive model of masculinity. This does not necessarily have to be dominant, patriarchal and violent: it can equally well be caring, tender and protective. But it is essentially *providing*. Within this model a man provides for his family and gets status and respect for his capacity to do this. He brings home the bacon or the goose to get the other half cooked. His children can admire and respect him for providing the means to support a comfortable home 'well-run' by 'his' wife and for treats at Christmas and other holiday times. This providing role relieves him from other parenting responsibilities. By venturing into the hard, competitive world of toilsome employment he gets privileges as well as pain.

So the family wage model has helped to unbalance men and to tie them to an instrumental role for their identity. Part of what makes many men feel masculine relates, therefore, to their providing role, and this may be equally important throughout all social levels. Similarly, part of being masculine is to seek and hold power, to be in control and to favour action as a way of coping in the outside competitive world. Women, who were initially disadvantaged by the separation of spheres, have a greater capacity to be flexible, to switch between different styles, modes and types of work and to engage in different tasks in parallel, if not simultaneously on occasions. This makes men more vulnerable: they are unable to be heroic and to get out of their personal troubles through heroic acts in the wider world. Work is now increasingly person-centred and their confidence in their capacity to 'lock-in' to people may be misplaced. They may feel threatened by insecurities both at home and at work.

Indeed, men may now be learning to envy women who appear more able to balance home, work and family. Men cannot manage to be fathers or grandfathers as effectively as women can be mothers and grandmothers. The child comes from the mother, and no matter how much the father shares in the birth experience, it may seem second best. The child who is quietened by the breast and not by the dummy may also help to make the father appear second best, a supernumerary support worker rather than a truly equal parent. Men may find it more difficult to respond to their own and to others' emotions. They are less skilled and practised at being caring and nurturing. They are less used to supporting others, since in a competitive market society they have become better at undermining others to achieve a competitive advantage. All this may lead them to envy women at a deep level, and envy can lead to depression. This in turn can lead to an envy of those who are not depressed, which can, in turn, lead to more depression.

This is, of course, a gross exaggeration and generalization of a complex set of issues, but it may well be that most men experience women's growing success in all spheres as a kind of threat they are reluctant to acknowledge. The change from a division of labour based on dependency to a division of labour based on competitive negotiation places greater strains on men than on women. As Chodorow (1987), Johnson (1988) and others have shown, men's insecurities may be partly based on their uneasy relationship with their mothers from whom they must make a psychological break without that being transformed into a generalized misogyny.[4]

In the final years of the twentieth century the 'normal' pattern of core male workers in secure employment providing for 'their' families is giving way to what was previously a female pattern of a succession of jobs of varying durations and terms of service. This so-called feminization of male employment has far-reaching implica- tions – it may mean that the economic base for an increasing number of households shifts from one settled 'career' to two unsettled sequences of jobs – or no career or jobs whatsoever.

This deposing of the centrality of the male from the sphere of employment is unlikely to be matched by a deposing of women from the major responsibility for child-care and the domestic sphere. Women seek and expect support from society so that they may combine effectively work in and outside employment: both instru- mental and expressive activities, 'family-friendly' work practices such as job-sharing, flexible working and time off to care for children or old people have been less than enthusiastically promoted by the British government and, where they have, they have been directed more at women than at men. One of the extraordinary failures in public policy in the Western world over the last twenty years has been in relation to unemployed men. Despite all the evidence that full employment based on a male chief earner will never return and that women's skills are as much or more in demand in the flexible work-forces of a society in which only about 15 or 16 per cent of manual workers are engaged in manufacturing industry, little has been done to wean men from their vulnerable dependence on employment. Manual workers believed that the sacrifice they made by giving their bodies and souls to employment justified their lack of involvement in the domestic sphere. Their bodies became machines subordinated to the demands of work. The mythology of the British Labour Party and the Trades Unions is based on this physical sacrifice. Manual workers were defined by their accommodation to the awfulness of the noise, dirt and sweat of toil. Their pride and dignity arose out of seeing fine ships launched or knowing that they were keeping the home fires burning.

All that is gone for ever. Women do not feel they are making sacrifices in the same way – the sacrifices they make are different. They do not feel they are what they do, as men might. The idea that people's identities are defined by their occupations is crumbling. People are increasingly acquiring personalized life trajectories. Women's life trajectories composed of mixes of full-time work, mothering, part-time work, caring, maybe self-employment and, almost certainly, periods of unemployment provide a balance between expressive and instrumental activities. They may want to be full-time workers and full-time mothers at the same time, but they are better prepared for the compromises they have to make. But not so men – the government provides little support or encouragement or anything but training and skills for them to return to full-time employment.

As I conclude this book there is much public discussion in America and Britain about why, despite the economic indicators showing clear signs of a recovery from recession, people do not respond positively to opinion polls. Why, the commentators ask, are Americans so unappreciative of their good fortune? Why has the 'feel-good factor' slumped? The public opinion polls suggest a decline in national self-confidence and, perhaps, a foreboding that endlessly growing prosperity is a thing of the past. Maybe the American people are coming to terms with living after success more rapidly than their leaders. Whatever may be the case, the combination of the collapse of both traditional work identities and of gender identities is likely to lead to a new politics based on flexible security. The contours of this new order are not clear but it is sure to be based on more people coming to terms with being demoted and spending the later part of their active lives at a lower social and economic level than when they were younger. Typically organiz-

ations make their middle managers redundant rather than re-
negotiating their contracts to part-time or to less senior positions.
The expectations of a career ladder dies hard among the senior
salariat. However, as the feminization of employment proceeds
apace, men between forty and sixty are going to find themselves
increasingly as part-time workers with younger women and men as
their managers or supervisors.

One possible scenario for the twenty-first century, presented
brilliantly by Henri Mendras some years ago, would involve substantial geographical mobility through the life course. Young people
spend the first ten or fifteen years of their lives in the *grandes
agglomerations* of France, Italy, Spain or Britain and then they
migrate with their young children to what Mendras calls Le Pays de
L'Utopie Rustique (PUR) which would develop in the Massif
Central and south-west France, in southern Italy, Wales, Scotland,
Ireland and so on. These quasi-independent communities would be
based on labour-intensive agriculture and craft-work, based on
ecologically sound principles and aiming at a balanced and sustaina-
ble mode of life. With elegant wit, Mendras (1979) compares and
contrasts different PURs in France which adopt different principles
and practices of self-government, focus on different high-quality
products, such as paté or brandy, and incorporate a sophisticated
understanding of traditional and contemporary culture into their
distinctive ways of life.

This is a charming and beguiling fantasy which does not pretend
to be any more than that. It does, nonetheless, have considerable
sociological insight and recognizes the untapped quality of remote
areas in certain European countries – especially, of course, France.
The exciting aspect of this work is that it brings together a kind of
downward social mobility as a desirable alternative to urban success
when coupled with geographical mobility and a change in the ideals
and goals of success through the life course. Whether people would
be able to shift from the dynamic individualist compulsion to achieve
wealth and conventional success early in life, to a more balanced
and collective style later in life is questionable, but those who drop
out of what they call the rat-race to work at home or to engage in
less stressful work are doing just that.

Mendras's Utopia achieves balance through geographical mobility
and the splitting of economic life into fast-track and branch-line
ways of doing work. Marx's Utopia, which is sketched at the
beginning of this chapter, mixed different forms of work through a
day. Alternative ways of achieving balance could operate through

the week – intensive employment for three or four days followed by quite alternative forms of work or play – or through the year – as with various forms of part-time work or, as some would think, certain kinds of occupations such as farming or academic pursuits. But more typically the balance is achieved through the life course, as people mix employment of different styles and skills for different durations, parenting, caring, education or retraining, being unemployed, taking rests between jobs and so on. The permutations that are possible, particularly for women, are varied and little explored.

However, as I suggested above, the greatest challenge is for men after success. In general they are receiving very little support and understanding for the changes they are forced to undergo. The experience of and response to unemployment has not provided the support and opportunities for them to explore new ways of channelling their desires and needs into specifically masculine ways of being rather than doing. By being a certain kind of man through pleasing women, the so-called 'new man' still remains attached to his mother and still fears his independence and masculinity. If he remains tied to his mother he is not free to grow. The new, more androgynous, male must still assert his distinctive masculinity in some way, and his difficulty in doing this through his work creates tensions and anxieties.

Perhaps the reason for the lack of the feel-good factor in America and Britain that was mentioned above is that economic recovery is simply not enough. People have economic worries to be sure. In general it was ever thus. But the shifts in the spheres of work *and* love simultaneously may be especially hard to bear. These changes are cross-cut by age, social status, ethnicity, race, religion and much else besides. However, when identity is not securely fixed by either community, class, kin or gender, widespread anxiety is to be expected. Curiously these strains and dilemmas do not appear to be so acute among the younger generation, although on this more evidence is needed. Unattached graduates in their twenties can afford to be more cavalier about switching jobs, taking sabbatical years and turning their backs on the putative success of their parents. Young people in less privileged positions cannot afford such a carefree attitude. Unable to live on their own or to share flats like young urban professionals, their only route away from the parental home is to set up home with a partner. This mismatch between an increasingly flexible labour market and a rigid housing market creates stress and misery. At this level the idea of success is more about survival.

This exploration of success is bound to end ambiguously. The fear of success confused the Greeks as much as it confused some of the subjects of this book. But one thing is certain: the old male-dominated career and power-based version of success is dying. After that form of success, I suggest, a new form based on balance will emerge. It may take many generations for that form of success to be socially understood and appreciated. But if the economic fix has failed it is surely time to think about the social fix, however elusive it may be to find.

Appendix on 'Method'

Much of what I say in this book is not easily falsifiable and so, in a strict Popperian sense, it will not pass muster as *echt* social science. However, I have been thinking about the same issues for about thirty-five years, so that may serve as the basis for a research programme, albeit a personal, individual and underfunded one. I cannot remember why I became so puzzled and fascinated by the fact that people worked so hard – particularly the managers I met when I was in my late twenties. I am not sure that I know now, but I feel I have continued to open up the issue which has troubled me over the intervening years.

Of course, when doing research one is often thinking about one's own life as much as that of others: it is a delusion common to sociologists that they can expect to do otherwise. I am my own research instrument. (Just as well the ESRC Data Archive has not got to the point of locking up researchers so that they can be immediately available for in-depth interviewing by others.)

As I have explained in the text, my initial concern was to explore the styles of work of the rich and successful as a way of relating organizational and occupational cultures to different patterns of motivation. I hoped to make a contribution to the sociology of motivation. I aimed to explore vocabularies of motives, both those that were presented as salient for respondents and others that were perceived to be acceptable to others. In particular, I was interested in balances of constraint and choice between different spheres of work – the duties and obligations associated with family, friends and kin, the narrowly defined employment or self-employment and the 'extra' public, professional or private work that was associated with employment but not demanded by it. Hence, in planning the questions I proposed to ask or the issues I hoped to explore, I focused on critical incidents that might reveal these individual work strategies. In the late 1980s people were building up 'side bets', in Howard Becker's phrase, as a way of coping with a more career-risky environment. How, I wondered, is risk handled? How close to the heat of the action are people prepared to go and yet ensure that they do not get burnt? Were people developing banking mentalities in an 'Age of Insurance'? Maybe one response to the entrepreneurial pressures of the time was to make private plans to insure against the untoward.

In summary, therefore, my questions were centred around the themes of a new Puritanism, ideas of success, new vocabularies of motives and explorations of 'choice' and 'constraint'. There were also the more obvious questions which encouraged the respondent to introduce himself or herself in terms of social background, educational and career experience, ambitions and perceptions of how other people saw them. Everyone was asked to describe for, as it were, a man from Mars, what exactly they did, and this was explored in considerable detail. I asked deceptively simple questions such as 'What are you paid to do?', or 'For whom do you work?' as ways of exploring all forms of work and its relation to competing and conflicting reference groups. I was particularly concerned to explore incentives and their relationship to identities, so I asked a number of questions about self-expression, self-respect and recognition. As a way of locating submerged identities, I asked about how putative free time or a sabbatical would be used, how the respondents felt about their day's work: what gave them the greatest pleasure or joy and what gave them the greatest anxiety. What, if anything, might keep them awake at night. What kind of critical decision might cause them the greatest discomfort? I generally concluded by asking what was the best thing that had happened to them – and the worst.

It would give a false impression for me to reproduce any interview guide, since it varied considerably from respondent to respondent. Some issues were explored in much more detail with some rather than others. However, the preceding remarks give some indication at least of my lines of questioning.

Finding respondents did not present a problem. It did cross my mind initially that in finding a sample of successful people I could simply write about those whom I knew at school and university who have gone on to greater things – the hard-nosed manager appointed to the old SSRC with whom I used to go camping, the Conservative minister whom I managed as a cabaret artist, the distinguished member of the House of Lords who was my partner in a school play, the chap on the next staircase in college who is one of the most dramatic business successes of his generation, the fellow athlete at school who made the British Olympic team. It was a tempting thought and I am sure that for old times' sake they would have agreed to be interviewed. However, an ego-centred sample is just that, so I went for chums of chums or people I met at parties instead.

Sociologists typically do not use the phrase 'chums of chums' but dress up their less than random procedures with pretentious talk of the network and snowball technique or similar. It has also become very fashionable to reveal all the mistakes and false starts that have been made, as a way of disarming criticism and of appearing highly reflexive and self-aware. Almost every conceivable method of gathering information is now documented and training manuals are provided for the edification of graduate students. Sage Publications, for example, has published some thirty-five volumes in the Qualitative Research Methods Series. These are short texts of less than a hundred pages each and costing over sixteen pence a page in hardback and about eight pence a page in paperback. Qualitative research attempts to replace statistical rigour with what is invariably described as insightful ethnography, case studies, apt illustrations, in-depth interviews, vignettes and other more subtle methods that are neatly categorized and codified in the textbooks. One study, which involved talking to exceptionally beautiful women on how they felt about being beautiful, was the basis for a text on in-depth interviewing (Douglas 1985).

It is clear that with the escalating cost of large-scale empirical research and the difficulty of getting funding for research which does not seem to be obviously of benefit to wealth-creating users, Methods Are Resembling Saloon Bar Sociology (MARSBARS). Furthermore, as researchers increasingly work from home, with the consequent need to operate without support staff, it is easy to see why MARSBARS.

My chosen method was to adopt a form of *purposive sampling* which, for the benefit of future textbook writers, I would like to distinguish from arbitrary or capricious sampling. Unlike those ethnographers who spend much time with respondents who are unbelievably tedious and confusing, I tried to find productive and cost-effective respondents and, by and large, the purposive sampling method was very successful. I interviewed in all twenty respondents on two occasions and one respondent on one occasion. I talked with five of the twenty one on other occasions informally. One respondent was so defensive that the interview was of only very limited value, and hence I did one more than my target number. Women comprised a quarter of my respondents but since they provided a rather different quality and style of information much of this has been held back for a separate publication.

The occupations of those I interviewed were architect, artist, bankers (2), barrister, Civil Servants (3), general, management consultant, musician, senior managers in industry (2), sociologist, solicitor, surgeon, a television producer, the chairman and owners of three large companies and a vice-chancellor. This book draws on interviews with half of those interviewed. This is not because the other half are less interesting; it is simply that in order to do justice to the richness and diversity of the material I considered it better to explore ten cases in more depth and to use the other material in a different context elsewhere. It may seem odd to some people that at least half my empirical research remains yet to be discussed. Such under-utilization is probably the case in most research projects. Far more material is gathered than is ever used or reported on, although this point is not always recorded. Pious statements about the material being available for scholars in the E.S.R.C. Data Archive, appears to absolve researchers from any charge of wasteful data collection. However, it may not be long before the research auditors of the Funding Council start to inspect the incidence of under-utilized or unused data lying about in box files or tapes. The fear of acquiring an unusable data mountain encouraged me to stop before my twenty-second interviewee, who had been recommended by both a Conservative and a Labour MP whom I had approached for advice. The one on my list whom I did not therefore interview in 1991 was Tony Blair. While it is gratifying to recognize the perception and skill of my sample selection advisers, it is galling that a misguided commitment to parsimony led to the loss of an 'after success' interview that would surely come to have historical, if not sociological, importance.

The interviews I carried out between 1988 and 1990 would be termed unstructured interviews in a textbook. However, I would prefer to call them restructured interviews, since the purpose for which the data was used was reformulated during and after they were collected. It is arguably the case that my research material is all the more powerful and robust since neither interviewer nor respondents was completely clear how the interviews would be used. Since neither party was in a position to be sure what it was they were doing, this may appear to be a neat way of obviating bias. Critics of social research, such as Peter Winch (1958), have alerted us to be always suspicious of data which we collected precisely for the purpose for which they are used, since, unlike the situation in the natural sciences, the producers of social science data have minds of their own.

Unquestionably the men and women I interviewed certainly did have minds of their own and on occasions I was aware that their thinking was more cogent and clearly articulated than my own. Perhaps the most successful person in the conventional sense was a woman whose replies were a model of clarity so that my attempt to tamper with her transcript made her lucid account more confused. As I end this book I am already planning the next, based on the material I have not yet used.

Most of the successful people I interviewed were younger than me, which may have been a help in asking some of the more personal and probing questions. Some respondents deferred to me partly, perhaps, because I am a professor and partly because they assumed that I knew more than they did about the topic of the interview. Some were very anxious to justify to me that they were, indeed, a success, and hoped that I would reinforce their own belief in themselves. Some had already been interviewed for the press or television and had a kind of party-piece success story that I had to penetrate and deconstruct. Some of the early interviews were more focused on styles of work. The surgeon and the architect were highly articulate about this, as also was the professional musician. The management consultant discussed the issues about work and success as one colleague to another. This, as with some others, was more a conversation than an interview. One of the debilitating aspects of this kind of research is that the interview material is of such great intrinsic interest that cutting it up into pieces as illustrative supports for an argument constructed by the author does substantial violence to the nature of the data.

Most reports of research projects in the 1990s are obliged to make obsequious reference to charitable institutions, research councils, governments departments and the like who provided the funds. This research was funded by a small seed-corn grant from the University of Kent which was entirely used to pay for the transcription of the taped interviews. The uninitiated will consider this to be a very cost-effective piece of research. However, the *cognoscenti* of social science research will recognize a disaster when they see one. I brought no outside funds to the university; I employed no research assistants and did not have to pay for interviewers, coders and data processing and analysis. Since I am on a half-time appointment at the university and since my paid time is taken up with teaching, my research is done in my capacity as an independent writer and consultant for which purposes I am registered with the Inland Revenue under Schedule D. The expenses involved in travelling to respondents, postage, telephone and stationery were claimed against future putative earnings as a freelance writer. However, the book, when published will appear as part of the submission of the university's Sociology Department to the Research Assessment Exercise which is a crucial element in the level of funding that is later received by the university. Assuming that my research efforts help in some way to increase the level of grant received by the university then, perhaps, the Inland Revenue should consider looking elsewhere than at my very modest royalties for recouping the losses which I have occurred over the period of preparing for and writing this book.

Since some people are very interested in how social research gets funded I have enlarged a little on this topic. The more MARSBARS, the more qualitative research will seek to hide that fact by introducing teams of skilled interviewers, transcribers and specialists in computer-assisted analysis of qualitative data such as the NUDIST programme. In this way grants can be attracted to universities with the essential 40 per cent overheads attached. In fact, people such as myself should cease being researchers and become managers. In this way we would be wealth creators for the university and provide employment for many flexible part-time workers with other commitments. Researching and writing this book without a proper research grant thus appears both selfish and anti-social: indeed, not using up a research grant almost disqualifies it from being considered seriously as sociological research.

Notes

Preface and Acknowledgements

1 *Financial Times*, 7 July 1994, based on data drawn from the *Employment Gazette*.

Chapter 1
Introduction: Mortality, the Individual and Society:
The Dialectics of Anxiety and Success

1 These questions have been most illuminatingly explored in Anthony Giddens, *Modernity and Self-Identity: Self and Society in the Late Modern Age* (Cambridge, 1991), and *The Transformation of Intimacy: Sexuality, Love and Eroticism in Modern Societies* (Cambridge, 1992). I have been heavily influenced by these two books and had they not been readily available I would have repeated many of the arguments developed by Giddens as an essential introduction to what is to follow.
2 Matthew Arnold, *Dover Beach* (1867).

Chapter 2
Success in Shame Cultures and Guilt Cultures

1 'Growing Rich Again', *The Economist*, 9 April 1988, pp. 13–14.
2 See, for example, Pliny, *Natural History*, 33: 50, 4; Juvenal, *Satires*, X 41; Tertullian, *Apologeticus*, 33.
3 The author is director of geo-economics at the Centre for Strategic and International Studies in Washington.

4 R. Lattimore (trans. and ed.), *The Odes of Pindar* (Chicago, 1947), *Olympia* 5.
5 Walter Blanco (trans. and ed.), *Herodotus, The Histories* (New York and London: W. W. Norton & Co, 1992), I: 29–32, p. 12.
6 Ibid., pp. 13–14.
7 See n. 2.
8 T. Gilby (trans. and ed.), *St Thomas Aquinas: Philosophical Texts* (London: Oxford University Press, 1951), No. 821.
9 Ibid., No. 1002.
10 Ibid., No. 877.
11 Karl Marx Economic and Philosophical Manuscripts (trans. T.B. Bottomore), in E. Fromm, *Marx's Concept of Man* (New York, 1961), p. 109.
12 There is a large and growing literature on this topic but see, in particular, Z. Bauman, *Legislators and Interpreters* (Cambridge, 1987); and K. Kumar, *The Rise of Modern Society* (Oxford, 1988), Part I.

Chapter 3
Managing without Success: 1960–1990

1 The infelicities of Mr Mant's prose style suggests one form of expertise that is badly needed.
2 N. Cohen, 'Nobody is Safe', *Independent on Sunday*, 24 October 1993, p. 17.
3 My first experience of working with managers was acting as a tutor for a staff course arranged by AEI (Associated Electrical Industries) in Oxford colleges in the early 1960s. I later lectured on the annual course for managers held at Madingley Hall, Cambridge and organized by the University Board of Extra-Mural Studies. A sample of managers attending the Madingley courses in the middle 1960s provided the main source for R. E. and J. M. Pahl, *Managers and Their Wives* (London, 1971).
4 These latter interviews were carried out in 1988. This was a very minor part of a large ESRC-funded project comparing London and New York. Little was known in detail about the life-style of the so-called 'Yuppies' (young, urban professionals). I interviewed a group of eight merchant bankers, investment analysts and corporation lawyers who had all graduated from the same Oxford college. My account 'St Matthew's and the Golden Handshake' was published in an abbreviated form, in *Kent Bulletin*, 14 (Canterbury, 1990), pp. 32–6. Perhaps if I am able to interview them again in 1998, ten years on, I might have something of more general interest to report.
5 See, for example, Acton Society Trust, *Management Succession*, (London, 1956) and R. V. Clements, *Managers: A Study of Their Careers in Industry* (London, 1958).
6 I was fortunate to be able to participate on a very informal basis with

older and more senior men on these courses. I watched, fascinated, as men from different 'tribes' or parts of the 'same organization' mixed in the Oxford pubs. Old-style research scientists in baggy tweeds met brash consumer-oriented Hotpoint salesmen for the first time. In those days 'management training' was considered to be as effectively done through swapping anecdotes at the bar as in learning fancy book-keeping. However, they did all play a business game in a reasonably competitive way. When the syndicate that won was shown to have done so by being advised by one of its salesmen members to invest heavily in advertising, the exercise lost all credibility for at least half the course!

7 There is a delightful, mocking irony in the description of Rabbit's busy day:

> As soon as he woke up he felt important, as if everything depended upon him. It was just the day for Organizing Something, or for Writing a Notice Signed Rabbit, or for Seeing What Everybody Else Thought About It. It was a perfect morning for hurrying round to Pooh, and saying, 'Very well, then, I'll tell Piglet', and then going to Piglet, and saying, 'Pooh thinks – but perhaps I'd better see Owl first'. It was a Captainish sort of day, when everybody said, 'Yes, Rabbit' and 'No, Rabbit, and waited until he told them.

Such a story could be happily read aloud by most professional middle-class people in mid-century with a slightly superior self-satisfied feeling. Few of their children would ever think *their* Daddy could ever be like that. Now, the Head of Quality Development at a new University, spending pre-planned quality time with his children might well feel he is being mocked. At least I hope he would.

8 Probably the best ethnography, unfortunately underestimated by most sociologists, is A. Barr and P. York, *The Official Sloane Ranger Handbook* (London, 1982). Reviewed by W. G. Runciman, 'Henry and Caroline', *London Review of Books*, 5/6 (Apr. 1983), pp. 3–4.

9 This was an astonishing experience about which, I am ashamed to say, I have published very little. See, however, R. E. Pahl and J. T. Winkler, 'The Economic Elite: Theory and Practice', in P. Stanworth and A. Giddens (eds), *Elites and Power in British Society* (Cambridge, 1974), pp. 102–22.

10 This was all happening as *Managers and Their Wives* was being published and parts were being serialized in *the Observer*. Seeing what was happening all around me I realized I had written about a world we have lost. The early 1970s were also heady days for the women's movement and, however accurate the title, my co-author Jan Pahl found the lack of a more vigorous feminist critique of the position of the wives in our book embarrassing. Had we waited as long between the gathering of the data and the writing of the book as I have done with this one, it would have been a very different, and probably better, book.

11 *The Economist*, 'The Coming Entrepreneurial Revolution: A Survey', 25 December 1976, pp. 41–65.
12 There is a large literature on this theme. Much is summarized in R.E. Lane, *The Market Experience* (Cambridge, 1991). The classic study is still R. Blauner, *Alienation and Freedom* (Chicago, 1964).
13 C. Cooper, *Executive Families Under Stress* (Englewood Cliffs, N. J., 1982); P. Evans and F. Bartolomé, *Must Success Cost So Much?* (London, 1980). More recently Cary Cooper and Anne Ferguson surveyed the Chief Executive Officers of 118 of the biggest European Community and Scandinavian businesses, based on turnover, together with ninety-three of their spouses. David Miller, group personnel director of the textiles group Coats Viyella, is quoted as saying that 'senior executives had adapted to working punishing hours and they may yet adapt to spending even less time with their families'. Twenty-three per cent of this sample were considering leaving top management and finding another job. (C. Cooper and A. Ferguson, 'Top people fear for their families', *Independent on Sunday*, 4 November 1990, Business Section, p. 24.)
14 For example, R. Goffee and R. Scase, *Women in Charge* (London, 1985); S. Carter and T. Cannon, *Women as Entrepreneurs* (London, 1992); T. Coe, *The Key to the Men's Club* (London, 1992); M. Davidson and C. Cooper, *The Woman Manager* (London, 1992); Industrial Society, *Women's Training, Career and Development Opportunities; Barriers, Initiatives and Agenda for Action* (London, 1993); M. Tauton (ed.), *Women in Management: The Second Wave* (London, 1994).

Chapter 4
Styles of Success in Business

1 D. McLellan, *Marx's Grundrisse* (St Albans, 1973), chapters 25 and 26. See also the quotation at the head of chapter 9 below and E. Fromm, *Marx's Concept of Man* (New York, 1961).

Chapter 7
Working for Self-identity

1 See, for example, C. Morris, *The Discovery of the Individual, 1050–1200* (London, 1972); B. Morris, *Western Concepts of the Individual* (New York and Oxford, 1991); N. Rose, *Governing the Soul* (London, 1989); C. Taylor, *Sources of the Self* (Cambridge, 1989); A. Giddens, *Modernity and Self Identity: self and society in the late modern age* (Cambridge, 1991); A. P. Cohen, *Self-Consciousness* (London, 1994).
2 Loane's other works include *An Englishman's Castle* (1909) and *The*

Next Street but One (1907); Carolyn Steedman, *Landscape for a Good Woman* (London, 1985).

3 See J. Clifford and G. E. Marcus, *Writing Culture* (Berkeley and London, 1986) and C. C. Ragin and H. S. Becker (eds), *What is a Case?* (Cambridge, 1992). See also the Appendix to this book.

4 I had been a member of the University Grants Committee's Social Studies Sub-Committee during the 1980s and had met most of the forty or so vice-chancellors of what are now known in Britain as the 'older universities', to distinguish them from the upgraded polytechnics which became universities in the 1990s. On the different ways in which my interviewees responded to me – see the Appendix to this book.

5 There was something very Victorian about this compulsion which echoes the writings of Samuel Smiles and others. For example in his *Lives of the Engineers* (London, revised edition 1874) Smiles describes the character of John Rennie who designed and superintended the construction of many of the London bridges, the Sheerness docks, the Plymouth breakwater and many other schemes. 'He himself held that life was made for work; and he could never bear to be idle. Work was with him not only a pleasure, it was almost a passion. He sometimes made business appointments at as early an hour as five in the morning, and would continue incessantly occupied until late at night' (p. 377).

6 F. Cioffi, 'Information, Contemplation and Social Life', *Royal Institute of Philosophy Lectures* 4 (1969–70) pp. 103–31; J. Ditton (ed.), *The View from Goffman* (London and Basingstoke 1980); T. Burns, *Erving Goffman* (London, 1991); P. Manning, *Erving Goffman and Modern Sociology* (Cambridge, 1992).

7 This may be changing. In the autumn of 1994 Zygmunt Bauman wrote a pamphlet, *Alone Again*, published by *Demos* an independent Think Tank in London and Anthony Giddens contributed three articles on policy for the Labour Party in *New Statesman and Society*. Nevertheless, this is a very modest start.

Chapter 8
From Hoccleve's Complaint to the Anxious Class

1 W. H. Auden, *The Age of Anxiety* (London, 1948), cf.

2 A. Giddens 'What's Left for Labour? *New Statesman and Society*, xxx (September 1994), pp. 37–40 at p. 38.

3 'Tradition, as it were, is the glue that holds modern societies together; but once one rejects functionalism it is no longer clear what makes the glue stick', A. Giddens, 'Living in a Post-Traditional Society', in U. Beck, A. Giddens and S. Lash (eds), *Reflexive Modernization* (Cambridge, 1994), p. 62.

4 See also Penelope Leach, *Baby and Child from Birth to Age Five* (London, 1977; rev. edn, Harmondsworth, 1989).

5 U. Beck, *Risk Society* (London, 1992); C. Campbell, *The Romantic Ethic and the Spirit of Modern Consumerism* (Oxford, 1987); Z. Bauman, *Intimations of Postmodernity* (London, 1992), esp. chapter 2, 'Sociological Responses to Modernity'; R. E. Pahl, *Divisions of Labour* (Oxford, 1984); L. Morris, *The Workings of the Household* (Cambridge, 1990).

6 E. Gellner, *Postmodernism, Reason and Religion* (London and New York, 1993); Z. Bauman, *Modernity and Ambivalence* (Cambridge, 1991); Beck et al., *Reflexive Modernization*; Giddens, *Modernity and Self Identity* (Cambridge, 1991).

7 Thomas Hoccleve, 'The Regement of Princes', in Bernard O'Donoghue (ed.), *Thomas Hoccleve, Selected Poems* (Manchester, 1982), p. 21.

8 Hoccleve, 'The Regement of Princes', l.41–2.

9 Ibid., ll. 78–84.

10 Ibid., l. 122.

11 Hoccleve's *Complaint* ll. 158–61 and 183–194, in J. A. Burrow, *English Verse 1300–1500* (Harlow, 1977).

12 Hoccleve's *Complaint* l. 9 et seq.

13 For a general introduction to panel studies together with some preliminary results from the British Household Panel Study see N. Buck et al. (eds.), *Changing Households: The British Household Panel Study 1990–1992* (Colchester, 1994). Some discussion of these results appears at pp. 169–70, 173–4.

14 *Sunday Times*, 26 June 1994.

15 Ibid.

16 Ibid.

17 W. Hutton, *Guardian*, 2 August 1994. See also the previous piece by John Gray, 'On the Edge of the Abyss', *Guardian*, 18 July 1994.

18 W. Hutton, *Guardian*, 2 August 1994.

19 *Daily Mail*, 6 September 1994.

20 *Evening Standard* (London), 5 September 1994.

21 *The Times*, 6 September 1994.

22 Reported in the *Financial Times*, 3 May 1994.

23 *Department of Employment Gazette*, April 1993 reporting on the 1991 census of employment.

24 In general on this topic see M. Anderson, 'The Emergence of the Modern Life Cycle in Britain', *Social History*, 10/1 (1985), pp. 69–87; P. Laslett, *A Fresh Map of Life* (London, 1989); The Carnegie Foundation, *Life, Work and Livelihood in the Third Age* (Folkestone, 1993); J. Willman, 'With a greyer picture of the future in mind', the *Financial Times*, 8 March 1994.

25 As someone who teaches on this topic at university, I can always get anecdotal evidence of the most complex set of intergenerational and multiple-coupling relationships from at least one member of each seminar group that I teach. Serious scholarly work on this issue remains to be done, but I have a high expectation that everyone reading

this will recognize such complexities in others' lives, if not in their own.

26 These sentiments appear regularly at the Annual Conferences of the Conservative Party and many journalistic articles in those newspapers that support it. See M. Durham, *Sex and Politics: the family and morality in the Thatcher years* (London, 1991). More recently, see the set of pamphlets from the Institute of Economic Affairs, N. Dennis and G. Erdos, *Families without Fatherhood* (London, 1992); J. Davies (ed.), *The Family: is it just another lifestyle choice?* (London, 1993); N. Dennis, *Rising Crime and the Dismembered Family* (London, 1993).

Chapter 9
Seeking Balance

1 See also M. Reynolds, *The Learned Lady in England, 1650–1760* (London, 1920).

2 For a general introduction see F. Herrmann, *The English as Collectors* (New York, 1972); see especially the introduction, pp. 3–54. The standard source book giving short biographies of most collectors is F. Lugt, *Les Marques de Collections* (Amsterdam, 1921) and *Les Marques de Collections: Supplément* (The Hague, 1956). The introduction to the sales or catalogues of specific collections are often illuminating. See, for example, the catalogue of the collection of J. Skippe (b. 1742) of Upper Hall, Ledbury with an introduction by A. E. Popham (London: Christies 20–1, November 1958) or the description of the collection of William Mayor of Bayswater Hill (London, 1875).

3 L. Stone, *The Crisis of the Aristocracy 1558–1641* (Oxford, 1965); and *The Family, Sex and Marriage in England 1500–1800* (London, 1977); G. Mingay, *English Landed Society in the Eighteenth Century* (London, 1963); M. Girouard, *Life in the English Country House* (New Haven, 1978); A.S. Turberville, *Johnson's England* (Oxford, 1933).

4 See also, for a recent, challenging and authoritative approach to this issue, A. Jukes, *Why Men Hate Women* (London, 1993).

Bibliography

Acton Society Trust 1956: *Management Succession* (London).

Adkins, A. W. H. 1972: *Moral Values and Political Behaviour in Ancient Greece* (London: Chatto and Windus).

Aers, D. 1988: *Community, Gender and Individual Identity* (London: Routledge).

Anderson, M. 1985: 'The Emergence of the Modern Life Cycle in Britain', *Social History*, 10/1.

Auden, W H. 1948: *The Age of Anxiety* (London: Faber and Faber).

Barr, A. and York, P. 1982: *The Official Sloane Ranger Handbook* (London: Ebury Press).

Bauman, Z. 1987: *Legislators and Interpreters* (Cambridge: Polity Press).

— 1991: *Modernity and Ambivalence* (Cambridge: Polity Press).

— 1992: *Intimations of Postmodernity* (London: Routledge).

— 1993: *Postmodern Ethics* (Oxford: Basil Blackwell).

— 1994: *Alone Again: Ethics after Certainty* (London: Demos).

Beck, U. 1992: *Risk Society* (London: Sage Publications).

— et al. 1994: *Reflexive Modernization* (Cambridge: Polity Press).

Bell, D. 1976: *The Cultural Contradictions of Capitalism* (London: Heinemann).

Berger, P. 1966: 'Identity as a Problem in the Sociology of Knowledge', *European Journal of Sociology*, 7.

Blanco, W. (trans. and ed.) 1992: *Herodotus, The Histories*, (New York and London: W. W. Norton & Co.).

Blauner, R. 1964: *Alienation and Freedom* (Chicago: University of Chicago Press).

Bradbury, M. 1977: *The History Man* (London: Arrow Books).

Buck, N. et al. (eds) 1994: *Changing Households: The British Household*

Panel Study 1990–1992 (Colchester: the ESRC Centre on Micro Social Change at the University of Essex).

Burns, T. 1991: *Erving Goffman* (London: Routledge).

Calhoun, C. (ed.) 1994: *Social Theory and the Politics of Identity* (Oxford: Basil Blackwell).

Campbell, C. 1987: *The Romantic Ethic and the Spirit of Modern Consumerism* (Oxford: Basil Blackwell).

The Carnegie Foundation 1993: *Life, Work and Livelihood in the Third Age* (Folkestone: Bailey Management Services).

Carter, S. and Cannon, T. 1992: *Women as Entrepreneurs* (London: Academic Press).

Chodorow, N. 1987: *Feminism and Psychoanalysis* (Cambridge: Polity Press).

Cioffi, F. 1969–70: 'Information, Contemplation and Social Life', *Royal Institute of Philosophy Lectures*, 4.

Clark, A. 1968: *The Working Life of Women in the Seventeenth Century* (London: Frank Cass Reprint). (Originally published in 1919.)

Clements, R.V. 1958: *Managers: A study of their careers in industry* (London: Allen and Unwin).

Clifford, J. and Marcus, G. E. 1986: *Writing Culture* (Berkeley and London: University of California Press).

Coe, T. 1992: *The Key to the Men's Club* (London: Institute of Management).

Cohen, A. P. 1994: *Self-Consciousness* (London: Routledge).

Cooper, C. 1982: *Executive Families Under Stress* (Englewood Cliffs, NJ: Prentice Hall).

Cornwall, A. and Lindisfarne, N. (eds) 1994: *Dislocating Masculinity* (London: Routledge).

Coward, R. 1993: *Our Treacherous Hearts* (London: Faber and Faber).

Dahrendorf, R. 1973: *Homo Sociologicus* (London: Routledge).

Davidson, M. and Cooper, C. 1992: *The Woman Manager* (London: Paul Chapman Publishing).

Davies, J. (ed.) 1993: *The Family: is it just another lifestyle choice?* (London: IEA).

Davis, J. 1977: *People of the Mediterranean* (London: Routledge and Kegan Paul).

Dennis, N. and Erdos, G. 1992: *Families without Fatherhood* (London: IEA).

—— 1993: *Rising Crime and the Dismembered Family* (London: IEA).

Department of Employment Gazette, 101/4, April 1993.

Dinnerstein, D. 1976: *The Mermaid and the Minotaur* (New York: Harper and Row).

Ditton, J. (ed.) 1980: *The View from Goffman* (London: Macmillan).

Dodds, E. R. 1951: *The Greeks and the Irrational* (Berkeley and Los Angeles: University of California Press).

Douglas, J. 1985: *Creative Interviewing* (London: Sage Publications).

Drabble, M. 1978: *The Ice Age* (London: Penguin Books).

Durham, M. 1991: *Sex and Politics: the family and morality in the Thatcher years* (London: Macmillan).

Durkheim, E. 1952: (trans. J. A. Spaulding and G. Simpson) *Suicide* (London: Routledge and Kegan Paul).

Ehrenreich, B. 1990: *Fear of Falling* (New York: HarperCollins).

Evans, P. and Bartolomé, F. 1980: *Must Success Cost So Much?* (London: Grant McIntyre).

Finch, J. 1987: 'The Vignette Technique in Survey Research', *Sociology*, 21/1.

—— 1989: *Family Obligations and Social Change* (Cambridge: Polity Press)

—— and Mason, J. 1993: *Negotiating Family Responsibilities* (London: Tavistock/Routledge).

Firth, R. 1936: *We the Tikopia* (London: Allen and Unwin).

Fowles, J. 1977: *Daniel Martin* (London: Jonathan Cape).

Freud, Sigmund (ed. A. Richards) 1977: *Case Histories*, Penguin Freud Library, vol. viii (Harmondsworth: Penguin Books).

Freden, B. 1963: *The Feminine Mystique* (London: Gollancz).

Fromm, E. (trans. T. B. Bottomore) 1961: *Marx's Concept of Man* (New York: Ungar Publishing Co.).

—— 1944: 'The Individual and Social Origin of Neurosis', *American Sociological Review*, 9/4.

Furstenberg, Jr, F. 1990: 'Divorce and the American Family', *Annual Review of Sociology*.

Fussell, G. E. and K. R. 1953: *The English Countrywoman* (London: Andrew Melrose Ltd). (Reprinted Bloomsbury Books, 1985.)

Gellner, E. 1993: *Postmodernism, Reason and Religion* (London and New York: Routledge).

George, M. 1973: 'From "Goodwife" to "Mistress": the transformation of the female in bourgeois society', *Science and Society*, 37/2.

Giddens, A. 1991: *Modernity and Self-Identity: self and society in the late modern age* (Cambridge: Polity Press)

—— 1992: *The Transformation of Intimacy: sexuality, love and eroticism in modern societies* (Cambridge: Polity Press).

—— 1994: 'Living in a Post-Traditional Society', in Beck et al. (eds), *Reflexive Modernization* (Cambridge: Polity Press).

Gilby, T. (trans. and ed.) 1951: *St. Thomas Aquinas: Philosophical Texts* (London: Oxford University Press).

Girouard, M. 1978: *Life in the English Country House* (New Haven: Yale University Press).

Gittins, D. 2/1993: *The Family in Question* (London: Macmillan).

Glass, D. et al. 1954: *Social Mobility in Britain* (London: Routledge).

Goffe, R. and Scase, R. 1985: *Women in Charge* (London: Allen and Unwin).

Goldner, F. H. 1965: 'Demotion in Industrial Management', *American Sociological Review*, 714–24.

Goldthorpe, J. H. et al. 1980, 2/1987: *Social Mobility and Class Structure in Modern Britain* (Oxford: Clarendon Press).

Gouldner, A. W. 1965: *Enter Plato* (New York: Basic Books).

Gutman, H. G. 1988: 'Work, Culture and Society in Industrializing America 1815–1919', repr. in R. E. Pahl (ed.), *On Work* (Oxford: Basil Blackwell).

Hall, C. 1992: *White, Male and Middle Class* (Cambridge: Polity Press).

Hall, P. et al. 1987: *Western Sunrise* (London: Allen and Unwin).

Handy, C. 1994: *The Empty Raincoat* (London, Hutchinson).

Harrison, B. and Bluestone, B. 1988: *The Great U-Turn Corporate Restructuring and the Polarizing of America* (New York: Basic Books).

Herrman, F. 1973: *The English as Collectors* (New York: W.W. Norton).

Hoccleve T.: *Complaint*, in J. A. Burrow 1977: *English Verse 1300–1500* (Harlow: Longman).

—— : 'The Regement of Princes', in B. O'Donoghue (ed.) 1982: *Thomas Hoccleve, Selected Poems* (Manchester: Carcanet Press).

Hoggart, R. 1988: *A Local Habitation* (London: Chatto and Windus).

Homans, G. 1961: *Social Behaviour: its elementary forms* (London: Routledge).

Horney, K. 1950, 2/1991: *Neurosis and Human Growth* (New York: W .W. Norton).

Huber, R. M. 1971: *The American Idea of Success* (New York: McGraw Hill).

Humphries, J. 1977: 'Class Struggle and the Persistence of the Working Class Family', *Cambridge Journal of Economics*, 1.

Industrial Society 1993: *Women's Training, Career and Development Opportunities: barriers, initiatives and agenda for action* (London: Industrial Society Report).

Inkson, K. and Coe, T. 1993: 'Are Career Ladders Disappearing?' (London: Institute of Management).

Institute of Employment Research 1993: *Review of Economy and Employment, Occupational Studies, Managerial Professional and Technical Occupations* (University of Warwick).

Johnson, M. 1988: *Strong Mothers, Weak Wives* (Berkeley: University of California Press).

Jones, M. 1983: 'Ritual, Drama and the Social Body in the Late Medieval English Town', *Past and Present*, 98.

Jukes, A. 1993: *Why Men Hate Women* (London: Free Association Books).

Kerr, C. et al. 1960: *Industrialism and Industrial Man* (London: Heinemann).

Klein, M. 1988: *Envy and Gratitude* (London: Virago Press).

Kumar, K. 1988: *The Rise of Modern Society* (Oxford: Basil Blackwell).

Land, H. 1980: 'The Family Wage', *Feminist Review*, 6.

Lane, R. E. 1991: *The Market Experience* (Cambridge: Cambridge University Press).

Laslett, P. 1989: *A Fresh Map of Life* (London: Weidenfeld).

Lattimore, R. (trans. and ed.) 1947: *The Odes of Pindar* (Chicago: University of Chicago Press).

Leach, P. 1977, R/1989: *Baby and Child from Birth to Age Five* (Harmondsworth: Penguin Books).

Loane, M. E. 1907: *The Next Street but One* (London: Edward Arnold).

—— 1908: *From Their Point of View* (London: Edward Arnold).

—— 1910: *Neighbours and Friends* (London: Edward Arnold).

—— 2/1909: *An Englishman's Castle* (London: Edward Arnold).

Lugt, F. 1921: *Les Marques de Collections* (Amsterdam: Vereenigde Drukkerijen).

—— 1956: *Les Marques de Collections: Supplément* (The Hague: Martinus Nijhoff).

Luttwak, E. 1994: 'Why Fascism is the Wave of the Future', *London Review of Books*, 16/7 (7 April).

Lynn, K. S. 1955: *The Dream of Success: a study of the modern American imagination* (London: Constable & Co. Ltd.).

McCann, G. 1988: *Marilyn Monroe* (Cambridge: Polity Press).

Macdonald, M., 1981: *Mystical Bedlam: madness, anxiety and healing in seventeenth-century England* (Cambridge: Cambridge University Press).

McFarlane, A. 1970: *The Family Life of Ralph Josselin: a seventeenth-century clergyman* (Cambridge: Cambridge University Press).

MacIntyre, A. 1981: *After Virtue: a study in moral theory* (London: Duckworth).

Mack, P. 1992: *Visionary Women: ecstatic prophecy in seventeenth-century England* (California: University of California Press).

McLellan, D. 1973: *Marx's Grundrisse* (St Albans: Paladin).

Manning, P. 1992: *Erving Goffman and Modern Sociology* (Cambridge: Polity Press).

Mant, A. 1969: *The Experienced Manager – a major resource* (London: British Institute of Management).

Massey, D. et al. 1992: *High-Tech Fantasies* (London: Routledge).

May, R. R/1977: *The Meaning of Anxiety* (New York: W.W. Norton).

Medcalf, S. 1981: 'Inner and Outer', in S. Medcalf (ed.), *The Later Middle Ages* (London: Methuen).

Mendras, H. 1979: *Voyage au pays de l'utopie rustique* (Le Paradou: Editions Actes/Sud).

Merton, R. K. 1957: *Social Theory and Social Structure* (Glencoe, Illinois: The Free Press).

Miller, A. 1949: *Death of a Salesman* (Cresset Press).

Milne, A. A. 1928, R/1965: *The House at Pooh Corner* (London: Methuen).

Mingay, G. 1963: *English Landed Society in the Eighteenth Century* (London: Routledge).

Morris, B. 1991: *Western Concepts of the Individual* (New York and Oxford: Berg).

Morris, C. 1972: *The Discovery of the Individual, 1050–1200* (London: SPCK).

Morris, L. 1990: *The Workings of the Household* (Cambridge: Polity Press).

Morton, A. 1992: *Diana: her true story* (London: O'Mara Books).

Newbould, D. and Jackson, A. S. 1972: *The Receding Ideal* (Liverpool: Guthstead Ltd).

Newman, K. S. 1988: *Falling from Grace: the experience of downward mobility in the American middle class* (New York: Free Press).

—— 1988: 'Uncertain Seas, Cultural Turmoil and the Domestic Economy', in A. Wolfe (ed.), *America at Century's End* (Berkeley: University of California Press).

Newson, J. and E. 1965: *Infant Care in an Urban Community* (Harmondsworth: Penguin Books).

Nisbet, R. A. 1966: *The Sociological Tradition* (New York: Basic Books).

Ollman, B. 1971: *Alienation* (Cambridge: Cambridge University Press).

Pahl, J. 1994: 'Like the Job, Hate the Organization: social workers and managers in social services', in R. Page and J. Baldock (eds), *Social Policy Review*, 6 (University of Kent, Social Policy Association).

Pahl, R. E. 1984: *Divisions of Labour* (Oxford: Basil Blackwell).

—— 1990: 'St Matthew's and the Golden Handshake', *Kent Bulletin*, 14 (Canterbury: The University of Kent).

—— and J. M. 1971: *Managers and their Wives* (London: Allen Lane, The Penguin Press).

—— and Winkler, J. T. 1974: 'The Economic Elite: theory and practice', in P. Stanworth and A. Giddens (eds), *Elites and Power in British Society* (Cambridge: Cambridge University Press).

Parkin, F. 1971: *Class Inequality and Political Order* (London: McGibbon and Kee).

Parsons, T. 1951, R/1953: *The Social System* (Glencoe, Illinois: The Free Press; London: Tavistock).

Parsons, T. and Shils, E. A. (eds) 1951: *Towards a General Theory of Action* (Boston: Harvard University Press).

Pearson, L. 1962: *Popular Ethics in Ancient Greece* (California: Stanford University Press).

Peristiany, J. G. (ed.) 1965: *Honour and Shame* (London: Weidenfeld and Nicolson).

Ragin, C. C. and Becker, H. S. (eds) 1992: *What is a Case?* (Cambridge: Cambridge University Press).

Raphael, F. 1976: *The Glittering Prizes* (Harmondsworth: Penguin Books).

Raynor, J. 1969: *The Middle Class* (Harlow: Longman).

Reid, D. A. 1976: 'The Decline of Saint Monday 1766–1876', *Past and Present*, 71.

Reynolds, M. 1920: *The Learned Lady in England 1650–1760* (London).

Le Rider, J. 1993: *Modernity and Crises of Identity: culture and society in fin-de-siècle Vienna* (Cambridge: Polity Press).

Riley, D. 1988: *'Am I that Name?' Feminism and the category of 'women' in history* (London: Macmillan) quoted in M. Barrett and A. Phillips (eds) 1992: *Destabilizing Theory* (Cambridge: Polity Press).

Roper, M. 1994: *Masculinity and the British Organization Man since 1945* (Oxford: Oxford University Press).

Rose, D. et al. 1984: 'Economic Restructuring: the British experience', *Annals of the AAPSS*, 475.

Rose, J. 1991: *The Haunting of Sylvia Plath* (London: Virago).

Rose, N. 1989: *Governing the Soul* (London: Routledge).

Runciman, W. G. 1983: 'Henry and Caroline', *London Review of Books*, 5/6 (April).

Ruzicka, W. J. 1973: *The Nightmare of Success: the fallacy of the super-success dream* (Los Altos, California: Peninsula Publications).

Scase, R. and Goffee, R. 1989: *Reluctant Managers* (London: Unwin Hyman Ltd).

Seidler, V. J. 1994: *Unreasonable Men: masculinity and social theory* (London: Routledge).

Seymour, M. C. 1981: *Selections from Hoccleve* (Oxford: Clarendon Press).

Slater, P. 1968: *The Glory of Hera* (Boston: Beacon Press).

Sloterdijk, P. 1984: 'Cynicism – the twilight of consciousness', *New German Critique*, 33 (autumn).

Smiles, S. 1874: *Lives of the Engineers* (London: John Murray).

—— 1905: *Self Help* (London: John Murray, 1905). (1st edn 1859.)

Sofer, C. 1970: *Men in Mid-Career: a study of British managers and technical specialists* (Cambridge: Cambridge University Press).

Somers, M. R. and Gibson, G. D. 1994: 'Reclaiming the Epistemological "Other": narrative and the social constitution of identity' in C. Calhoun, (ed.), *Social Theory and the Politics of Identity* (Oxford: Basil Blackwell).

Stacey, J. 1990: *Brave New Families* (New York: Basic Books).

Steedman, C. 1985: *Landscape for a Good Woman* (London: Virago).

Stone, L. 1965: *The Crisis of the Aristocracy 1558–1641* (Oxford: Clarendon Press).

—— 1977: *The Family, Sex and Marriage in England 1500–1800* (London: Weidenfeld and Nicolson).

Tausky, Z. C. and Dubin, R. 1965: 'Career Anchorage: managerial mobility motivations', *American Sociological Review*, 725–35.

Tauton, M. (ed.) 1994: *Women in Management: the second wave* (London: Routledge).

Tawney, R. H. 1926, R/1938: *Religion and the Rise of Capitalism* (Harmondsworth: Penguin Books).

Taylor, C. 1989: *Sources of the Self* (Cambridge: Cambridge University Press).

Thompson, E. P. 1967: 'Time, Work Discipline and Industrial Capitalism', *Past and Present*, 38.

Thompson, J. A. K. 1955: *The Ethics of Aristotle* (Harmondsworth: Penguin Books).

Thompson, P. 1990: 'The Power of Family Myths', in R. Samuel and P. Thompson (eds), *The Myths We Live By* (London: Routledge).

Tresemer, D. 1977: *Fear of Success* (New York and London: Plenum Press).

Turberville, A. S. 1933: *Johnson's England* (Oxford: Clarendon Press).

Versnel, H. S. 1970: *Triumphus: an inquiry into the origin, development and meaning of the Roman triumph* (Leiden: E. J. Brill).

Weber, M. 1930: *The Protestant Ethic and the Spirit of Capitalism* (London: Unwin University Books).

White, H. 1973: *Metahistory: the historical imagination in nineteenth-century Europe* (Baltimore: Johns Hopkins University Press).

Whyte, W. H. 1957: *The Organization Man* (London: Jonathan Cape).

Wilkinson, H. 1994: *No Turning Back* (London: Demos).

Wilson, P. and Pahl, R. E. 1988: 'The Changing Sociological Construct of the Family', *Sociological Review*, 36/2.

Winch, P. 1958: *The Idea of a Social Science and Its Relation to Philosophy* (London: Routledge).

Wright, P. 1987: 'Excellence', *London Review of Books* (21 May).

Wrong, D. 1977: *Skeptical Sociology* (London: Heinemann).

Index